This book reflects the important findings of cutting-edge research. It demonstrates the frightening scale of organised crime investment in the legitimate economy, and the negative effects of this phenomenon. Tracing and recovering the proceeds of crime remains a major strategic challenge for law enforcement agencies across Europe, so this publication is as timely as it is important.

Rob Wainwright, *Director of Europol*

This timely book is a must-read for academics and practitioners who want to know more about criminal infiltration and the various ways in which criminal activities and the legitimate economy are intertwined in a wide array of European countries.

Edward R. Kleemans, *Full Professor (Chair of Serious and Organized Crime and Criminal Justice), VU University Amsterdam, the Netherlands*

New criminals have moved away from the Dickensian den of thieves and now reside in posh city centre offices. With the aid of accountants, lawyers and financial experts they devise new extortion rackets and malpractices that are threatening the fabric of state and society. This interdisciplinary book presents meticulously researched case studies to show how the criminal elites operate under the guise of business and professionalism. It is a must-read for students, scholars and policy-makers.

Prem Sikka, *Professor of Accounting, Essex Business School, University of Essex*

Organised Crime in European Businesses

The infiltration of organised crime in the legitimate economy has emerged as a transnational phenomenon. This book constitutes an unprecedented study of the involvement of criminal groups in the legitimate economy and their infiltration in legal businesses, and is the first to bridge the research gap between money laundering and organised crime. It analyses the main drivers of this process, explaining *why, how* and *where* infiltration happens.

Building on empirical evidence from the Netherlands, Slovenia, Spain, Sweden, the UK, Ireland, Italy, France and Finland, *Organised Crime in European Businesses* is divided into four parts. Part I explores the infiltration of legitimate businesses to conceal and facilitate illicit trafficking. Part II examines the infiltration of legitimate businesses to develop fraud schemes. Part III focuses on the infiltration of legitimate businesses to control the territory and influence policy makers. Part IV concludes by considering the research and policy implications in light of these findings.

Bringing together leading experts and detailed case studies, this book considers the infiltration of organised crime in legitimate business around Europe. It is an ideal resource for students and academics in the fields of criminology, economics and sociology, as well as private sector practitioners, public officials and policy makers.

Ernesto U. Savona is Professor of Criminology at the Università Cattolica del Sacro Cuore, Italy. He is also Director of Transcrime, the Joint Research Centre on Transnational Crime of the Università Cattolica del Sacro Cuore.

Michele Riccardi is Adjunct Professor of Business Economics at the Università Cattolica del Sacro Cuore, Italy, and senior researcher at Transcrime.

Giulia Berlusconi is Postdoctoral Fellow at the Faculty of Political and Social Sciences, Università Cattolica del Sacro Cuore, Italy, and researcher at Transcrime.

Routledge Studies in Crime and Society

Organised Crime in European Businesses

Edited by
Ernesto U. Savona,
Michele Riccardi and
Giulia Berlusconi

Routledge
Taylor & Francis Group

LONDON AND NEW YORK

First published 2016
by Routledge
2 Park Square, Milton Park, Abingdon, Oxon OX14 4RN

and by Routledge
711 Third Avenue, New York, NY 10017

First issued in paperback 2018

Routledge is an imprint of the Taylor & Francis Group, an informa business

© 2016 Ernesto U. Savona, Michele Riccardi and Giulia Berlusconi

The right of the editors to be identified as the authors of the editorial matter, and of the authors for their individual chapters, has been asserted in accordance with sections 77 and 78 of the Copyright, Designs and Patents Act 1988.

British Library Cataloguing-in-Publication Data
A catalogue record for this book is available from the British Library

Library of Congress Cataloging-in-Publication Data
A catalog record for this book has been requested

ISBN 13: 978-1-138-49947-8 (pbk)
ISBN 13: 978-1-138-19109-9 (hbk)

Typeset in Times New Roman
by Wearset Ltd, Boldon, Tyne and Wear

Contents

Figures

Tables

Contributors

Branko Ažman, MA, is a senior lecturer at the Faculty of Criminal Justice and Security, University of Maribor. His research interests include English terminology in criminal justice and security, teaching methodology, and AI.

Giulia Berlusconi, PhD Criminology, is a postdoctoral fellow at Università Cattolica del Sacro Cuore, Faculty of Political and Social Sciences. Since the academic year 2013–2014 she has been lecturer on a module on organised crime of the bachelor course on Sociology of Deviance at Università Cattolica. She has been a researcher at Transcrime – Joint Research Centre on Transnational Crime (www.transcrime.it) – since 2010. Her fields of interest include organised and economic crime, social network analysis and maritime piracy. She participated and currently participates in several research projects, including project ARIEL on organised crime infiltration in legal businesses (www.arielproject.eu).

Stefano Bonino, PhD, is a lecturer in Criminology in the Department of Social Science at Northumbria University. He was previously research fellow at Durham University where he worked on EU co-funded project ARIEL.

Diana Camerini, MSc Economics and Social Science and BSc Economics of Financial Institutions and Markets at Bocconi University of Milan, has been a researcher at Transcrime since February 2014. Her research focuses on the application of quantitative methods (econometrics and applied statistics) to economics, criminology and social sciences. She has been involved in research projects in the area of money laundering risk assessment (project IARM) and organised crime investments (project OCP – Organized Crime Portfolio, www.ocportfolio.eu). She was previously research assistant at Bocconi University (2011–2013) and at Synergia Srl (2012–2014).

Yulia Chistyakova, PhD, is senior lecturer in Criminology in the School of Humanities and Social Science at Liverpool John Moores University where she researches and teaches policing in Eastern Europe and organised crime. She was previously research fellow at Durham University where she worked on EU co-funded project OCP – Organised Crime Portfolio.

Katja Eman, PhD, is assistant professor of Criminology at the Faculty of Criminal Justice and Security, University of Maribor, Slovenia. Her research interests focus on green criminology, environmental crime, organised crime, white-collar crime, crime prevention, crime mapping, and crime and legitimacy.

Joras Ferwerda holds a Bachelor in Economics and Law, a Master in Economics and Social Science and a PhD in Economics from the Utrecht University School of Economics in the Netherlands. He is currently assistant professor of the Economics of the Public Sector Chair at the Utrecht University School of Economics in the Netherlands and affiliated with VU University Amsterdam for an EU co-funded research project. His publications focus on money laundering and other financial economic crimes. He has been involved in research projects financed, among others, by the Dutch Ministry of Finance, Justice and Interior Affairs, European Commission (DG Home and DG Justice) and OLAF, the European Anti-Fraud Office.

Lorella Garofalo has been researcher at Transcrime since 2011. She received a Master's degree in Applied Social Science, with honours, from the Faculty of Sociology of the Università Cattolica del Sacro Cuore in Milan with a dissertation on the 'Ndrangheta organisational structure in Northern Italy. Her research interests include organised crime and economic crime, Italian mafias, illegal markets, extortion and social network analysis. She has participated in several research projects, including project CEREU (2014–2016), project ARIEL (2014–2015) and project 'Gli investimenti delle mafie – Mafia investments' (2013).

Valentina Giampietri is a researcher at Transcrime. Her research focuses on organised crime infiltration of legitimate businesses, extortion racketeering and illicit proceeds of opiates trafficking. She has contributed to various research projects, including UNODC project Drug Money: the illicit proceeds of opiates trafficked on the Balkan route, EU co-funded project ARIEL and project CEREU, Countering Extortion and Racketeering in the EU.

Jarmo Houtsonen, PhD, is a senior researcher and Director for Development at the Police University College of Finland, where he manages the project portfolio and project office. His research interest covers policing sciences and internal security, and his latest publications include the restructuring of police administration in Finland, investigation of narcotics offences, recruitment into criminal groups and citizens' obedience to law.

Lars Korsell, PhD, is a lawyer and criminologist. He has a doctoral degree in criminology (economic crime) at Stockholm University and works as a researcher at Brå (the Swedish National Council for Crime Prevention), the Organised and Economic Crime Research Division. He has a background as a judge at both administrative and penal/civil courts as well as courts of appeal. As a legal advisor, he has a long experience in different ministries and governmental committees. He has been responsible for many research projects and has published several books, reports and articles in the field of economic and organised crime. Besides these areas, he has done several works on cultural heritage crime. At the moment, he is involved in projects on money laundering, corruption, the development of economic crime and crime control in Sweden and different aspects of organised crime.

Pilar Laguna is Dean of the Law and Social Sciences School and Associate Professor at the Business Administration Department, Rey Juan Carlos University, Spain. She has a PhD in Finance and a Diploma in Military Studies (Spanish Centre for Advanced National Defence Studies). Currently, she is KPMG-URJC Chair on Financial and Forensic Research, Vice-president of the Association of Graduates on National Defence Higher Studies, member of the Board of the Spanish Atlantic Treaty Association, Vice-president of the Spanish Association of Directors, and Director of the International Business Program and the Student Exchange Program with Bordeaux. She has participated in several international projects on security and defence topics, and organised international seminars on National Security and Terrorism.

Jerónimo Márquez is a PhD student at the Rey Juan Carlos University, Spain. He received a BA in Business Administration at the Rey Juan Carlos University, a Bachelor's degree in Business Administration at the University of Nevada, Las Vegas (UNLV), an MSc in Organizational Management from the University Rey Juan Carlos and an MSc in Anti-Money Laundering and Counter Terrorist Financing from the University of Vic, Spain. He is a member of the professional business fraternity Alpha Kappa Psi and the Golden Key International Honour Society. In recent years, he has focused on organised crime, illegal markets and money laundering activities and their impact on the legitimate economy.

Maja Modic, PhD, is assistant professor of Security Studies at the Faculty of Criminal Justice and Security, University of Maribor, Slovenia. Her current research interests include policing, migration and policing, police–residents relationships and legitimacy of policing.

Jesús Palomo is associate professor at the Business Administration Department, Rey Juan Carlos University, Spain. He has a PhD in Computer Sciences and Mathematical Modelling (Honourable Mention Award ISBA-L.S. Savage), an MA in Business Administration and an MSc in Management Computer Sciences (with Distinction). Previously, he has been visitor researcher at Georgetown University, NATO Defense College, CNR (Consiglio Nazionale delle Ricerche), Italy, Duke University, University of California at Santa Cruz, National Institute of Environmental Health Sciences and the Danish Institute of Social Research. He has published more than 50 research papers, books and book chapters, and has directed more than 10 international projects on security and defence, including EU-funded projects CEART (Centre of Excellence in Asset Recovery and Training), OCP (Organised Crime Portfolio), TIE (Tackling Illegal Economy) and NATO-SPS project UNSCR1325

Reload. His main research interests focus on decision sciences, data analysis, security and defence economics and statistics.

Sarianna Petrell has a Master of Arts in European History from Leiden University. She has worked as a strategic analyst in the National Bureau of Investigation of Finland for five years concentrating on different crime areas. She worked as a researcher in the Police University College of Finland where she participated in EU co-funded project OCP (Organised Crime Portfolio), on organised crime investments in Europe.

Michele Riccardi, MSc Accounting & Financial Economics, University of Essex, UK and MA International Relations, Università Cattolica Sacro Cuore, Italy, is adjunct professor of Business Economics at the Università Cattolica in Milan and senior researcher at Transcrime. His research focuses on organised crime, financial crime, money laundering, management of confiscated assets and manipulation of corporate information. He has contributed to several international projects, including project IARM (www.transcrime.it/iarm), OCP (www.ocportfolio.eu), EBOCS (www.ebocs.eu) and BOWNET. He is an expert member of the Asset Recovery Offices Platform of the European Commission and of the EU CEPOL money laundering working group. He has been a consultant for the Italian CSF, Financial Security Committee, in the ML/TF national risk assessment and for the latest FATF mutual evaluation of Italy.

Helena Rönnblom currently works as analyst at the anti-fraud unit, Swedish National Board for Study Support. In her previous position as researcher at Brå (the Swedish National Council for Crime Prevention, the Organised and Economic Crime Research Division) her primary fields included multi-agency approaches to organised crime and organised crime infiltration in legitimate businesses. Within these fields, she used mixed method approaches such as participatory observation, interviews, field studies, script analysis and quantitative data analysis. She also worked in project ARIEL. Prior to her work at Brå, she worked as an advisor in public financing for small and medium size businesses. She holds a Master's degree in Political Science at Uppsala University, Sweden.

Ernesto U. Savona is professor of Criminology at the Università Cattolica del Sacro Cuore, Milan, and director of Transcrime – Joint Research Centre on Transnational Crime (www.transcrime.it). He is editor-in-chief of the *European Journal on Criminal Policy and Research* and has been a member of expert groups within the United Nations, the European Commission, Europol and other institutions at national and international level. He has researched and published extensively on organised and economic crime, corruption, crime statistics and criminal justice systems. He has coordinated numerous research projects at national and international level, including EU co-funded projects OCP on the investments of organised crime in Europe (www.ocportfolio.eu) and ARIEL on criminal infiltration in legitimate businesses (www.arielproject.eu).

Johanna Skinnari is a criminologist and works as senior researcher and project manager at Brå (the Swedish National Council for Crime Prevention), the Organised and Economic Crime Research Division. She has managed and been involved in research projects on various topics including extortion against business owners, corruption from organised crime against public officials, organised crime investments, organised crime infiltration in business sectors (e.g. EU co-funded project ARIEL), tax crimes, fraud and money laundering. Currently she is the project manager of two research projects. The largest one is on unlawful influence (threats, harassment, violence, criminal damage and corruption) against public officials in 13 agencies, ranging from police officers and customs officers to bailiffs and judges. It is based on qualitative interviews and a web survey completed by 46,000 officials.

Boštjan Slak is researcher and part-time member of the Chair of Criminal Investigation at the Faculty of Criminal Justice and Security, University of Maribor (Ljubljana, Slovenia). His research interests focus on integrity, white-collar and organised crime, media portrayal of criminal investigations and media influence on the criminal investigation process.

Cristina Soriani is researcher at Transcrime and PhD student in Criminology at the Università Cattolica del Sacro Cuore. Her research focuses on money laundering, organised crime and seizure and confiscation of proceeds of crime in particular companies. She has contributed to various research projects on these topics including EU co-funded project OCP (Organised Crime Portfolio) and to the study 'Gli investimenti delle mafie – Mafia investments', funded by the Italian Ministry of Interior in 2012. As intern at Europol, she has contributed to a comparative analysis of seized and confiscated assets across EU countries and to the study of different forms of money laundering by organised crime groups in Europe.

Brigitte Unger, born in Austria in 1955, has studied economics at the Vienna University of Economics and Business Administration and at the Wirtschaftsuniversitaet Wien, where she also became Full Professor. Since 2002 she holds the Chair of Public Sector Economics at the Utrecht University School of Economics in the Netherlands. Her publications are on corporatism, economic policy, tax competition, money laundering and other financial and economic crimes. She estimated money laundering in the Netherlands for the first time in 2006, and has published three books and several academic articles on money laundering. Furthermore, she is consultant of the Dutch Ministry of Finance, the European Commission (DG Justice and DG Home), the UNODC and EUROSTAT on money laundering issues.

John Walker began working life with rocket science and regional economic analysis, but a 1973 analysis of urban dysfunction, using geospatial and statistical methods to analyse police crime reports at a time when police were still using pins on maps, led to a career in analysing crime trends and the economics of crime. Subsequently he developed mathematical models for forecasting trends in crime, widely used as the basis for strategic planning in the Australian criminal justice systems, and adapted standard economic models, including the gravity model of trade, to the analysis of transnational organised crime and money laundering, regarded as a seminal contribution to understanding the proceeds of crime and money laundering flows. He has worked as a consultant to the UNODC (United Nations Office on Drugs and Crime), the IMF (International Monetary Fund), the European Union and the World Bank, as well as most of Australia's law enforcement and justice agencies.

David Wall, PhD, is professor of Criminology in the Centre for Criminal Justice studies, School of Law, University of Leeds (UK) where he researches and teaches cybercrime, organised crime, policing and intellectual property crime. Until August 2015 he was professor of Criminology at Durham University where he was the UK principal investigator for the EU co-funded projects OCP (Organised Crime Portfolio – www.ocportfolio.eu) and ARIEL (www.arielproject.eu).

Abbreviations

AGRASC	Agence de Gestion et de Recouvrement des Avoirs Saisis et Confisqués (French Agency for the Management and the Recovery of Seized and Confiscated Assets)
AJPES	Agencija Republike Slovenije za javnopravne evidence in storitve (Agency of the Republic of Slovenia for Public Legal Records and Related Services)
AML	Anti-money laundering
ANBSC	Agenzia Nazionale per l'amministrazione e la destinazione dei Beni Sequestrati e Confiscati alla criminalità organizzata (Italian National Agency for the Management of Seized and Confiscated Assets from Organised Crime)
ARIEL	Assessing the Risk of the Infiltration of Organized Crime in EU MSs Legitimate Economies: a Pilot Project in five EU Countries
ARO	Asset recovery office
BKA	Bundeskriminalamt (German Federal Criminal Police Office)
BMC	Bandidos Motorcycle Club
Brå	Brottsförebyggande rådet (Swedish National Council for Crime Prevention)
BTP	Bâtiments et Travaux Publics (construction and public procurements)
CDD	Customer Due Diligence
CICO	Centro de Inteligencia Contra el Crimen Organizado (Spanish Centre of Intelligence against Organised Crime)
CIS	Commonwealth of Independent States
CITCO	Centro de Inteligencia contra el Terrorismo y el Crimen Organizado (Spanish Centre of Intelligence against Terrorism and Organised Crime)
CMC	Cannonball Motorcycle Club
CSD	Centre for the Study of Democracy
DIA	Direzione Investigativa Antimafia (Italian Antimafia Investigations Directorate)
DNA	Direzione Nazionale Antimafia (Italian National Antimafia Directorate)

EBM	Ekobrottsmyndigheten (Swedish Economic Crime Authority)
EMCDDA	European Monitoring Centre for Drugs and Drug Addiction
EU	European Union
FATF	Financial Action Task Force
FIU	Financial Intelligence Unit
GDF	Guardia di Finanza (Italian Financial Guard)
GDO	Grande Distribuzione Organizzata (Mass retail trade channels)
GRETA	Group of Experts on Action against Trafficking in Human Beings
HAMC	Hells Angels Motorcycle Club
HMRC	Her Majesty's Revenue and Customs
HO.RE.CA.	Hotels, restaurants and catering industry
HPAC	Heating, piping and air conditioning
ICT	Information, communication and technology
IMF	International Monetary Fund
INHESJ	Institut National des Hautes Études de la Sécurité et de la Justice (French National Institute for Advanced Studies in Security and Justice)
IRCP	Institute for International Research on Criminal Policy
ISF	Inspektionen för socialförsäkringen (Swedish Social Insurance Inspectorate)
KYC	Know Your Customer
LEA	Law enforcement agency
MAVUS	Method for Assessment of the Vulnerability of Sectors
METRIC	Monitoraggio dell'Economia Trentina contro il Rischio Criminalità (Monitoring the Trentino economy against the risk of crime)
MOVUS	Modello Vulnerabilità Settori (Model to assess the Vulnerability of Sectors)
MPI	Mafia Presence Index
MTIC	Missing Trader Intra-Community
NBI	National Bureau of Investigation
NCA	National Crime Agency
NUTS	Nomenclature of Territorial Units for Statistics (Eurostat)
OC	Organised crime
OCG	Organised crime group
OCP	Organised Crime Portfolio (name of the project)
OCTA	Organised Crime Threat Assessment
OMCG	Outlaw motorcycle gang
ONDRP	Observatoire National de la Délinquance et des Réponses Pénales (French National Supervisory Body on Crime and Punishment)
PACA	Provence–Alpes–Côte d'Azur
PATJA	Finnish Police Information System
PIAC	Plateforme d'Identifications des Avoirs Criminels (French Criminal Asset Identification Platform)
PNSD	Plan Nacional sobre Drogas (Spanish National Plan on Drugs)

PPO	Public Prosecution Office
R&D	Research and development
SIRASCO	Service d'Information de Renseignement et d'Analyse Stratégique sur la Criminalité Organisée (French Organised Crime Intelligence Agency)
SOC	Serious and Organised Crime
SOCTA	Serious and Organised Crime Threat Assessment
SOU	Statens offentliga utredningar (Swedish Governmental committee of inquiry)
SRL	Società a responsabilità limitata (Italian limited liability Company)
STRJD	Service Technique de Recherches Judiciaires et de Documentation
TAV	Treno Alta Velocità (Italian High-Speed Railway)
TRACFIN	Traitement du Renseignement et Action contre les Circuits FINanciers clandestins (French Unit for the Treatment of Information and Action Against Illicit Financial Circuits)
UAE	United Arab Emirates
UB	United Brotherhood
UNAFEI	United Nations Asia and Far Eastern Institute
UNODC	United Nations Office on Drugs and Crime
USA	United States of America
VAT	Value added tax
VLT	Video Lottery Terminal
WEF	World Economic Forum

Introduction

Ernesto U. Savona

In his article entitled 'Paragons, Pariahs, and Pirates: A Spectrum-Based Theory of Enterprise', written in the 1980s, Dwight Smith said:

> If instead of those differences we recognize a common thread of enterprise, and understand that it takes place across a spectrum including legal and criminal businesses, then a single, unifying perspective can take shape. The distinctions along that spectrum are exemplified by three kinds of business-men: the paragon, the pariah, and the pirate.
>
> (Smith, 1980, p. 358)

Dwight Smith's article was the result of deep analysis of the role of La Cosa Nostra in the United States. Its development followed Bell's ladder (Bell, 1953, p. 133) and the role of legitimate businesses versus criminal ones. There were few cases in which the dividing line between the two types of business (criminal and legitimate) was clear in the development of a criminal family; more frequent were cases in which that line was not distinguishable (contemporary criminal and legitimate activities).

This book has the ambition of continuing this analysis by framing it within the international development of organised crime 15 years after the UN Convention against Transnational Organized Crime. This convention marked the end of the approach based on the equivalence between organised crime and violence and the start of a process of looking for broader consequences. Part of this process is study of the impact of organised crime upon the economy. Such analysis began at the end of the last century with the investigation of money laundering, and it continues today within a broader framework that considers the *infiltration* of organised crime into the legitimate economy.

Why is this issue – the involvement of criminal groups in the legitimate economy – the most important one for the current debate on organised crime? There are two answers: because of its significant consequences for the economic and social systems, and because of the difficulty of recognising it.

The consequences of criminal infiltration of the legitimate economy are not as obvious as those of homicides, but they are harmful and permanent. They mainly concern the transparency of financial markets and their regulation. The first of these consequences is the distortion of competition rules. The infiltration of a business through employment of a quantity of criminal money is not just a laundering scheme; it is something more important, because the infiltrated business will enjoy the advantages of cash not borrowed on the financial market. That means unfair competition with those businesses that engage in the same activity but bear the costs of loan repayments. Besides this specific consequence there are others related to the infiltration process that may be summarised as follows.

First, the multiplier effect on crime that a criminal organisation generates on entering the legitimate business and conducting relations with other entrepreneurs, administrators, or politicians. This power easily leads to fraud and the corruption of public officials and law enforcement officers; offences frequently associated with the violation of fiscal, employment and environmental regulations.

Second, the harm which society suffers from the infiltration of organised crime. It is difficult to quantify this harm. Attempts have been made by considering the presence of organised crime as a factor that deteriorates some social and economic aspects of the society such as employment, prices, and others (Wharton Econometric Forecasting Associates Inc., 1986).

As regards the identification of this phenomenon, the book defines the infiltration of organised crime in the legitimate economy as a process that moves through several steps. Some of these steps are recognisable from what this book defines as *sentinel crimes*. These are the crimes that most often occur and facilitate this process: for example, extortion, corruption, and money laundering, frequently associated with other offences and violations. These steps change according to the legal framework, the size of enterprises, their business activities, and the different legitimate managerial practices that occur under different economic, social and political conditions. All these variables define the skeleton of the infiltration process.

These various elements also explain why the criminal infiltration process is difficult to interrupt and dismantle: because of its complexity and low recognisability. This complexity constitutes a major challenge for researchers and investigators. Their action is preliminary to another challenge: finding effective remedies that reduce the infiltration risk and maintain the regulation of legitimate enterprises efficiently. The risk that controls on the infiltration process may reduce the efficiency of the business system is real.

The main questions are the following: How to determine that infiltration is occurring or has occurred? How to interrupt and dismantle it? What policies should be adopted to facilitate the understanding and dismantling of this phenomenon?

The first of these questions receives partial answers in this book. Further research is needed to gain better understanding of the risk factors related to the infiltration process. The second question refers to law enforcement and its capacity to recognise the process, detect the crimes committed, and identify the perpetrators and their relationships. The third question relates to the first two: the better the understanding of the risk factors, the more investigative activity will be able to recognise it, with the consequence that more information is provided to policy makers to develop more effective policies.

The chapters of this book may provide the reader with some answers to the above questions. Given the heterogeneity of the infiltration phenomenon and in the absence of systematic data, the case studies approach used in this book seems to be the one most productive of information.

Two introductory chapters presenting the problem of infiltration and the relations of the criminal world with the legitimate one are followed by three sections in which the infiltration process is classified according to the goals pursued by criminals. The main question addressed is this: *Why do criminals infiltrate legitimate businesses?* The answers are these: to facilitate illicit trafficking, to develop fraud schemes, to control the territory, and to influence policy makers. They pertain to the experience of specific countries but they could be extended to others and be informative, even if partial. The book concludes with suggestions for further research and emphasis on the need for better policies.

References

Bell, D. (1953). Crime as an American way of life. *The Antioch Review*, *13*(2), 131–154.

Smith, D. C. (1980). Paragons, pariahs, and pirates: A spectrum-based theory of enterprise. *Crime & Delinquency*, *26*(3), 358–386.

Wharton Econometric Forecasting Associates Inc. (1986). *The impact: Organized crime today*. Washington, DC: President's Commission on Organized Crime.

1 Organised criminals and the legal economy

Giulia Berlusconi

The relationship between organised crime and the legal economy

The complex relationship between organised crime groups and the legal economy has been discussed by several authors (Anderson, 1979; Arlacchi, 1983, 2007; Catanzaro, 1986, 1988; Cressey, 1969; Fiorentini & Peltzman, 1995; Ianni & Reuss-Ianni, 1972).

Some authors argue that criminal organisations need to engage in legal activities because investment opportunities in the illegal markets are insufficient to reinvest the money accumulated with illicit activities. After a portion of the profits has been allocated to the organisation's management costs, investment in other illegal activities is usually the first option for criminals (Barresi, 1999; Ruggiero, 1996, 2010). However, investment opportunities in illegal markets may be insufficient. Criminal organisations thus need to diversify their investments by engaging in legal activities, and the proceeds of illegal activities are laundered through investments in the legal economy (Catanzaro, 1988; Centorrino & Signorino, 1997).

Other authors suggest that infiltration of the legal economy is a constant feature of criminal organisations that diversify their investments between legal and illegal markets. Therefore, infiltration in the legal economy is not conditional upon a sufficient accumulation of profits from illegal activities; rather, it is a typical feature of organised crime (Fantò, 1999; Santino, 2006). Criminal organisations launder money of illicit origin, and they also reinvest money which has already been laundered. Once the money has been invested in the legal economy, organised crime groups act like other entrepreneurs by complying with the normal market rules (Edelhertz & Overcast, 1994).

The first interpretation is in favour of a chronological nexus between the presence of criminal organisations in illegal and legal markets, whereas the second interpretation envisages a two-way process. The literature suggests that the legal and illegal economy cannot be clearly separated. In fact, economic activities are distributed along a continuum whose extremes are criminal activities and completely legal ones (Ruggiero, 2008; Smith, 1975, 1980). Between these two extremes lie several other possible ways in which organised criminals engage in activities that are formally legal yet organised and managed illegally. The legal sectors in which criminal entrepreneurs operate, together with illegal activities, define the criminal economy as a whole (Becchi & Rey, 1994).

The organised crime and money laundering literature provides insights into the relationship between criminal organisations and the legal economy (e.g. Savona & Riccardi, 2015; van Duyne, von Lampe, van Dijck & Newell, 2005). These studies concern the complex relationship between legal and illegal markets, and the investments by criminal organisations in the legitimate economy. Attention has recently also been paid to infiltration by organised crime groups of legal businesses. Some scholars have focused on legal businesses and their exploitation by criminal organisations. This entails examining the drivers of – or the reasons for – infiltration, the locations and business sectors of the businesses targeted, the process of infiltration, and the strategies used to control and manage infiltrated businesses (Savona & Berlusconi, 2015).

Organised crime and legal businesses

The relationship between organised crime groups and legal businesses is a complex one. The involvement of organised criminals in the management of a legal company may vary; and the same applies to the level of direct control exercised over the business. On the one hand, legal businesses may be owned and directly managed by criminal entrepreneurs. On the other hand, organised criminals may create a partnership with the legal entrepreneur; and illegal and legal capital may coexist in financing the business activities (Di Bono, Cincimino, Riccardi & Berlusconi, 2015; Fantò, 1999; Sarno, 2015).

Legal entrepreneurs may be motivated to cooperate with the criminal organisation by the fear of retaliation; or they may actively decide to take part in illicit activities to obtain economic benefits. The members of the criminal organisation benefit from the relationship with legal entrepreneurs as well. This is particularly the case when the business activity of the criminal group is linked to the activities of the legal company, e.g. in the case of a licensed pharmacy used to sell illegal drugs (Bruinsma, Denkers & Alberts, 2015; Riccardi, Dugato, Polizzotti & Pecile, 2015; Sciarrone, 2009).

Besides passive cooperation motivated by the fear of retaliation, a form of active cooperation may result from an agreement between the legal entrepreneur and the members of a criminal organisation. Organised criminals generally approach collusive entrepreneurs whose businesses are of interest to them, and they offer them an opportunity to expand their businesses and increase the financial rewards. If the business owners consider cooperation with the criminal groups to be convenient, they are likely to facilitate the process of infiltration of their own companies (Berlusconi, 2015; Sciarrone, 2009).

Especially in the case of passive cooperation by the legal entrepreneur, extortion and coercion are typical methods of infiltration in legal markets. However, an analysis of case studies on criminal infiltration in legal businesses has revealed that the use of violence and threats, as well as corruption, is not common and generally involves Italian mafia groups (Savona & Berlusconi, 2015). In most case studies in which legal entrepreneurs are involved, the evidence suggests that they have been either collusive or unaware of the illicit activities conducted by the members of the criminal organisation (Berlusconi, 2015). For instance, Rönnblom, Skinnari and Korsell (2015) report a case in which the organised criminals pretended to acquire a business by signing the documents to change the board members, but never submitted them to the Companies Registration Office. As a consequence, the legal entrepreneur, who was unaware that the property had not been transferred, became a straw man for the criminal organisation in his own company (Berlusconi, 2015; Rönnblom et al., 2015).

An analysis of case studies on infiltrated businesses in Europe has shown that targeting businesses in economic difficulties facilitates the infiltration process, since the owners of the companies are eager to sell their shares before leading their business to bankruptcy (Berlusconi, 2015). Usury also multiplies the opportunities to infiltrate the private sector (Bertoni & Rossi, 1997). The lack of regulation of the financial system that provides an early warning system, low capitalisation of family-run companies, and the segmentation of the credit market are factors that make businesses with certain characteristics more vulnerable to financial crises and, therefore, vulnerable to organised crime. These companies are mainly small traders and service companies, craftsmen and small family firms (Bertoni & Rossi, 1997).

When these businesses are unable to obtain bank loans and are therefore in financial difficulties, criminal organisations may take the place of banks and offer their usurious loans. These loans enable the criminal groups to infiltrate the companies in difficulties until they can take them over (Ciconte, 2008). Despite evidence of the use of violence, threats, extortion or usury, in many cases the infiltration process seems to be quite straightforward in that it involves one member of the criminal group regularly starting a new business or acquiring an already-existing one from a legal entrepreneur. This process can be facilitated in some countries by the scant requirements needed to set up a company or the lack of regulation on the process of acquiring a business (Berlusconi, 2015).

Once infiltrated, businesses can be subject to different types of control and management. Shell companies, whose main purpose is the concealment of illegal activities, often do not perform any kind of productive activity, since the creation of wealth through the production and sale of goods or services is not one of the objectives for which they have been created (Catanzaro, 1988). As a consequence, they are characterised by no or minimum productive activities, which may result in low revenues (Transcrime, 2013). Low profits may also be due to the fact that infiltrated businesses often face economic difficulties, either because of a specific choice by organised criminals to target companies close to bankruptcy or as a consequence of bad management by the members of the criminal group (Di Bono et al., 2015).

Businesses infiltrated in order to commit frauds tend to present low levels of fixed assets, indicating that they are unlikely to invest the capital in buildings, machinery and other means of production (Di Bono et al., 2015; Schneider,

2004; Transcrime, 2013). By contrast, organised criminals prefer high levels of current assets and cash because they help them liquidate the business in the event of a law enforcement investigation and avoid the risk of asset confiscation. Should the criminals be aware of a financial investigation (e.g. thanks to a tip-off or some other disclosure), they may try to sell the company assets before these are seized by the judicial authority, and move the resulting liquidity to safer places (e.g. offshore bank accounts) (Catanzaro, 1988; Di Bono et al., 2015).

Finally, infiltrated companies – and particularly those used to launder the profits of illicit activities – generally show low levels of financial debts, indicating that they do not resort to banks and other financial institutions for loans to finance their activities (Di Bono et al., 2015; Transcrime, 2013). At the same time, criminal groups need to conceal the origin of the money used to finance the infiltrated businesses. Possible options include the creation of complex corporate schemes to account loans as debts towards companies of the same group, or towards subsidiaries, shareholders and parent companies. Debts to suppliers and other debts, in fact, may be used to conceal the injection of illicit proceeds into businesses controlled by criminal groups (Di Bono et al., 2015; Transcrime, 2013).

The drivers of criminal infiltration in legitimate businesses

Organised crime groups are induced to infiltrate legitimate businesses by several drivers. The maximisation of profit can coexist with other drivers, such as political, social and cultural motivations. The objective of organised criminals in the legal economy is, in fact, to maximise the benefits, which include benefits other than economic (Becker, 1968). A recent analysis of case studies on criminal infiltration of legal businesses in five European countries has helped identify several drivers of infiltration, including money laundering, profit through formally legal activities, profit through frauds, and concealment of illegal activities (Savona & Berlusconi, 2015).

Criminal groups may infiltrate legal businesses for more than one reason at a time; and different drivers of infiltration may intersect. For instance, the use of legal businesses to conceal illegal activities may lead criminals to use the same businesses to legitimise illicit profits (Riccardi, 2014; Transcrime, 2013; Wall & Bonino, 2015). A similar variety in the drivers of organised crime infiltration of legal businesses can also be found in the chapters of this book. At the same time, drivers of criminal infiltration are not necessarily all present at the same time; and depending on the specific situation, one may prevail over the others.

Organised crime groups active in the Netherlands, Sweden, and the United Kingdom have been found to infiltrate businesses mainly in order to commit frauds (Bruinsma et al., 2015; Rönnblom et al., 2015; Wall & Bonino, 2015). For instance, Swedish organised criminals use businesses to provide restaurants and small shops with untaxed alcohol and cigarettes. The fact that alcohol and tobacco are subject to excise tax enables large-scale tax fraud when the goods are imported legally and then resold to restaurants and kiosks without paying taxes. Having control over or running a business with a licence to import alcohol or tobacco is thus an opportunity to carry out excise tax fraud (CSD, 2015; Rönnblom et al., 2015).

Most of the Slovenian case studies have concerned legal businesses infiltrated to conceal illegal activities, mainly prostitution. These cases confirm the criminals' interest in bars and night clubs with the purpose to perpetrate forced prostitution. The bars give the outward impression of legitimate businesses providing dance routines for their customers; meanwhile, forced prostitution occurs in the background. Evidence of human trafficking has also been found in connection with the provision of women to be employed in such bars (Meško et al., 2015; see also Chapter 4 in this book). On the contrary, evidence of infiltration to gain social consensus or to control the territory has not been found in Slovenia.

In Italy, some case studies have considered organised crime groups investing in legal business entities in order to maximise their social consensus and to control a particular market of the local economy. Organised criminals may decide to infiltrate businesses operating in sectors that provide goods and services to the population (e.g. education, health care) and create new jobs to promote a respectable image of themselves in contrast with that of mere criminals (Fantò, 1999; Ravenda, Argilés-Bosch & Valencia-Silva, 2015; Sciarrone, 2009). Italian mafias also infiltrate sectors with high territorial specificity (e.g. hotels and restaurants, gas and water supply, construction) to control an area physically and to create strategic collusive relationships with politicians and local entrepreneurs (Giampietri & Sarno, 2015; Riccardi, 2014; see also Chapter 8 in this book).

Organised crime groups may invest money in legal businesses to launder the profits from criminal activities, especially through money service and cash-intensive businesses such as bars and restaurants, and retail trade (Dvoršek, 1995; Meško et al., 2015; Organised Crime Task Force, 2013; Rönnblom et al., 2015; Wall & Bonino, 2015). However, in some countries, such as Slovenia, most organised criminals seem to be minimally involved in money laundering through legal businesses (Meško et al., 2015), confirming that many criminals simply use the profits from illicit activities to fund a lavish lifestyle (van Duyne, 1996).

Criminal groups may have direct or indirect control of the businesses used to launder money (RKP, 2012a). Such businesses may be used by criminals as layers to hide the proceeds of crime and conceal incoming and outgoing illicit flows (Riccardi, 2014). In the case of commercial activities, inflated bills and accounting manipulation may enable criminals to justify the money earned from illicit activities (Becchi & Rey, 1994; Bini, 1997; Gratteri, 2011).

Banks and other financial institutions are required to report suspicious transactions to their country's Fiscal Intelligence Unit (EU Parliament and the Council, 2015). In some countries, the probability of such transactions being reported has increased over the years (Brå, 2011a). As a consequence, the interest of criminal groups has shifted, and currency exchange offices have started to be targeted either by recruiting their employees or by starting new businesses in this sector (Brå, 2008, 2011a, 2011b; EBM, 2013; Noroozi & Lind, 2013; RKP, 2013).

Another driver of criminal infiltration of legal businesses is profit from legal – or formally legal – activities (Garofalo & Berlusconi, 2015; Savona & Berlusconi, 2015). Criminal groups may target legal businesses to acquire their assets, or they may invest in businesses to obtain considerable earnings and benefit from their profitability (Brå, 2012; Rönnblom et al., 2015). Sectors with low levels of technological innovation and professional skills are particularly attractive because of low research and development costs (Becchi & Rey, 1994). Companies active in business sectors characterised by public subsidies and public contracts, such as renewable energy and waste disposal, may also be vulnerable to infiltration by criminals aiming to maximise their profits through formally legal business activities. In fact, criminal groups may use legal businesses to gain public contracts and increase their profits (Fantò, 1999; Meško et al., 2015; Transcrime, 2013).

Unlike shell companies used as covers for illicit activities, these businesses engage in production activities and are profit oriented, although organised criminals often have unrealistic ideas about a company's profitability and underestimate the costs (Becchi & Rey, 1994; Bini, 1997; Brå, 2007, 2012; Catanzaro, 1988; Costantino & Fiandaca, 1986). Legal activities are only formally legal when their profitability is linked to illicit activities such as the discouragement of competition or irregularities in the labour market, e.g. when a company is targeted because it is a business competitor of other infiltrated businesses (Arlacchi, 1983; Brå, 2012).

Legal businesses may also be used by criminal groups to gain profits from, and conceal, illicit activities such as fraud and the trafficking of illegal goods (Rönnblom et al., 2015; Wall & Bonino, 2015). Legal businesses may be facilitators or crucial in committing crimes such as insurance or VAT frauds. In Sweden, cases have been found of social welfare fraud through legitimate companies (Rönnblom et al., 2015; see also Chapter 6 in this book). Legal businesses in the United Kingdom have instead been found to be used mainly to organise and perpetrate crash-for-cash and VAT frauds involving a complex scheme of legal shell companies (Wall & Bonino, 2015; see also Chapter 7 in this book). Organised criminal groups, in fact, may control legal businesses and exploit them to commit various types of corporate fraud (e.g. insurance fraud, insolvency and bankruptcy-related fraud) and fiscal fraud (e.g. VAT and tax fraud, benefit fraud) (Bruinsma et al., 2015; Garofalo & Berlusconi, 2015; Rönnblom et al., 2015; Wall & Bonino, 2015).

Benefit fraud, for instance, is particularly common in countries with advanced social welfare systems that provide a variety of benefits such as sickness and unemployment benefits to employees (Brå, 2011b; ISF, 2011; RKP, 2012b; see also Chapter 6 in this book). In this framework, organised criminals may infiltrate legal businesses in order to receive subsidies from the state to create new job opportunities. Or they may hire employees from among their family members and friends, drive the business into bankruptcy, and have public institutions pay the employees' benefits for the months following the bankruptcy (Rönnblom et al., 2015). Fake documentation such as medical certificates may also be produced by employees with the help of doctors so that they can qualify for sickness benefits and defraud the state (Brå, 2011b).

Furthermore, legal businesses may provide cover for criminal groups' illegal activities (Mills, 2013; Silverstone, 2011; von Lampe, 2006). Organised criminals may use legal businesses to conceal illicit activities such as drug trafficking or prostitution. For instance, the members of a criminal organisation may use the vehicles and storehouses of their transport company to conceal and smuggle illegal goods (Palomo, Márquez & Ruiz, 2015). In particular, transportation companies have proved particularly suitable for hiding the illicit trafficking of drugs (Bruinsma et al., 2015; Ferwerda & Unger, 2015; Palomo et al., 2015; see also Chapters 3 to 5 in this book). Similarly, restaurants may facilitate the sale of untaxed alcohol, and bars and clubs may be used to cover prostitution rings (Brå, 2006; Dvoršek, 1995; Korsell, Skinnari, & Vesterhav, 2009; Meško et al., 2015; see also Chapter 4 in this book).

Bars and cafés, grocery stores, luxury companies, and hairdressing salons are also used as covers for heroin and cocaine dealing and trafficking. Bars can also be used as centres for illegal gambling, whereas clothing companies and shops can become covers for the production and retail of counterfeit goods (Hales & Hobbs, 2010; Meško et al., 2015). Infiltrated businesses may also be exploited to perform transactions which would otherwise be considered suspect and to conceal them as production costs (Anderson, 1979; Fiorentini, 2000).

Cultural and personal reasons may also induce criminal groups to infiltrate legal businesses, and they may influence the choice of the business sector (Garofalo & Berlusconi, 2015; Savona & Riccardi, 2015; Transcrime, 2013). Criminals may invest in certain businesses because they are close to their culture, education background or family tradition. This may explain, for instance, the infiltration of vehicle repair garages, sex shops and tattoo parlours by some Nordic motorcycle gangs (Petrell & Houtsonen, 2015a; see also Chapter 10 in this book) or the acquisition of companies engaged in the wholesale of typical local food products by Camorra groups (Riccardi, 2014).

Criminal groups may infiltrate legal companies to create new jobs and to assign subcontracts to other enterprises, thus maximising their social consensus (Arlacchi, 2007; Becchi & Rey, 1994; Bini, 1997; Fantò, 1999). Mafia organisations are particularly interested in obtaining social consensus from the local population. They consequently seek to infiltrate strategic sectors such as education and health care. For the same reason, these groups may also target labour-intensive and territorial-specific business sectors to create new jobs (Fantò, 1999; Ravenda et al., 2015; Sciarrone, 2009). The improper use of legal businesses to create employment for friends or relatives, however, is not restricted to Italian mafias. A Swedish study found cases of criminals being hired by a business and receiving a salary after threatening the owner (Brå, 2012).

The use of legal businesses to maximise social consensus may also help criminals gain status within both the legal and the criminal spheres. Indeed, running or controlling a legal company may legitimise a person as a legal entrepreneur rather than a criminal, thus strengthening his influence over the community (Brå,

2007, 2012). Running a legal company in certain business sectors may also be positively regarded by criminals. This is the case, for instance, of restaurants, which can be used by organised criminals to meet co-offenders to plan future operations and to cover illicit activities (Brå, 2007; Korsell et al., 2009; Rönn-blom et al., 2015; Transcrime, 2013).

There is also evidence of organised crime infiltration of legal businesses to control the territory and exert influence over policymakers. This is particularly the case in Italy (Giampietri & Sarno, 2015; see also Chapter 8 in this book), whereas other countries seem to be characterised by a variety of criminal actors targeting diverse sectors to meet varying needs (Petrell & Houtsonen, 2015b; Riccardi & Salha, 2015; see also Chapters 9 and 10 in this book). Criminal organisations may aim to achieve control over a particular sector of the local economy through participation in legal market activities, e.g. by infiltrating the public construction industry and manipulating subcontracts (Fantò, 1999; Savona, 2010). Mafia organisations typically aim to control a portion of the territory, especially when they operate in regions with a traditional mafia presence. The control of the territory can be achieved by infiltrating the legal economy in sectors with a high territorial specificity – e.g. construction, hotels and restaurants – and fostering collusive relationships with local administrators and politicians (Berlusconi, 2014; Riccardi, 2014).

A recent study on criminal infiltration of legal businesses in Sweden (Rönn-blom et al., 2015) has found that the drivers of infiltration also include acquiring status within the criminal or legal sphere, and gaining access to stolen or illicit goods markets. The former is linked with social consensus.

The distinction among different drivers of criminal infiltration of legal businesses is useful for analytical purposes. However, it does not imply that criminal organisations infiltrate legal businesses to fulfil one driver at a time. For instance, the same infiltrated business may be used to launder the profits from illicit activities and earn revenues from legal activities (Anderson, 1979; Fantò, 1999; Fiorentini, 2000). Furthermore, these drivers constitute the reasons why organised crime groups may infiltrate legal businesses. The choice of a particular territory and business sector, as well as the business to be targeted, are influenced by both their characteristics and the drivers of infiltration (Garofalo & Berlusconi, 2015).

This book collects current knowledge on organised crime infiltration of legitimate businesses in eight European countries: Finland, France, Italy, the Netherlands, Slovenia, Spain, Sweden, and the United Kingdom. For each country, it focuses on specific drivers of infiltration, identifying the territories and business sectors targeted by criminal groups, and their vulnerabilities to infiltration. The structure of the book reflects the variety of drivers of infiltration. The book is in fact divided into four parts, three of which present current knowledge on criminal infiltration of the legal economy in eight European countries. On the basis of the information collected for each country, Chapters 11 and 12 discuss the development of a methodology to measure the impact of infiltration on the European legitimate economy and to assess the risk of infiltration across territories and business sectors, respectively.

References

Anderson, A. G. (1979). *The business of organized crime: A Cosa Nostra family*. Stanford: Hoover Institute Press.

Arlacchi, P. (1983). *La mafia imprenditrice. L'etica mafiosa e lo spirito del capitalismo*. Bologna: Il Mulino.

Arlacchi, P. (2007). *La mafia imprenditrice. Dalla Calabria al centro dell'inferno*. Milano: Il Saggiatore.

Barresi, F. (1999). *Mafia ed economia criminale. Analisi socio-criminologica e giuridica di un'economia sommersa e dei danni arrecati all'economia legale*. Roma: EdUP.

Becchi, A., & Rey, G. M. (1994). *L'economia criminale*. Roma: Laterza.

Becker, G. S. (1968). Crime and punishment: An economic approach. *Journal of Political Economy, 76*(2), 169–217.

Berlusconi, G. (2014). Italian mafia. In G. Bruinsma & D. Weisburd (Eds.), *Encyclopedia of criminology and criminal justice* (pp. 2699–2706). New York, NY: Springer.

Berlusconi, G. (2015). The step-by-step process of infiltration. In E. U. Savona & G. Berlusconi (Eds.), *Organised crime infiltration of legitimate businesses in Europe: A pilot project in five European countries* (pp. 83–89). Trento: Transcrime – Università degli Studi di Trento.

Bertoni, A., & Rossi, E. (1997). I rapporti tra impresa criminale e l'economia legale di riferimento. La gestione del patrimonio cumulato con attività criminose. In A. Bertoni (Ed.), *La criminalità come impresa*. Milano: EGEA.

Bini, M. (1997). Il polimorfismo dell'impresa criminale. In A. Bertoni (Ed.), *La criminalità come impresa*. Milano: EGEA.

Brå. (2006). *Häleri. Den organiserade brottslighetens möte med den legala marknaden* (No. 2006:6). Stockholm: Brottsförebyggande rådet.

Brå. (2007). *Vart tog alla pengarna vägen? En studie av narkotikabrottslighetens ekonomihantering* (No. 2007:4). Stockholm: Brottsförebyggande rådet.

Brå. (2008). *Slutrapport: RPE Servicefunktioner, ett kontroll och kartläggningsprojekt* (No. 2008:2). Stockholm: Brottsförebyggande rådet.

Brå. (2011a). *Penningtvätt. Rapportering och hantering av misstänkta transaktioner* (No. 2011:4). Stockholm: Brottsförebyggande rådet.

Brå. (2011b). *Storskaliga skattebrott. En kartläggning av skattebrottslingens kostnader* (No. 2011:7). Stockholm: Brottsförebyggande rådet.

Brå. (2012). *Otillåten påverkan mot företag. En undersökning om utpressning* (No. 2012:12). Stockholm: Brottsförebyggande rådet.

Bruinsma, G., Denkers, A., & Alberts, S. (2015). The Netherlands. In E. U. Savona & G. Berlusconi (Eds.), *Organised crime infiltration of legitimate businesses in Europe: A pilot project in five European countries* (pp. 45–49). Trento: Transcrime – Università degli Studi di Trento.

Catanzaro, R. (1986). Impresa mafiosa, economia e sistemi di regolazione sociale: Appunti sul caso siciliano. In G. Fiandaca & S. Costantino (Eds.), *La legge antimafia tre anni dopo. Bilancio di un'esperienza applicative* (pp. 177–194). Milano: Franco Angeli.

Catanzaro, R. (1988). *Il delitto come impresa. Storia sociale della mafia*. Padova: Liviana.

Centorrino, M., & Signorino, G. (Eds.). (1997). *Macroeconomia della mafia*. Roma: La Nuova Italia Scientifica.

Ciconte, E. (2008). *'Ndrangheta*. Soveria Mannelli: Rubbettino.

Costantino, S., & Fiandaca, G. (Eds.). (1986). *La legge antimafia tre anni dopo. Bilancio di un'esperienza applicativa*. Milano: Franco Angeli.

Cressey, D. R. (1969). *Theft of the nation: The structure and operations of organized crime in America*. New York, NY: Harper and Row.

CSD. (2015). *Financing of organised crime*. Sofia: Center for the Study of Democracy. Retrieved from www.csd.bg/artShow.php?id=17368.

Di Bono, L., Cincimino, S., Riccardi, M., & Berlusconi, G. (2015). Management strategies of infiltrated businesses. In E. U. Savona & G. Berlusconi (Eds.), *Organized crime infiltration of legitimate businesses in Europe: A pilot project in five European countries* (pp. 102–112). Trento: Transcrime – Università degli Studi di Trento.

Dvoršek, A. (1995). Organizirani kriminal v Sloveniji. *Zbornik Strokovno Znanstvenih Razprav, XVIII*, 146–152.

EBM. (2013). *Ekobrottsmyndighetens lägesbild 2013*. Stockholm: Ekobrottsmyndigheten.

Edelhertz, H., & Overcast, T. D. (1994). *The business of organized crime: An assessment of organized crime business-type activities and their implications for law ernforcement*. Loomis, CA: Palmer Press.

EU Parliament and the Council. (2015). Directive on the prevention of the use of the financial system for the purposes of money laundering or terrorist financing, Pub. L. No. 2015/849 (2015).

Fantò, E. (1999). *L'impresa a partecipazione mafiosa. Economia legale ed economia criminale*. Bari: Edizioni Dedalo.

Ferwerda, J., & Unger, B. (2015). Organised crime investments in the Netherlands. In E. U. Savona & M. Riccardi (Eds.), *From illegal markets to legitimate businesses: The portfolio of organised crime in Europe* (pp. 196–201). Trento: Transcrime – Università degli Studi di Trento.

Fiorentini, G. (2000). Organized crime and illegal markets. In B. Bouckaert & G. De Geest (Eds.), *Encyclopedia of law & economics* (Vol. 5). Cheltenham: Edward Elgar Publishing.

Fiorentini, G., & Peltzman, S. (1995). *The economics of organised crime*. Cambridge: Cambridge University Press – CEPR.

Garofalo, L., & Berlusconi, G. (2015). Drivers of infiltration. In E. U. Savona & G. Berlusconi (Eds.), *Organised crime infiltration of legitimate businesses in Europe: A pilot project in five European countries* (pp. 78–82). Trento: Transcrime – Università degli Studi di Trento.

Giampietri, V., & Sarno, F. (2015). Italy. In E. U. Savona & G. Berlusconi, *Organised crime infiltration of legitimate businesses in Europe: A pilot project in five European countries* (pp. 37–44). Trento: Transcrime – Università degli Studi di Trento.

Gratteri, N. (2011). Scuola 'Ndrangheta. In S. Danna (Ed.), *Prodotto interno mafia. Così la criminalità organizzata è diventata il sistema Italia* (pp. 43–71). Torino: Einaudi.

Hales, G., & Hobbs, R. (2010). Drug markets in the community: A London borough case study. *Trends in Organized Crime, 13*(1), 13–30.

Ianni, F. A. J., & Reuss-Ianni, E. (1972). *A family business: Kinship and social control in organized crime*. New York, NY: Russell Sage Foundation.

ISF. (2011). *Bidragsbrott och skattebrott. Välfärdens dubbla kriminalitet* (No. 2011:12). Stockholm: Inspektionen för socialförsäkringen & Brottsförebyggande rådet.

Korsell, L., Skinnari, J., & Vesterhav, D. (2009). *Organiserad brottslighet i Sverige*. Stockholm: Liber.

Meško, G., Sotlar, A., Dobovšek, B., Eman, K., Modic, M., Ažman, B., & Slak, B. (2015). Slovenia. In E. U. Savona & G. Berlusconi (Eds.), *Organised crime infiltration* of legitimate businesses in Europe: A pilot project in five European countries (pp. 50–56). Trento: Transcrime – Università degli Studi di Trento.

Mills, C. (2013). *Waste system open to organised crime. Report into Derry dumping.* Belfast: Northern Ireland Environment Agency.

Noroozi, E., & Lind, K. (2013, 1 September). Organiserad brottslighet på växlingskontoren. *SR P4 Nyheter*. Retrieved from http://sverigesradio.se/sida/artikel.aspx?programid=96&artikel=5403002.

Organised Crime Task Force. (2013). *Annual Report & Threat Assessment: Organised crime in Northern Ireland.* Belfast: Department of Justice.

Palomo, J., Márquez, J., & Ruiz, N. (2015). Organised crime investments in Spain. In E. U. Savona & M. Riccardi (Eds.), *From illegal markets to legitimate businesses: The portfolio of organised crime in Europe* (pp. 202–209). Trento: Transcrime – Università degli Studi di Trento.

Petrell, S., & Houtsonen, J. (2015a). Finland. In E. U. Savona & M. Riccardi (Eds.), *From illegal markets to legitimate businesses: The portfolio of organised crime in Europe* (pp. 166–171). Trento: Transcrime – Università degli Studi di Trento.

Petrell, S., & Houtsonen, J. (2015b). Organised crime groups in Finland. In E. U. Savona & M. Riccardi (Eds.), *From illegal markets to legitimate businesses: The portfolio of organised crime in Europe* (pp. 95–100). Trento: Transcrime – Università degli Studi di Trento.

Ravenda, D., Argilés-Bosch, J. M., & Valencia-Silva, M. M. (2015). Detection model of legally registered mafia firms in Italy. *European Management Review*, *12*(1), 23–29.

Riccardi, M. (2014). When criminals invest in businesses: Are we looking in the right direction? An exploratory analysis of companies controlled by mafias. In S. Caneppele & F. Calderoni (Eds.), *Organized crime, corruption and crime prevention* (pp. 197–206). New York, NY: Springer.

Riccardi, M., Dugato, M., Polizzotti, M., & Pecile, V. (2015). *The theft of medicines from Italian hospitals, Transcrime Research in Brief – N.2/2015.* Trento: Transcrime – Joint Research Centre on Transnational Crime.

Riccardi, M., & Salha, A. (2015). Organised crime groups in France. In E. U. Savona & M. Riccardi (Eds.), *From illegal markets to legitimate businesses: The portfolio of organised crime in Europe* (pp. 101–106). Trento: Transcrime – Università degli Studi di Trento.

RKP. (2012a). *Finanspolisens årsrapport 2011* (No. 1). Stockholm: Rikskriminalpolisen.

RKP. (2012b). *Polisens lägesbild av organiserad brottslighet 2012* (No. 2). Stockholm: Rikskriminalpolisen.

RKP. (2013). *Finanspolisens årsrapport 2012.* Stockholm: Rikskriminalpolisen.

Rönnblom, H., Skinnari, J., & Korsell, L. (2015). Sweden. In E. U. Savona & G. Berlusconi (Eds.), *Organised crime infiltration of legitimate businesses in Europe: A pilot project in five European countries* (pp. 57–67). Trento: Transcrime – Università degli Studi di Trento.

Ruggiero, V. (1996). *Economie sporche: L'impresa criminale in Europa.* Torino: Bollati Boringhieri.

Ruggiero, V. (2008). 'E' l'economia, stupido!' Una classificazione dei crimini di potere. *Questione Giustizia*, *3*, 188–208.

Ruggiero, V. (2010). Organized crime: Between the informal and the formal economy. *Global Consortium on Security Transformation*, *4*, 1–33.

Santino, U. (2006). *Dalla mafia alle mafie: scienze sociali e crimine organizzato.* Soveria Mannelli: Rubbettino.

Sarno, F. (2015). Control strategies of infiltrated businesses. In E. U. Savona & G. Berlusconi (Eds.), *Organised crime infiltration of legitimate businesses in Europe: A pilot project in five European countries* (pp. 90–101). Trento: Transcrime – Università degli Studi di Trento.

Savona, E. U. (2010). Infiltration of the public construction industry by Italian organised crime. In K. Bullock, R. V. Clarke, & N. Tilley (Eds.), *Situational prevention of organized crimes* (pp. 130–150). Cullompton: Willan Publishing.

Savona, E. U., & Berlusconi, G. (Eds.). (2015). *Organised crime infiltration of legitimate businesses in Europe: A pilot project in five European countries*. Trento: Transcrime – Università degli Studi di Trento.

Savona, E. U., & Riccardi, M. (Eds.). (2015). *From illegal markets to legitimate businesses: The portfolio of organised crime in Europe*. Trento: Transcrime – Università degli Studi di Trento.

Schneider, S. (2004). The incorporation and operation of criminally controlled companies in Canada. *Journal of Money Laundering Control, 7*(2), 126–138.

Sciarrone, R. (2009). *Mafie vecchie, mafie nuove: Radicamento ed espansione*. Roma: Donzelli.

Silverstone, D. (2011). From Triads to snakeheads: Organised crime and illegal migration within Britain's Chinese community. *Global Crime, 12*(2), 93–111.

Smith, D. C. (1975). *The mafia mystique*. New York, NY: Basic Books.

Smith, D. C. (1980). Paragons, pariahs, and pirates: A spectrum-based theory of enterprise. *Crime & Delinquency, 26*(3), 358–386.

Transcrime. (2013). *Progetto PON Sicurezza 2007–2013. Gli investimenti delle mafie*. Milano: Transcrime – Joint Research Centre on Transnational Crime.

van Duyne, P. C. (1996). *Organized crime in Europe*. Commack, NY: Nova Science Publishers.

van Duyne, P. C., von Lampe, K., van Dijck, M., & Newell, J. L. (Eds.). (2005). *The organised crime economy: Managing crime markets in Europe*. Nijmegen: Wolf Legal Publishers.

von Lampe, K. (2006). The cigarette black market in Germany and in the United Kingdom. *Journal of Financial Crime, 13*(2), 235–254.

Wall, D., & Bonino, S. (2015). United Kingdom. In E. U. Savona & G. Berlusconi (Eds.), *Organised crime infiltration of legitimate businesses in Europe: A pilot project in five European countries* (pp. 67–74). Trento: Transcrime – Università degli Studi di Trento.

2 Measuring organised crime infiltration in legal businesses

Michele Riccardi and Giulia Berlusconi

Measuring organised crime infiltration in legal businesses requires addressing several issues. Building on Black, Vander Beken and De Ruyver (2000) and von Lampe (2004), three methodological steps can be identified. First, key concepts – the notion of *organised crime* and that of *infiltration* – must be defined and specified through a set of inclusion rules. Second, key concepts must be operationalised into variables to be used for their measurement. Third, the variables must be linked to available empirical data. This chapter first discusses the challenges in defining, operationalising and measuring *organised crime* (hereafter OC); it then focuses on how to define and operationalise *infiltration* in legitimate businesses. It describes the strengths and weaknesses of existing measures and explores further directions in terms of research and data collection.

Defining and measuring organised crime

Defining organised crime

One of the main issues in organised crime research is the lack of a common definition, together with the complexity of the phenomenon to be described (von Lampe, 2004). Many definitions have been developed by international organisations, law enforcement agencies and scholars (Adamoli, Di Nicola, Savona & Zoffi, 1998; Albanese, 2000; Finckenauer, 2005; Hagan, 2006; Kenney & Finckenauer, 1995; van Dijk, 2007). However, there is no agreed-upon definition of what organised crime is (van Duyne & van Dijck, 2007).

The design of empirical or operational definitions requires determining what should be included in the measurement and what should be excluded: in other words, identifying the unit of measurement. Counting units include either activities or actors (van Duyne & van Dijck, 2007). The former approach focuses on certain types of criminal activities and illegal markets; the latter on the criminal groups active in those markets (Paoli, 2002; von Lampe, 2004). As a consequence, some studies measure groups, whereas others measure activities (Zoutendijk, 2010). Albanese (2008), for instance, proposed a model to assess the risk of organised crime in a given area, and he treated illicit markets as units of analysis. He argued that, if illegal activities are properly assessed and ranked, targeting these activities will make it possible to tackle the high-risk organised crime groups involved.

The recent EU-funded OCP and ARIEL rescarch projects (Savona & Riccardi, 2015; Savona & Berlusconi, 2015),[1] which analysed organised crime investments and infiltration in the European economy, adopted a 'mixed' approach which considered both the actors and the illicit activities in which they were involved. Building on Europol SOCTA 2013 (Europol, 2013), the projects defined an organised crime group as:

> any criminal actor – from large organisations to loose networks of collaborating criminals – that falls under the definition provided by the EU Framework Decision on the Fight against Organised Crime (2008/841/JHA)[2] and/ or is involved in serious crimes as identified by art. 83(1) of the Treaty on the Functioning of the European Union.[3]
>
> (Savona & Riccardi, 2015; Savona & Berlusconi, 2015)

Such broad definitions of organised crime have been criticised for their vagueness (Calderoni, 2008; Finckenauer, 2005; Hagan, 2006; Maltz, 1996; von Lampe, 2004; Zoutendijk, 2010). However, they make it possible to include a variety of criminal organisations and actors, not just crime syndicates, and to take account of the differences among European countries, also in terms of organised crime legislation (Savona & Riccardi, 2015; Savona & Berlusconi, 2015; von Lampe, 2004).

Measuring organised crime

Despite the challenges in defining and operationalising key concepts, in recent years numerous exercises have been conducted to measure organised crime at local, national and international level. Measuring organised crime has manifold benefits. It helps to understand the scope of the problem within and across territories, thus facilitating the allocation of resources and priorities for interventions. In the case of repeated measures over time, it also makes it possible to identify trends and to evaluate the effectiveness of countermeasures (von Lampe, 2004).

Most attempts to measure organised crime are made by governments and law enforcement agencies, rather than scholars (von Lampe, 2004). The first exercises were annual situation reports on organised crime, such as the one published by the German federal police agency Bundeskriminalamt (BKA) since 1992 (Zoutendijk, 2010). These reports are based on information on ongoing criminal investigations, and they provide details on organised crime cases, the types of offences, the offenders (e.g. their nationality), and the estimated profits (von Lampe, 2004).

Over the years, there has been a shift from the measurement of organised crime to the assessment of its *threat*. In threat assessments, the nature and the extent (seriousness) of a phenomenon, not just its presence, must be evaluated (van Duyne & van Dijck, 2007; van Duyne, 2006). Organised crime threat assessments (OCTA) have been released by several agencies including Europol (Europol, 2013, 2011, 2009), the Dutch National Police Intelligence Service (IPOL, 2014), and the UK Serious and Organised Crime Agency (National Crime Agency, 2014). However, these studies have been criticised by some scholars because they lack common definitions (von Lampe, 2004) or because they do not meet the requirements of reliability and validity (Zoutendijk, 2010). This also applies to the limited number of academic studies in this field (e.g. Albanese, 2001; Vander Beken, 2004) because also in this case definitions of key concepts are missing or operational definitions are too vague (Zoutendijk, 2010).

In order to take full account of the complexity of the phenomenon, some authors (Savona, Dugato & Garofalo, 2012; Dugato, De Simoni & Savona, 2014) have proposed measures of organised crime which consider not only dimensions related to its activity (e.g. groups and illegal activities) but also the enablers that facilitate or impede such activity, and the responses by the state and civil society. For each dimension, several variables have been identified to create composite indicators of the presence of organised crime groups in a given territory (Dugato et al., 2014). Yet these scholars, rather than measuring organised crime, have assessed its *risk*. Adopting the taxonomy proposed by the Financial Action Task Force for money laundering risk assessment (FATF, 2013), they have focused not only on the *threat* (organised crime itself) but also on the contextual *vulnerabilities* and, to a lesser extent, on their *consequences* (or impact) on society and the economy. Another example in this regard is the risk-based methodology developed by the Ghent University Crime Research Group, which was conceived as an improvement of the Belgian Annual Report on Organised Crime (Black et al., 2000). This method also considers the environmental factors related to organised crime (e.g. socio-economic and political factors), and identifies their impact on the likelihood of threat and potential harm.

Composite indicators, such as the one developed by Dugato et al. (2014), are increasingly used by scholars and law enforcement agencies to measure organised crime. In 2013 Transcrime developed the 'Mafia Presence Index' (now under update) to assess, through proxies like mafia homicides and confiscated assets, the presence of mafia groups across Italian provinces (Calderoni, 2014; Transcrime, 2013). Similarly, van Dijk (2007) measured the level of organised crime across countries through the so-called 'Composite Organized Crime Index', which combined data on the perceived prevalence of organised crime in the country, instrumental violence, grand corruption, money laundering, and black economy.

Defining and measuring infiltration in legal businesses

Defining and operationalising infiltration

After defining and operationalising the concept of organised crime, it is necessary to specify the notion of *infiltration*. In most European countries criminal infiltration of legal businesses is not criminalised per se. Therefore, neither legal definitions of the phenomenon nor police or judicial data are available. Infiltration is not an individual offence, but rather a process encompassing a range of offences: for example, corruption of public officials, money laundering, intimidation and extortion of entrepreneurs or market abuse infractions. These *sentinel crimes* are not always present at the same time; they may occur at different stages of the infiltration process and may vary across time and places. Police or judicial data are usually available on sentinel crimes, but recombining them into single cases of infiltration is very difficult – and meaningless without a script of the infiltration mechanism.

One of the first attempts to define and schematise the process of organised crime infiltration in legitimate businesses was made by Savona and Berlusconi (2015) for the ARIEL project. They defined it as 'any case in which a natural person belonging to a criminal organisation or acting on its behalf, or an already infiltrated legal person, invests financial and/or human resources to participate in the decision-making process of a legitimate business' (Savona & Berlusconi, 2015, p. 19). The definition comprises four elements: a criminal organisation; a natural person belonging to a criminal organisation or acting on its behalf, or an already infiltrated legal person; the investment of financial and/or human resources; participation in the decision-making process of a legitimate business.

The first element is a criminal organisation. As mentioned, the authors built on the definition of organised crime adopted by Europol (2013) and also used by Savona and Riccardi (2015) in their study of the economics of OC in Europe (project OCP). The second element is the presence of a natural person belonging to a criminal organisation or acting on its behalf, or an already infiltrated legal person. The literature usually considers criminal organisations as collective bodies which take decisions (including investment choices) as a whole. Nevertheless, infiltration of legitimate businesses is carried out by individuals (or groups) who are members of the organisation or act as figureheads (e.g. relatives, lawyers, professionals) (Berlusconi, 2015; Levi, 2015; Sarno, 2015; Transcrime, 2013). It is not always possible to distinguish between cases of infiltration driven by personal motives and those dictated by the criminal group's strategy (Savona & Riccardi, 2015), although it is proven that the selection of sectors, territories and legal forms of investment may vary widely across different groups within the same organisation (Riccardi, 2014b; Transcrime, 2013). In some cases, infiltration is committed by another legal person (e.g. company, cooperative, foundation) already controlled by the criminal organisation or some of its members, and often employed as an additional *layer* to conceal the criminal beneficial ownership (Berlusconi, 2015; Sarno, 2015; Riccardi, Soriani & Standridge, 2015).

The third element concerns the technique of infiltration. Financial investment (such as acquisition of a share of the equity) is not an essential requirement because legitimate businesses can be infiltrated also by employing human resources, for example by appointing a member of the criminal organisation as company director or administrator in order to participate in (and eventually acquire control of) the business management. Criminals may rely on even more indirect strategies to influence legal entrepreneurs or managers and supervisors employed by a legal business: for example, violence and intimidation, extortion racketeering, or even usury. In this last case, the entrepreneurs resorting to criminal loans often abandon control of the business to their criminal financiers.

The fourth element that identifies criminal infiltration is participation in the decision-making process of the legitimate business. Organised crime, through a member, a straw man, or another legal person, is able to influence decisions on business strategies and future investments, as well as hiring, promotions and salary increases, subcontracting and supply contracts, security and controls. The influence over the decision-making process can be exerted through ownership of (a percentage of) the shares and/or control over the management. The control can be exercised by a member of the criminal organisation (internal direct control), a straw man acting on behalf of the organisation or an already infiltrated legal business (internal indirect control), or through intimidation, violence, or corruption of a manager or a supervisor employed by the business (external control). Cases of internal and external control over the management can be extended to include low-level employees, provided that the employee takes decisions on hiring and promotions, subcontracting and supply contracts, or security and controls, even at the local unit level.

Infiltration vs. investment vs. money laundering

The concept of organised crime infiltration in part overlaps with the concept of organised crime *investment*, which is in turn related to the notion of money laundering. However, some differences can be identified, and they are now discussed.

In recent years, numerous studies (some gathered in this book) have analysed the so-called *portfolio* of investments of organised crime in various countries (see Levi, 2015 for a review): in Italy (Dugato, Giommoni & Favarin, 2015; Riccardi, 2014b; Transcrime, 2013), in the Netherlands (Ferwerda & Unger, 2015; Kruisbergen, Kleemans & Kouwenberg, 2015), in Spain (Palomo, Márquez & Ruiz, 2015; Steinko, 2012), in France (Riccardi & Salha, 2015), in Ireland (Soriani, 2015), in Finland (Petrell & Houtsonen, 2015), in Bulgaria (CSD, 2012) and at European level (Savona & Riccardi, 2015). The definition of 'investment' adopted by most of these studies is sufficiently broad to encompass

> any possession and/or acquisition of any type of asset in the legal economy (e.g. movable goods, registered assets, real estate properties, companies or their shares) by individuals belonging to a criminal group, acting on its behalf and/or involved in one of the criminal activities previously identified.
> (Savona & Riccardi, 2015, p. 26)

The first difference refers to the nature of the 'target': while organised crime investments may concern assets of any kind (e.g. real estate properties, cars, vehicles, jewels, bonds, and other movable assets), infiltration concerns only businesses of any type (from individual enterprises to limited companies, also including those listed on the stock exchange) operating in any type of business sector.[4] The second difference regards the *modus operandi*, i.e. the type of resource employed: while, as said, infiltration can exploit both financial and/or human resources, and does not necessarily lead to ownership of a (share of) the company, investments usually rely on the employment of monetary resources and imply the acquisition/possession of the asset (Savona & Riccardi, 2015).

It should be noted that in the cases of both organised crime *investment* and *infiltration*, when financial resources are employed, it is not always possible to identify the origin of the capital: it may be 'dirty' money (i.e. proceeds of illicit activities carried out by the criminal organisation or some of its members), laundered money (i.e. the proceeds of illicit activities carried out by the criminal organisation that have already been laundered before the investment) or 'clean' money (i.e. the proceeds of, at least formally, licit activities carried out by the criminal organisation or by some of its members, e.g. profits from other legal businesses or the gain from the sale of an inherited property).

The latter represents the main difference between investments and infiltration, on the one hand, and money laundering on the other. Criminals laundering money employ, by definition, 'dirty' capital. It is the result of a predicate offence, and it passes through a not necessarily sophisticated process – the *placement*, *layering* and *integration* scheme as defined by Reuter and Truman (2004) – in order to be enjoyed by the criminal while cleansing it and concealing its illicit origin. Organised crime infiltration in legitimate businesses may be driven by money laundering purposes, but not necessarily so (see Chapter 1 for a review of the drivers of infiltration). As a result, it does not 'represent full integration in the sense that the classic model of legitimation conceives it' (Levi, 2015, p. 290).

Measuring infiltration

Because of all these overlaps, to date the measurement of criminal infiltration of legitimate businesses has inevitably intersected with the analysis of criminals' investments and money laundering activities. But even when these are grouped together, the amount of empirical knowledge on the issue remains small. This section does not aim to review the findings of the empirical research on organised crime infiltration/investments/money laundering (see Levi, 2015); but rather to discuss the strengths and weaknesses of the methodological approaches and of the measures adopted by scholars in these studies.

Seized and confiscated assets

The first attempts to conduct empirical analysis of criminal infiltration were made in Italy (Riccardi, 2014b; Transcrime, 2013), and they used companies confiscated from mafia groups as *proxies* for infiltrated businesses (see Chapter 8). By using these data, researchers were able to study the geographical and sectorial distribution of businesses infiltrated by mafias, also measuring their correlation with contextual variables (e.g. industry profitability, level of tax evasion in the territory) (Riccardi, 2014b), their accounting and management strategies (Di Bono, Cincimino, Riccardi & Berlusconi, 2015; Donato, Saporito & Scognamiglio, 2013; Transcrime, 2013), their ownership structures (Riccardi et al., 2015; Sarno, 2015), and their interactions with competitors and suppliers (Gurciullo, 2014).

Seized and confiscated assets have been used as proxies for the portfolios of criminal groups in many countries. But the analyses have not been restricted to confiscated companies in that other types of goods have been considered as well: real estate properties, registered assets (e.g. cars, boats), movable goods (e.g. jewels, watches). Generally speaking, rather than analyses of the infiltration of businesses, they can be interpreted as studies on *investments* by criminal groups in the legal economy. Research analysing organised crime investments using data on confiscated assets has been conducted, for example, in Finland (Petrell & Houtsonen, 2015, see Chapter 10), France (Riccardi & Salha, 2015, see Chapter 9), Ireland (Soriani, 2015), Spain (Palomo et al., 2015), Netherlands (Ferwerda & Unger, 2015; van Duyne & Soudijn, 2009) and, again, Italy with respect to both businesses (Riccardi, 2014b; Transcrime, 2013) and real estate (Dugato et al., 2015).

Use of these data has made innovative contributions to study of the financial aspects of criminal organisations, but it has some limitations. First, it may lead to underestimations or overestimations of certain types of goods depending on the focus of law enforcement on certain crimes, the ease of taking certain types of assets into custody, and the legal instruments at the disposal of prosecutors (Transcrime, 2013, p. 95). Second, it does not allow comparisons to be made, since asset recovery regulation varies widely across regions and countries (Savona & Riccardi, 2015, p. 224). Third, it may furnish an outdated picture of criminal investments, because very long periods often elapse between the financial investigation and final forfeiture of the asset (Transcrime, 2013, p. 95). Fourth, it may not cover those types of criminal infiltration which do not require *ownership* of the asset. Moreover, good data are lacking: only a few countries, at least in the EU, produce systematic statistics on the asset recovery process, and only a few provide disaggregated information for each confiscated asset – the only information which allows in-depth statistical analysis (Europol Criminal Asset Bureau, 2015; Savona & Riccardi, 2015).

As a result, rather than providing a picture of the actual OC portfolio, confiscated goods may be a measure of how good prosecutors and police are in tracing and recovering criminal assets. For example, in most EU member states the majority of seized goods are cash and bank accounts, while confiscation of businesses is very rare. The reason for this, as suggested by some authors, is not a lack of interest among criminals in investing in companies, but the difficulties (and the lack of interest) of law enforcement in tracing them (Savona & Riccardi, 2015).

Personal holdings and expenditure patterns

An alternative, but less frequent, approach is to consider the personal holdings of offenders, or their expenditure patterns. Meloen et al. (2003) mixed police and financial records and conducted a detailed study on the composition of the holdings of 52 criminals in the Netherlands, distinguishing among hoardings (e.g. cash), consumption (e.g. vehicles), and investment goods (e.g. immovable properties, securities). This approach has yielded valuable insights into *where* offenders employ their illegal earnings, but it has not focused on how the ownership of these assets (including companies) was acquired.

In the UK, 222 prisoners convicted for drug crimes were interviewed to explore their patterns of consumption and laundering (Matrix Research & Consultancy, 2007). According to the responses, cases of laundering through legitimate businesses are very rare, while dirtiest cash is spent on lifestyle or to pay mortgages, or is reinvested in drug trafficking. A similar approach was adopted by Webb and Burrows (2009), who interviewed imprisoned human traffickers in the UK. Despite some evidence of criminal investments in shops, hotels and restaurants, the study did not provide information on how these businesses had been infiltrated. Also Petrunov (2011) studied the strategy of managing and laundering money acquired from human trafficking through interviewing 152 sex traffickers, sex workers, police officers and prosecutors in Bulgaria. But a focus on the infiltration process was lacking.

Figures on personal holdings and expenditure patterns have a strong potential, and they are less biased by regulatory asymmetries than are data on seizures and confiscations. However, they have drawbacks too. First, due to privacy reasons, it is very difficult to access the personal records of offenders (e.g. bank accounts, tax declarations, income statements). On the other hand, self-reported figures may be affected by survey bias and a lack of transparency by respondents. Second, this approach almost exclusively focuses on individual holdings and individual expenditures, while it does not take account of those which can be attributed to the criminal organisation as a whole. Third, personal holdings by definition concern only *owned* assets, so that consideration is not made of cases in which control is acquired and exercised through other means (e.g. straw men, managers, shell companies) which do not require a direct asset ownership.

Case studies

Overall, the two approaches discussed above have a major shortcoming: they make it possible to understand *where* (which type of asset, which business sector, which region) criminals employ their proceeds, but they do not explain *why* and *how*. For example, data on confiscated companies can reveal that a certain sector registers more cases of infiltration than others, but they do not provide information on either the purpose or the *modus operandi* followed by criminals to infiltrate them.

In order to address this gap, and the other issues presented above, researchers have often resorted to the analysis of case studies. This approach makes it possible to gather information not only on the type of asset or business sector involved but also on the nature of the criminal actor, on the technique used to infiltrate/launder money, on the purpose of the investment – in other words, on the entire infiltration/investment/money laundering process. Inevitably, the quantitative approach is sacrificed in favour of a more qualitative and narrative one, e.g. in the form of script analysis.

Case studies have been used to analyse a variety of money laundering and investment activities: for example, organised crime investments in the Netherlands (Kruisbergen et al., 2015, on 150 cases from the Dutch Organised Crime Monitor, equivalent to 1,196 assets); money laundering in Spain (Steinko, 2012, on cases taken from 363 court sentences) and in Germany (Suendorf, 2001, on 40 cases); the relationship among organised crime, money laundering and the real estate market in Canada (Schneider, 2004, on 150 cases); the ownership and management strategies of mafia-owned companies in Italy (Transcrime, 2013, on around 100 cases of infiltrated businesses); infiltration by organised crime of the wind power sector in Italy (Caneppele, Riccardi & Standridge, 2013, on about 15 cases) and by mafias in Northern Italy (Alessandri, Montani & Miedico, 2014). Moreover, case studies are quite successfully used by FATF in its reports on the types and trends of money laundering, and they are also often included by most European FIUs in their annual reports.

Information on cases is usually gathered from judicial files and court documents (as in Steinko, 2012), police investigation files (as in Schneider, 2004, or in Kruisbergen et al., 2015), and institutional reports, but also from academic literature, media and newspaper articles. Some studies rely on all these sources together (e.g. Savona & Berlusconi, 2015; Savona & Riccardi, 2015; Transcrime, 2013). Cases can be selected according to whether they include specific offences (e.g. 'money laundering', 'participation in a criminal association', 'possession of the proceeds of crime', depending on the focus of the study and on the relevant legislation), to the type of criminal actor involved, to the type of asset (e.g. real estate properties, companies), to a selected time range, or to specific monetary values.

Projects OCP (Savona & Riccardi, 2015) and ARIEL (Savona & Berlusconi, 2015), on which most of the chapters of this book are based, adopted a very similar methodological approach. The former applied it to the study of organised crime investments, and the latter to criminal infiltration of legitimate businesses. For example, Savona and Berlusconi (2015) collected evidence responding to the definition of *infiltration* presented in the previous section from a plurality of sources, including judicial files, institutional reports, LEA reports, academic studies, media and newspaper articles. The wide range of sources used was intended to address the gaps in terms of data availability across countries: for example, whereas cases can be easily found in LEA reports in Italy and Ireland, in Spain and the United Kingdom they cannot. The evidence gathered was coded in order to highlight aspects such as the geographic region of infiltration, the business sector, and the criminal organisation involved. It was then organised into a database structured so that each record represented a reference to one business sector or one region. As a result, the database included 2,380 references to OC infiltration (Savona & Berlusconi, 2015, p. 23). The strategy used by Savona and Riccardi (2015) for the collection of evidence of OC investments was similar.

A narrative approach based on the analysis of case studies makes it possible to go beyond numbers and to gain a more comprehensive understanding of the infiltration process. However, it can be questioned because individual cases are not necessarily representative of the phenomenon as a whole, as pointed out by Levi (2015, p. 280): 'it is not clear how (un)representative known cases are of unknown cases'; and they are not very useful for sound quantitative analysis. Moreover, differences in terms of regulation, data availability, and nature of the sources make it very difficult to produce cross-country comparisons. But criminal infiltration, like organised crime and money laundering, is transnational by nature, and cross-country biases are unavoidable challenges to be faced with in these kinds of studies.

Other methodological issues in measuring infiltration of legal businesses

Other methodological issues arise, in particular if the intention is to carry out financial statement analysis of infiltrated businesses. First, the literature shows that accounting manipulations are very likely in the case of companies owned by criminals and used to commit illegal activities such as money laundering or fraud (Di Bono et al., 2015; Transcrime, 2013). Therefore, company accounts do not often provide a true picture of the economic and financial situation of the infiltrated business. In particular income statements are more easily and more often falsified than balance sheets to minimise the taxable income.

Second, infiltrated companies may change their management strategy over time, and this behaviour may be reflected in accounting terms. For example, criminals may start disinvesting and liquidating companies' assets as soon as they suspect that they are under investigation (Di Bono et al., 2015; Donato et al., 2013; Riccardi, 2014a). When confiscated companies are analysed, researchers should pay attention also to the effects produced by judicial administration on a company's accounts. For this reason, the study of infiltrated companies should not focus only on a certain point in time; ideally, it should cover a time range broad enough to span from the infiltration to the investigation, and then to seizure of the business. Unfortunately, historical records in business registers are not easy to find, nor are financial statements or ownership data, so that retrospective analysis of infiltrated companies is often very challenging (Savona & Berlusconi, 2015; Transcrime, 2013).

Future directions in research and data collection

Organised crime infiltration in companies is a complex phenomenon, and its study is still pioneering. It is more advanced in some regions (e.g. Italy) which have experienced mafia intrusion in the legal economy for decades; it is less developed in other countries which are still asking what infiltration is and whether it really constitutes a crime. And as for any other exploratory study, it would be wrong to focus on only one future direction of research. Instead, it is suggested that all the following areas should be improved in order to extend the 'arsenal' at the disposal of scholars and practitioners in this field.

Improving the identification of cases of infiltration

Cases of organised crime infiltration in legal businesses could be identified more precisely through better specification of the *sentinel crimes* involved in the infiltration process: money laundering, market manipulation, public or private corruption, etc. A script analysis of the already collected cases could help to identify these offences, also taking account of differences in terms of regulation and legal definitions across countries. Following the script, and adopting a bottom-up approach, those judicial cases including the sentinel crimes identified (or a combination of them) could be more easily recognised and thus collected; and then constitute the basis for gathering further information on the infiltration (e.g. ownership data on the infiltrated businesses, financial accounts).

Focusing on sentinel crimes, rather than cases themselves, would have two main advantages: first, it would shift the attention from actors to activities, thus circumventing the never-ending debate on *what organised crime is* while focusing on what criminals do. Second, it would be more useful for practitioners (prosecutors, investigators, lawyers, professionals) because it would offer them a legal basis to apply the research findings in their everyday activities.

Improving the availability of judicial files and of data on confiscated assets

This approach would be effective only if access to judicial files is improved. In most European countries, court sentences and other judicial documents can be obtained from individual prosecutors, but this does not guarantee a systematic and comprehensive collection of all the relevant cases. Instead, access to centralised databases of judicial files should be improved and opened to researchers; and the tools for searching across these datasets should be strengthened, for example by enabling multiple queries per type of criminal offence, nationality of the offender, type of asset involved, and monetary value.

EU agencies should foster also the collection of better statistics on seized and confiscated assets (in line with Art. 11 of Directive 2014/42/EU) and guarantee access to researchers. Previous reports have highlighted that these data across EU member states are lacking and of a poor quality (Savona & Riccardi, 2015; Europol Criminal Asset Bureau, 2015). In particular, microdata (i.e. per each individual asset) should be made available to researchers so that sounder statistical analysis is possible.

Exploring new methodological approaches and new sources of information

As said, quantitative analysis of hard data (e.g. statistics on confiscated companies, personal holdings of offenders) is not sufficient to gain full understanding of the drivers and the *modi operandi* of criminal infiltration in legitimate companies. It is necessary to mix such analysis with a more narrative approach that looks at the *story* of the infiltration, the actors involved, and the contextual factors.

To this end, 'softer' information on the cases identified should be collected: for example, by expanding the interviews to include offenders, prosecutors, investigators, entrepreneurs (both victims and facilitators of infiltration), professionals, and other intermediaries. Individual interviews, focus groups or surveys could be set up for this purpose; or existing ones (e.g. surveys on offenders' illegal earnings) could be adapted for this scope.

In order to improve the financial analysis of infiltrated businesses, approaches typical of business studies – primarily forensic accounting and corporate governance – could be adopted. In parallel, the analysis of company accounts could be enriched by means of interviews with managers, judicial administrators and suppliers so as to circumvent accounting manipulations and obtain a more accurate picture of the economic performance and the management strategy of infiltrated companies (Di Bono et al., 2015).

Moving from analysis of past cases to assessment of the risk of infiltration

Finally, a risk assessment approach could be adopted also in the study of criminal infiltration in legal businesses, in the same way as it has been successfully applied to other fields such as money laundering or corruption (see Chapter 12). Adopting the FATF taxonomy used in money laundering risk assessment (see Dawe, 2013; FATF, 2013) to evaluate the risk of criminal infiltration would require identifying and measuring the *threats* of infiltration, the *vulnerabilities* which facilitate it (e.g. loopholes in the regulation, weaknesses in the business structure of a company or of a sector), and the impact (*consequences*) that infiltration would have on the market, the economy, and the society as a whole.

The risk could be assessed by considering risk factors on various dimensions: territory, business sector, management strategy, ownership structure (see Chapter 12). And it could be customised according to the nature of the end-user. This approach would make it possible to transfer the results of the research on criminal infiltration into tools useful for the everyday activities of practitioners: for example, intermediaries (banks, notaries, lawyers) subject to AML obligations to conduct customer due diligence; or public bodies (e.g. municipalities, regional governments) to assess the risk of infiltration in (and manipulation of) public procurements; or LEA and ARO agencies to identify the companies on which to focus investigation and monitoring.

Notes

1 Project OCP – Organised Crime Portfolio (www.ocportfolio.eu) – was co-funded by the European Commission, DG Home Affairs and carried out in 2012–2013 by an international consortium coordinated by Transcrime, Joint Research Centre on Transnational Crime (www.transcrime.it). Project ARIEL – Assessing the Risk of the Infiltration of Organized Crime in EU MSs Legitimate Economies: a Pilot Project in 5 EU Countries (www.arielproject.eu) – was also co-funded by the European Commission and coordinated by Transcrime in 2014–2015.

2 Art. 1 of the EU Framework Decision on the Fight against Organised Crime defines a criminal organisation as:

> a structured association, established over a period of time, of more than two persons acting in concert with a view to committing offences which are punishable by deprivation of liberty or a detention order of a maximum of at least four years or a more serious penalty, to obtain, directly or indirectly, a financial or other material benefit.

> (Council of the European Union, 2008)

3 Art. 83(1) of the Treaty on the Functioning of the European Union (TFEU) identifies 'serious crimes' as: 'terrorism, trafficking in human beings and sexual exploitation of women and children, illicit drug trafficking, illicit arms trafficking, money laundering, corruption, counterfeiting of means of payment, computer crime and organised crime' (European Union, 2012). In addition to these, Savona & Riccardi (2015) covered further criminal activities (namely illicit trade in tobacco products, counterfeiting, illegal gambling and match fixing, extortion racketeering, usury, fraud and organised property crime) which are not listed in the TFEU but were considered by the authors relevant to the study of the economics of organised crime groups in Europe (Savona & Riccardi, 2015, p. 26).

4 In truth, infiltration can also target other types of legal entities and organisations, such as public administration agencies, city councils or regional governments. In Italy, for example, city councils may be dissolved and put under the administration of the Interior Ministry as a result of a decree proving their *infiltration by mafia groups* (on the basis of Art. 143 D.Lgs 267/2000).

References

Adamoli, S., Di Nicola, A., Savona, E. U., & Zoffi, P. (1998). *Organized crime around the world*. Helsinki: European Institute for Crime Prevention and Control.

Albanese, J. S. (2000). The causes of organized crime: Do criminals organize around opportunities for crime or do criminal opportunities create new offenders? *Journal of Contemporary Criminal Justice*, *16*(4), 409–423.

Albanese, J. S. (2001). The prediction and control of organized crime: A risk assessment instrument for targeting law enforcement efforts. *Trends in Organized Crime*, *6*(3), 4–29.

Albanese, J. S. (2008). Risk assessment in organized crime: Developing a market and product-based model to determine threat levels. *Journal of Contemporary Criminal Justice*, *24*(3), 263–273.

Alessandri, A., Montani, E., & Miedico, M. (2014). *Espansione della criminalità organizzata nell'attività d'impresa al nord*. Milano: Università Bocconi.

Berlusconi, G. (2015). The step-by-step process of infiltration. In E. U. Savona & G. Berlusconi (Eds.), *Organised crime infiltration of legitimate businesses in Europe: A pilot project in five European countries* (pp. 83–89). Trento: Transcrime – Università degli Studi di Trento.

Black, C., Vander Beken, T., & De Ruyver, B. (2000). *Measuring organised crime in Belgium: A risk-based methodology*. Antwerp: Maklu.

Calderoni, F. (2008). A definition that could not work: The EU Framework Decision on the fight against organised crime. *European Journal of Crime, Criminal Law and Criminal Justice*, *16*(3), 265–282.

Calderoni, F. (2014). Measuring the presence of the mafias in Italy. In S. Caneppele & F. Calderoni (Eds.), *Organized crime, corruption and crime prevention* (pp. 239–249). New York, NY: Springer.

Caneppele, S., Riccardi, M., & Standridge, P. (2013). Green energy and black economy: Mafia investments in the wind power sector in Italy. *Crime Law and Social Change*, *59*(3), 319–339.

Council of the European Union. (2008, 11 November). Council Framework Decision 2008/841/JHA of 24 October 2008 on the fight against organised crime. Retrieved from http://eur-lex.europa.eu/LexUriServ/LexUriServ.do?uri=OJ:L:2008:300:0042:0045: EN:PDF

CSD. (2012). *Serious and organised crime threat assessment 2010–2011*. Sofia, Bulgaria: Center for Study of Democracy.

Dawe, S. (2013). Conducting national money laundering or financing of terrorism risk assessment. In B. Unger & D. van der Linde (Eds.), *Research Handbook on Money Laundering* (pp. 110–126). Cheltenham: Edward Elgar Publishing.

Di Bono, L., Cincimino, S., Riccardi, M., & Berlusconi, G. (2015). Management strategies of infiltrated businesses. In E. U. Savona & G. Berlusconi (Eds.), *Organized crime infiltration of legitimate businesses in Europe: A pilot project in five European countries* (pp. 102–112). Trento: Transcrime – Università degli Studi di Trento.

Donato, L., Saporito, A., & Scognamiglio, A. (2013). *Aziende sequestrate alla criminalità organizzata: Le relazioni con il sistema bancario* (Occasional Papers No. 202). Roma: Banca d'Italia.

Dugato, M., De Simoni, M., & Savona, E. U. (2014). *Measuring OC in Latin America. A methodology for developing and validating scores and composite indicators at national and subnational level*. Aguascalientes, Mexico: INEGI/UNODC. Retrieved from www. transcrime.it/pubblicazioni/measuring-oc-in-latin-america/.

Dugato, M., Giommoni, L., & Favarin, S. (2015). The risks and rewards of organized crime investments in real estate. *British Journal of Criminology*, *55*(5), 944–965.

European Union. (2012). Treaty on European Union and the Treaty on the Functioning of the European Union – Pub. L. No. 2012/C 326/01.

Europol. (2009). *EU organised crime threat assessment*. The Hague: Europol.

Europol. (2011). *EU organised crime threat assessment*. The Hague: Europol.

Europol. (2013). *EU organised crime threat assessment*. The Hague: Europol.

Europol Criminal Asset Bureau. (2015). *Survey Report: Statistical information on asset recovery in the EU 2010–2014*. Preliminary draft. The Hague: Europol.

FATF. (2013). *National money laundering and terrorist financing risk assessment*. Paris: The Financial Action Task Force.

Ferwerda, J., & Unger, B. (2015). Organised crime investments in the Netherlands. In E. U. Savona & M. Riccardi (Eds.), *From illegal markets to legitimate businesses: The portfolio of organised crime in Europe* (pp. 196–201). Trento: Transcrime – Università degli Studi di Trento.

Finckenauer, J. O. (2005). Problems of definition: What is organized crime? *Trends in Organized Crime*, *8*(3), 63–83.

Gurciullo, S. (2014). Organised crime infiltration in the legitimate private economy: An empirical network analysis approach. Retrieved from http://arxiv.org/abs/1403.5071.

Hagan, F. (2006). 'Organized crime' and 'organized crime': Indeterminate problems of definition. *Trends in Organized Crime, 9*(4), 127–137.

IPOL. (2014). *Nationaal Dreigingsbeeld 2008 Georganiseerde Criminaliteit.* Amsterdam: Dutch National Police Intelligence Service.

Kenney, D. J., & Finckenauer, J. O. (1995). *Organized crime in America.* Belmont, CA: Wadsworth.

Kruisbergen, E. W., Kleemans, E. R., & Kouwenberg, R. F. (2015). Profitability, power, or proximity? Organized crime offenders investing their money in legal economy. *European Journal on Criminal Policy and Research, 21*(2), 237–256.

Levi, M. (2015). Money for crime and money from crime: Financing crime and laundering crime proceeds. *European Journal on Criminal Policy and Research, 21*(2), 275–297.

Maltz, M. D. (1996). Criminality in space and time: Life course analysis and the micro-ecology of crime. In J. Eck & D. Weisburd (Eds.), *Crime and place.* Monsey, NY: Criminal Justice Press.

Matrix Research & Consultancy. (2007). *The illicit drug trade in the United Kingdom.* London: Home Office.

Meloen, J. D., Landman, R., De Miranda, H., van Eekelen, J., van Soest, S., van Duyne, P. C., & van Tilburg, W. (2003). *Buit en besteding: Een empirisch onderzoek naar de omvang, de kenmerken en de besteding van misdaadgeld.* Zoetermeer: Nationale Recherche Informatie.

National Crime Agency. (2014, 5 January). *National Strategic Assessment of Serious and Organised Crime 2014.* Retrieved from www.nationalcrimeagency.gov.uk/publications/207-nca-strategic-assessment-of-serious-and-organised-crime/file.

Palomo, J., Márquez, J., & Ruiz, N. (2015). Organised crime investments in Spain. In E. U. Savona & M. Riccardi (Eds.), *From illegal markets to legitimate businesses: The portfolio of organised crime in Europe* (pp. 202–209). Trento: Transcrime – Università degli Studi di Trento.

Paoli, L. (2002). The paradoxes of organized crime. *Crime, Law and Social Change, 37*(1), 51–97.

Petrell, S., & Houtsonen, J. (2015). Finland. In E. U. Savona & M. Riccardi (Eds.), *From illegal markets to legitimate businesses: The portfolio of organised crime in Europe* (pp. 166–171). Trento: Transcrime – Università degli Studi di Trento.

Petrunov, G. (2011). Managing money acquired from human trafficking: Case study of sex trafficking from Bulgaria to Western Europe. *Trends in Organized Crime, 14,* 165–186.

Reuter, P., & Truman, E. M. (2004). *Chasing dirty money.* Washington, DC: Institute for International Economics.

Riccardi, M. (2014a). The management of seized companies: Learning from the Italian experience. Presented at the 2nd Meeting of the European Commission Asset Recovery Office (ARO) Platform subgroup on Asset Management, Brussels.

Riccardi, M. (2014b). When criminals invest in businesses: Are we looking in the right direction? An exploratory analysis of companies controlled by mafias. In S. Caneppele & F. Calderoni (Eds.), *Organized crime, corruption and crime prevention* (pp. 197–206). New York, NY: Springer.

Riccardi, M., & Salha, A. (2015). Organised crime investments in France. In E. U. Savona & M. Riccardi (Eds.), *From illegal markets to legitimate businesses: The portfolio of organised crime in Europe* (pp. 172–177). Trento: Transcrime – Università degli Studi di Trento.

Riccardi, M., Soriani, C., & Standridge, P. (2015). When the mafia is beneficial owner: Control strategies of mafia-owned companies. Presented at the European Society of Criminology meeting, Porto.

Sarno, F. (2015). Control strategies of infiltrated businesses. In E. U. Savona & G. Berlusconi (Eds.), *Organised crime infiltration of legitimate businesses in Europe: A pilot project in five European countries* (pp. 90–101). Trento: Transcrime – Università degli Studi di Trento.

Savona, E. U., & Berlusconi, G. (Eds.). (2015). *Organised crime infiltration of legitimate businesses in Europe: A pilot project in five European countries*. Trento: Transcrime – Università degli Studi di Trento.

Savona, E. U., Dugato, M., & Garofalo, L. (2012). *A framework for the quantification of organized crime and assessment of availability and quality of relevant data in three selected countries of Latin America and the Caribbean*. Aguascalientes: INEGI/UNODC.

Savona, E. U., & Riccardi, M. (Eds.). (2015). *From illegal markets to legitimate businesses: The portfolio of organised crime in Europe*. Trento: Transcrime – Università degli Studi di Trento.

Schneider, S. (2004). Organized crime, money laundering and the real estate market in Canada. *Journal of Property Research*, *21*(2), 99–118.

Soriani, C. (2015). Organised crime investments in Ireland. In E. U. Savona & M. Riccardi (Eds.), *From illegal markets to legitimate businesses: The portfolio of organised crime in Europe* (pp. 178–182). Trento: Transcrime – Università degli Studi di Trento.

Steinko, A. F. (2012). Financial channels of money laundering in Spain. *British Journal of Criminology*, *52*(5), 908–931.

Suendorf, U. (2001). *Geldwäsche: Eine kriminologische Untersuchung*. Luchterhand: Neuwied und Kriftel.

Transcrime. (2013). *Progetto PON Sicurezza 2007–2013. Gli investimenti delle mafie*. Milano: Transcrime – Joint Research Centre on Transnational Crime.

Vander Beken, T. (2004). Risky business: A risk-based methodology to measure organized crime. *Crime, Law and Social Change*, *41*(5), 471–516.

van Dijk, J. (2007). Mafia markers: Assessing organized crime and its impact upon societies. *Trends in Organized Crime*, *10*(4), 39–56.

van Duyne, P. C. (2006). Introduction: Counting clouds and measuring organised crime. In P. C. Van Duyne, A. Maljevic, M. van Dijck, K. von Lampe, & J. L. Newell (Eds.), *The organisation of crime profit: Conduct, law and measurement* (pp. 1–16). Nijmegen: Wolf Legal Publishers (WLP).

van Duyne, P. C., & Soudijn, M. (2009). Hot money, hot stones and hot air: Crime-money threat, real estate and real concern. *Journal of Money Laundering Control*, *12*(2), 173–188.

van Duyne, P. C., & van Dijck, M. (2007). Assessing organised crime: The sad state of an impossible art. In F. Bovenkerk & M. Levi (Eds.), *The organized crime community: Essays in honor of Alan A. Block* (pp. 101–124). New York, NY: Springer.

von Lampe, K. (2004). Measuring organized crime: A critique of current approaches. In P. C. van Duyne, M. Jager, K. von Lampe, & J. L. Newell (Eds.), *Threats and phantoms of organised crime, corruption and terrorism: Critical European perspectives* (pp. 85–116). Nijmegen: Wolf Legal Publishers.

Webb, S., & Burrows, J. (2009). *Organised immigration crime: A post-conviction study*. London: Home Office. Retrieved from www.gov.uk/government/uploads/system/uploads/attachment_data/file/116627/horr15-keyimplications. pdf.

Zoutendijk, A. J. (2010). Organised crime threat assessments: A critical review. *Crime, Law and Social Change, 54*(1), 63–86.

Part I

Infiltrating legitimate businesses to conceal and facilitate illicit trafficking

3 Organised crime infiltration in the Netherlands

Transportation companies hiding transit crimes

Joras Ferwerda and Brigitte Unger

Organised crime and transit crime in the Netherlands: an overview

Because of its historical development and geographical location, the Netherlands is especially attractive for the through-flow of crime and vulnerable to transit crime. Here we understand transit crime in a very broad sense as the through-flow of criminal assets from an origin country where the crime has been committed to a destination country with the use of an in-between 'transit' country (Unger et al., 2006). In order to determine the role of transportation companies in drug trafficking and other forms of transit crime in the Netherlands, we shall first explore what makes the Netherlands so particularly attractive for drug trafficking and other transit crimes, what are the organised crime groups involved in illegal businesses, what types of transit crime are committed, and what is the magnitude of these transit crimes (Sections 1 and 2). Section 3 then shows the use of transportation companies by organised crime for drug trafficking and other forms of transit crime in the Netherlands.

What makes the Netherlands so particularly attractive for drug trafficking and other transit crimes? Already in the sixteenth and seventeenth century, Dutch 'merchant capitalism' was based on trading, shipping and finance, rather than on manufacturing or agriculture. Merchant capitalism included investments in high-risk ventures such as pioneering expeditions to the East Indies to engage in the spice trade. These ventures were soon consolidated in the Dutch East India Company (VOC), which established the Amsterdam Stock Exchange, subsequently renamed the Amsterdam *Bourse*, in 1602. This was the first stock exchange to formally begin trading in securities. Trade and ship building also helped Rotterdam become Europe's largest harbour (de Vries & van der Woude, 1997). Still today, the port of Rotterdam is the largest port in Europe, and until 2002 also functioned as the world's busiest port, only later to be surpassed by ports in Singapore, Dubai and China.

The trade and finance orientation of the Dutch, combined with their central geographical location on the North Sea amidst large European countries, a big harbour and an important airport, Schiphol, make the country attractive for legal as well as illegal trade and finance. Organised crime groups (hereafter OCGs) in the Netherlands have adjusted to the Dutch trading patterns and to the country's multi-ethnicity. They use mainly ethnical networks, which are established for specific criminal transaction purposes, rather than relying on strongly hierarchical structures (Kleemans, 2007). This is why 'mafia-type' organisations such as those present in Italy and the United States have not been identified (Kruisbergen et al., 2012).

The Netherlands has been an attractive through-flow country for crime (see Unger et al., 2006). The major criminal groups in the Netherlands engage in international smuggling activities (drugs trafficking, smuggling of illegal immigrants, human trafficking for sexual exploitation, firearms trafficking, trafficking in stolen vehicles) and other transnational illegal activities, such as money laundering, tax fraud and cigarette smuggling (Kruisbergen et al., 2012). Committed crimes, as mentioned above, are mostly transit in nature: organised crime groups are involved in international illegal trade using the same opportunity structure that facilitates regular Dutch economic activities.

In order further to investigate the types of transit crime in the Netherlands, their magnitude, and the role of organised crime in them, we were able to create a database on organised crime cases in the Netherlands. We are grateful to the Dutch Public Prosecution Office (hereafter PPO) for granting us access to its database to study what criminal groups are active in the Netherlands, on which illegal markets they operate, and how big these illegal markets are. After filtering out the most serious and relevant cases of organised crime, Ferwerda & Unger (2015a) ended up with 12,946 suspects in 4,397 cases between 2003 and 2014, on which our analysis below is based.[1]

Table 3.1 displays the prominence of multi-ethnicity. We identified 26 different categories of criminal groups based on the nationality of their members. Compared to domestic Dutch organised crime, the share of foreign criminal groups is, however, small. About two-thirds (68 per cent) of the crime cases are committed by domestic Dutch OCGs. The large variety of criminal groups with foreign nationality that is present, however, confirms the transnational nature of organised crime in the Netherlands. Among the foreign OCGs active in the Netherlands, two groups stand out: Turkish OCGs, which account for 8.3 per cent of the crime cases, and South American OCGs, which account for 4.6 per cent of the crime cases. All other foreign organised criminal groups are involved to a lesser extent. Notably, it is apparent that organised crime groups from Southern, Central and Eastern Europe are not markedly present.

The fact that Turkish OCGs seem to be relatively active is partly due to the fact that the Turks are the largest foreign community in the Netherlands, which in 2014 consisted of approximately 400,000 inhabitants.[2] Turkish-speaking OCGs, however, also have a history of smuggling and drug trafficking. In the 1970s, when many Turkish guest workers came to the Netherlands, there were criminals among them, hidden as guest workers in order to set up drug businesses. At that time, the so-called 'heroin trail', along which Turkish smugglers brought opium from the province of Afyon in Anatolia to Europe, was an important drug route (Yesilgöz & Bovenkerk, 2004a). Today, Turkey is a key

Table 3.1 Frequency of involvement in Dutch PPO cases per OCG, number and percentage of cases and suspects, 2003–2014

OCG classification	Cases		Suspects	
	N	%	N	%
Dutch OCGs	2,670	68.0	7,486	67.5
Turkish OCGs	326	8.3	766	6.9
South American OCGs	181	4.6	841	7.6
Middle Eastern OCGs	141	3.6	356	3.2
African OCGs	108	2.8	302	2.7
Other Asian OCGs	105	2.7	289	2.6
North African OCGs	84	2.1	239	2.2
Other Western European OCGs	67	1.7	116	1.0
Other Eastern European OCGs	38	1.0	95	0.9
British OCGs	33	0.8	97	0.9
Chinese OCGs	30	0.8	89	0.8
Colombian OCGs	27	0.7	125	1.1
Russian Georgian OCGs	26	0.7	48	0.4
Balkan OCGs	23	0.6	49	0.4
Bulgarian OCGs	14	0.4	28	0.3
North American OCGs	12	0.3	36	0.3
Romanian OCGs	9	0.2	38	0.3
Italian OCGs	8	0.2	20	0.2
Lithuanian OCGs	6	0.2	11	0.1
Albanian OCGs	4	0.1	16	0.1
Motorcycle gangs	4	0.1	27	0.2
Irish OCGs	3	0.08	11	0.1
French OCGs	2	0.05	2	0.02
Japanese OCGs	1	0.03	4	0.04
Mexican OCGs	1	0.03	3	0.03
Spanish OCGs	1	0.03	3	0.03
TOTAL	3,924	100	11,097	100

Source: authors' elaboration on Ferwerda and Unger (2015a, p. 121).

trans-shipment and storage point for criminal organisations to arrange the transport to the EU of heroin shipments trafficked mostly by land from Iran along the Balkan route (EMCDDA, 2015). Although Turkish organised crime groups have a patriarchal structure, they still differ from mafia-type organisations. 'The business is kept tightly shut and it is impossible to see from outside who is the boss' (Yesilgöz & Bovenkerk, 2004b, p. 597). The behaviour of the Turkish OCGs thus fits with the multi-ethnic network organisation typical of Dutch organised crime.

The high-ranking position of South Americans is, on the one hand, most likely due to Dutch colonial history, which established close, long-lasting ties with some of its former colonies. Dutch former colonies include Suriname, which became independent in 1975, and the Dutch Antilles, which used to be part of the Netherlands until 2010. Speaking the same language and sharing cultural and historical roots makes the Netherlands attractive for both legal and illegal South American business. On the other hand, the geographical location also matters. The Colombian mafia uses the Netherlands quite extensively for its drug business. Colombian and British OCGs are relatively more often involved in drug crimes than other OCGs. This confirms the findings of the 2015 World Drug Report (UNODC, 2015) and European Drug Report (EMCDDA, 2015) that the Netherlands is a transit country along the drug route from Colombia to the United Kingdom.

The Italian mafias rank relatively low. The KLPD (Dutch police) report on the 'Ndrangheta in the Netherlands concludes that there is at least one cell of the 'Ndrangheta operating in the country with at least 12 members, and that this cell is involved in, among others, drugs trade and smuggling, trafficking in firearms, money laundering and swindle companies (KLPD-DNR, 2011). Chinese criminals rank relatively low, and they are hardly ever mentioned in the media in the Netherlands. Even though 48 Chinese were killed between 1992 and 2007 – almost all of them in the criminal underworld – they hardly ever showed up in the statistics. The main crimes committed by Chinese OCGs in the Netherlands are drugs trade (via its harbour Rotterdam), extortion (of other Chinese), human trafficking, exploitation (of other Chinese) and illegal gambling (ACB Knowledge Centre, 2011). If the Chinese are the main victims of the Chinese OCGs and the Chinese hardly ever report crimes to the police (ACB Knowledge Centre, 2011), this might explain their relatively low presence in the Dutch PPO database.

As regards the types of criminal activities in which OCGs are involved, most cases refer to fraud, drugs, counterfeiting and human trafficking (Table 3.2). There is, however, some evidence that Dutch organised crime is more dominant in the illegal market of fraud (in 72 per cent of fraud cases) and in counterfeiting (in 67 per cent of counterfeiting cases), while foreign organised crime groups are more visible in crimes of a more international nature, such as drugs, firearms and human trafficking. Almost half of the drug business and of human trafficking involves foreign organised crime (46 per cent of the drug cases and 48 per cent of the firearms trafficking concern non-Dutch suspects). Moreover, Dutch organised crime is engaged to a very little extent in human trafficking (only 21 per cent of the cases concern Dutch suspects). For illicit trafficking in tobacco products and illegal gambling, there are not enough observations to draw firm conclusions.

Drug trafficking, transit crime and the role of legal businesses

To what extent is legal business infiltrated by crime, and in particular by transit crime? How are transportation companies misused by drug traffickers? Before discussing these connections, it is useful to provide a brief description of the structure and the magnitude of the drug market in the Netherlands.

Table 3.2 Frequency of OCG involvement in illicit markets in Dutch PPO cases, number of cases, 2003–2014

OCG classification	Drugs	Human trafficking	ITF[a]	ITTP[b]	Counterfeiting	Illegal gambling	Fraud
Dutch OCGs	166	26	11	3	147	4	1,815
Turkish OCGs	29	7	4		18		241
South American OCGs	22	9	1		15		106
Middle Eastern OCGs	6	13	2	1	8		91
African OCGs	8	15			9		51
Other Asian OCGs	7	16			6		54
North African OCGs	9	4		1	5		43
Other Western European OCGs	4	2		2	2		43
Other Eastern European OCGs	3	7		2	6		14
British OCGs	12						19
Chinese OCGs	1	12			2		6
Colombian OCGs	17		1				4
Russian Georgian OCGs	2	3					16
Balkan OCGs	6	1	1				9
Bulgarian OCGs		4					8
North American OCGs	2	2	1				4
Romanian OCGs		3		1			4
Italian OCGs	2						4
Lithuanian OCGs	2	1					2
Albanian OCGs	3						1
Motorcycle gangs	3						
Irish OCGs	1						2
French OCGs							1
Japanese OCGs	1						
Mexican OCGs							
Spanish OCGs	1						

Source: authors' elaboration on Ferwerda and Unger (2015a, p. 124).

Notes
a Illegal trafficking in firearms.
b Illegal trafficking in tobacco products.

The structure and the magnitude of drug trafficking in the Netherlands

Drug trafficking is the most profitable illegal activity in the Netherlands (measured by the estimated illegally obtained benefits per suspect, see Table 3.3), as it is in many other countries. Drug trafficking is also an important transit crime, since drug routes start in Asia or South America, and end in Europe or the US. Cocaine, which is almost exclusively cultivated in South America, is mostly smuggled through Africa or the Caribbean before reaching Europe, according to the 2015 World Drug Report (UNODC, 2015, p. 48). Opiates are almost exclusively produced in Myanmar and Afghanistan. Drug routes of Afghan opiates include the 'Northern route' through Central Asia to Russia, the 'Southern route' through Iran or Pakistan to Asia, and the 'Balkan route' through Iran and Turkey to Europe (UNODC, 2015, p. 48). The European Drug Report of June 2015 (EMCDDA, 2015) speaks of a north-west hub.

Belgium and the Netherlands are key landing points and distribution hubs for heroin consignments travelling by land, sea or air along the Balkan and Southern routes. Large heroin consignments are broken down into smaller batches and trafficked in multiple ways to other countries of Western Europe and to Scandinavia.

Table 3.3 Estimation of illegally obtained benefit per illegal market in Dutch PPO cases, 2003–2014

Illegal market	Number of suspects for which the illegally obtained benefit has been estimated	Total amount of estimated illegally obtained benefit (million euro)	Average illegally obtained benefit per suspect (million euro)
Drugs	95	300	3.2
THB[a]	45	18	0.41
ITF[b]	1	0.091	0.091
ITTP[c]	0	–	–
Counterfeiting	49	7.6	0.16
Illegal gambling	4	71	17.8
Fraud	251	284	1.1

Source: authors' elaboration on Ferwerda and Unger (2015a, p. 122).

Notes
a Trafficking in human beings.
b Illegal trafficking in firearms.
c Illegal trafficking in tobacco products.

Note that the illegally obtained benefit is not estimated for all suspects, so the totals reported in this table could only be interpreted as the lower boundary of the actual illegally obtained benefit. The reported average benefit is not the actual average benefit of this crime, because the database consists of only the most serious and big cases of the PPO (see Savona & Riccardi, 2015). Including all cases of the PPO would bring this average down. Moreover, the estimation of the illegally obtained profits could be done more often in bigger cases affecting the representativity of these figures.

The Netherlands, Morocco and Spain have been mentioned in individual drug seizures as the main departure or transit countries for cannabis over the past decade as a whole, and they continue to be so when considering more recent trends during the period 2010–2014.

(UNODC, 2015, p. 229)

As Table 3.3 shows, along with fraud, drugs are the most important illegal market in the Netherlands. This is in line with the findings in other EU countries such as Finland, France or Spain (e.g. Palomo, Márquez & Laguna, 2015, p. 128; Petrell & Houtsonen, 2015, p. 98; Riccardi & Salha, 2015, p. 101) and with former international research on the relative size of illegal markets (e.g. Reuter & Truman, 2004; Walker & Unger, 2009). Our database of relevant cases of organised crime – as discussed in Ferwerda and Unger (2015b) – features 95 drug cases with an average benefit per suspect of €3.2 million. The number of fraud cases is 251 with an average benefit per suspect of €1.1 million.

The total estimated illegally obtained benefit in the drugs market in the PPO database is almost €300 million between 2003 and 2014. The total size of the drugs market in the Netherlands has been estimated by Kilmer and Pacula (2009) to be around €600 million per year. Unfortunately, the PPO database does not allow differentiation among different drugs, although it is known that these have rather distinct markets, as we will briefly describe below before focusing on the infiltrated companies and business sectors.

Heroin

Imported heroin has historically been available in Europe in two forms, the most common being brown heroin (its chemical base form), originating mainly in Afghanistan and other countries in south-west Asia. Less common is white heroin (a salt form), which historically came from south-east Asia but is now also produced in Afghanistan and probably in neighbouring Iran and Pakistan. This region, sometimes referred to as the Golden Crescent, dominates production for the European market (EMCDDA, 2015). When compared with other EU countries, heroin is relatively cheap in the Netherlands. The street price of one gram of heroin is between €20 and €40. The wholesale price is estimated at €14,000 per kilo. The massive increase in demand for heroin in the last decade in the EU did not occur in the Netherlands (KLPD, 2012). According to the Trimbos-instituut the number of consumers in 2011 was estimated at between 17,300 and 18,100 (van Laar et al., 2012). Giommoni (2015, p. 45) estimates the annual revenues from heroin in the Netherlands in 2012 at about €54 million, which is lower than Kilmer and Pacula's (2009) estimate for 2005 of €78.6 million.

Cocaine

Cocaine use continues to decline in Western and Central Europe and North America, and cultivation of the coca bush is at its lowest since the mid-1980s

(UNODC, 2015). Nevertheless, cocaine is very popular in the Netherlands, with 55,000 users and a total consumption estimated at 1,660 kilos per year (UNODC, 2010). Its consumption increased heavily from 1998 to 2006, and stabilised thereafter (KLPD, 2012). The profits in this illegal market are very high. One kilogram of cocaine can be bought for about US$3,600 (about €3,200) in the source country and sold in the Netherlands for about US$20,000 (about €18,000) (KLPD, 2012). Giommoni (2015, p. 47) estimates that the annual revenues of the cocaine market in the Netherlands (2005) amount to about €85 million, which is slightly lower than the estimate by Kilmer and Pacula (2009), who evaluated the total size of the Dutch cocaine market at €101.7 million in 2005. If one also takes account of the fact that Rotterdam in the Netherlands and Antwerp in Belgium are the main import harbours for cocaine in Europe, OCGs that are active in the Netherlands and export cocaine to other countries may make larger proceeds than those estimated above, since they are calculated only on the basis of the internal consumption at the retail level.

Cannabis

Personal production and use of cannabis is tolerated in the Netherlands. Cannabis is sold in so-called 'coffee shops'. The production of more weed than for personal usage, however, is illegal and individuals doing so risk prosecution. The probability of getting caught producing weed beyond levels for personal use is actually relatively high, with estimates ranging between 30 and 50 per cent (Van der Heijden, 2006). The Netherlands is probably still the most important source country for seeds and cuttings, as well as growing technologies and knowledge (Europol, 2013). The Dutch cannabis market was estimated at 480 tons in 2011 (Jansen, 2012). Caulkins and Kilmer (Caulkins, Kilmer & Graf, 2013) estimate the size of the Dutch cannabis market at €305 million in 2005.

Amphetamine-type drugs

While the Netherlands is a through-flow country for many drugs, it is the most important producer country of ecstasy globally (Europol, 2013). The most widely consumed synthetic drugs in the Netherlands are ecstasy (about 1.4 per cent of the population in 2009) and amphetamine (used by 0.4 per cent of the population in 2009) (KLPD, 2012). Estimates of the production of synthetic drugs in the Netherlands varies between 66 and 1,343 million tablets (KLPD, 2012). Assuming a price of €3 per tablet (KLPD, 2012), the annual turnover of the Dutch ecstasy market lies between €198 million and €4 billion. Kilmer and Pacula (2009) estimate the size of the Dutch ecstasy market as much smaller, between €16 and €130 million.

Infiltrated companies and business sectors

The available information on infiltrated companies and business sectors is that included in the database on references to organised crime investments analysed by Ferwerda and Unger (2015b). This database includes cases collected from judiciary and police reports and other publicly available sources. In 613 among the 859 references to the Netherlands, the business sectors of infiltrated businesses could be identified. To give a reference point for the Dutch situation: according to the evidence collected by a multi-country comparative study, the business sectors most vulnerable to infiltration by organised crime groups are (see Riccardi, Soriani & Standridge, 2015, p. 156): bars and restaurants; construction; real estate activities; hotels; wholesale and retail trade, in particular of food products and of clothing; and transportation. Although this list of the business sectors most vulnerable to infiltration by criminal activities is similar across countries, and therefore quite general in nature, there are differences among countries. These may depend on many variables, including the country's business structure and entrepreneurial culture (e.g. criminal investments in agriculture and fishery are higher in Spain than in the Netherlands or Finland, see Palomo, Márquez & Ruiz, 2015), investment opportunities, and differences in terms of national administrative and regulatory systems.

Criminals in the Netherlands prefer to invest in sectors with which they are familiar (Kruisbergen et al., 2012). According to our database (see Ferwerda & Unger, 2015b), the most popular sectors for OCG investments are transportation and renting of motor vehicles, wholesale and retail trade, bars and restaurants, and hotels and other tourist accommodations.

The transportation sector is attractive for transit crime (see Section 3 below). Criminal goods can be transported and smuggled together with legal goods. Transportation and renting of motor vehicles is particularly attractive for motorcycle gangs and OCGs involved in illicit trafficking activities. Moreover, investing in this sector creates possibilities to use, for instance, trucks or ships belonging to the company for drugs trafficking, human trafficking or illicit trafficking in tobacco products (Kruisbergen et al., 2012).

Wholesale and retail trade are also attractive for transit crime. They constitute the biggest sector in the legal economy, so that they may be overrepresented in the investment portfolios of OCGs. Export-import businesses can be used for trading in both criminal and legal goods. This sector also offers many opportunities for money laundering. Fake invoices offer possibilities for trade-based money laundering. The sector also involves many cash transactions, which create money laundering opportunities. Bars, restaurants, hotels and other tourist accommodations are relatively cash intensive and attract criminal investment in order to launder money, thus enabling organised crime groups to hide illicit proceeds of crime. Kruisbergen, Kleemans, and Kouwenberg (2015, pp. 364–370) draw a similar conclusion regarding the sectors most vulnerable to infiltration by criminal activities after analysing 150 organised crime cases in the Netherlands.

Wholesale trade, retail trade and transportation are the legal business sectors most likely to be infiltrated by criminal groups involved in transit crime. Export and import companies can be used to export and import legal and illegal goods; and they can be used to issue or receive fake invoices in order to transfer illegal money and for other forms of trade-based money laundering. The transport sector is a very important sector to support this business. There is also some evidence that international OCGs in the Netherlands prefer to invest back in their country of origin (Ferwerda & Unger, 2015b, p. 198), but there is not sufficient data on international confiscations by the Dutch PPO to draw firm conclusions on this point. The regions with most criminal investments are located around Amsterdam with its international airport and Rotterdam with its international harbour (Ferwerda & Unger, 2015b, p. 196). This again supports the view that the Netherlands is an important country for transit crime.

The role of Dutch transportation companies in transit crimes

As mentioned above, the transport sector is attractive for criminals. Transportation means like cars can be stolen and sold abroad. Ships can be hijacked. Ship cargos can be stolen and redirected elsewhere. Trucks can be used for the transport of legal and illegal goods. Transportation and logistics companies can be used for the illicit trafficking of drugs, counterfeits, firearms or human beings. It is no coincidence that one of the preferred sectors for criminal investment is logistics (Riccardi et al., 2015): OCGs set up transportation companies as fronts, misusing companies' legitimate trucks or containers for illicit trade purposes (e.g. Kruisbergen et al., 2012; Van Koppen & De Poot, 2013). Transportation means can also be used to transport large amounts of cash money.

Transportation is a business which can also be used to hide illicit proceeds and money laundering through fake invoices and trade-based money laundering. Foreign shipping companies can be established in a country for transit crime. Airports and harbours are important strategic centres of transportation that criminals can try to bring under their control in order to be able to fly and ship criminal goods. They can also be abused for terrorist purposes. Europol (2009) warns that Dutch airports are used by OCGs for drug smuggling with methods like Transit-Point-Stacking and the so-called 'shotgun method'. With Transit-Point-Stacking the OCG files a flight plan consisting of multiple sequential flights in an effort to hide the initial origin of couriers. With the 'shotgun method' an attempt is made to overwhelm customs controls by having multiple couriers on a single flight; in one instance, 28 couriers were detected on the same flight.

Transportation companies can play a key role in control of the territory and may be related to cargo crimes (Kleemans, De Poot, Kalidien, Kouwenberg & van Nassou, 2007). Consideration of criminal careers in the Netherlands that originate from legal professions shows that most come from the trade business (Kleemans et al., 2007, p. 2). Transportation can be used as a front for illicit activity (e.g. using transport or shipping companies to hide the smuggling of drugs); and to 'launder' stolen products (e.g. fake wholesalers) (Kruisbergen et al., 2012). A recent example of this is the Acero-Krupy case. The Krupy (originally Crupi) family members in the Netherlands were not only active as drug dealers but were also involved in the flower growing and trade sector, controlling a vast segment of the Dutch market with typical mafia-methods. The Krupy brothers were also shareholders in an Italian wholesale trade business of flowers in Siderno, Calabria, and Latina, Lazio. Flowers from the Netherlands were sent to Italy through a network of import-export companies guaranteed by two Dutch companies founded by the two brothers. The two Dutch companies allowed the family and other 'Ndrangheta clans to launder huge amounts of money from drug trafficking, and to 'launder' stolen goods, such as 259 tons of chocolate, for a value higher than €7 million, stolen from the Italian branch of a major Swiss chocolate company and then resold in third countries such as Hungary (Anesi & Rubino, 2015).

Another example is described in Van Koppen and De Poot (2013, p. 81). After Edgar (a pseudonym) finished intermediate technical school at the age of 21, he started working as a car salesman at a Volkswagen dealer. After 10 years he switched to a job at a different car-dealing company, where he started trafficking drugs for criminals. Edgar declared that at his new job: 'You are approached by clients from all sides.' Thirty years later he is serving a 10-year sentence for holding a leading position in a crime group involved in drugs trade. Van Koppen and De Poot (2013, p. 82) also describe another relevant case. Daniel (a pseudonym), aged over 60, owned two trading companies that were concerned with bulk buying and selling. These companies used hangars to store goods. Initially, Daniel was approached by a foreigner with whom he had already done legal business. Daniel became involved in a criminal smuggling group, for which he organised cross-border transport. Daniel explained that '[i]f I hadn't owned a business, I would never have gotten involved.'

According to the 2015 World Drug Report (UNODC, 2015), the frequency of use of different modes of transportation used by drug traffickers has not changed a great deal over the past decade. Accounting for nearly half the reported individual drug seizures in the 2009–2014 period, trafficking by road and rail is the most common mode of transportation used by traffickers globally, along with trafficking by air. The average size of drug shipments intercepted on road and rail increased substantially from 68 kilograms between 2006 and 2008 to 107 kilograms between 2009 and 2014 (UNODC, 2015). Maritime trafficking is the least common in terms of individual seizure cases, accounting for only eight per cent of all reported cases in the past six years, but maritime seizures tend to be comparatively very large. With an average weight of 365 kilograms per seizure in the 2009–2014 period (compared with 250 kilograms in the 2006–2008 period), maritime seizures are by far the largest among the three modes of transportation. This confirms that interdiction of maritime shipments potentially has the greatest impact on the total quantities of drugs smuggled, as well as on trafficking flows and the availability of illicit drugs at the global level (UNODC, 2015).

The ports of Rotterdam in the Netherlands and Antwerp in Belgium are of particular importance for drug trafficking. Large containers can transport several tons of drugs. Police officers in the Netherlands and Belgium also report cases of criminals hacking ship containers in order to steal them. Containers with drugs are also hacked in order to steal them from other drug dealers.

The plot, which began in 2011, reportedly involved a mix of international drug gangs and digital henchmen: drug traffickers recruited hackers to penetrate computers that tracked and controlled the movement location of shipping containers arriving at Antwerp's port. The simple software and hardware hacks – using USB key loggers and more sophisticated purpose-built devices – allowed traffickers to send in drivers and gunmen to steal particular containers before the legitimate owner arrived.

(Pasternack, 2013)

All these cases show that the infiltration of transportation companies by criminal groups is higher in transit countries like the Netherlands than in other countries (Ferwerda & Unger, 2015b). According to the 2015 World Trade Report (UNODC, 2015, p. 48), Belgium and the Netherlands remain important transit points for heroin trafficking to the United Kingdom via heavy goods vehicles and ferries. This also makes the transport sector in these countries more vulnerable than in other countries.

The seizure of boats, trucks and other transport-related assets

Evidence collected by Savona & Riccardi (2015) shows that also those registered assets related to transport, such as cars or boats, play an important role in the portfolio of OCGs and in terms of asset seizures. These registered assets are instrumental to many illicit activities (e.g. boats for drug transportation), as well as status-symbols for criminal group members and a reflection of the criminal group's culture (e.g. 'choppers' for motorcycle gangs). In particular, they are central for the transportation of illicit goods of any kind.

Boats are widely used, for example, to transport trafficked persons and drugs. In particular, cargo ships are often used to traffic counterfeit goods, illicit drugs, stolen assets and illicit tobacco products (Transcrime, 2015; UNICRI, 2011; WCO, 2014). The evidence collected and discussed above shows that OCGs may directly control cargo companies, e.g. in the Netherlands for drug trafficking (Kruisbergen et al., 2012, 2015). Registered assets also serve prestige purposes: cases of seizure from OCGs of Ferrari, Lamborghini and other luxury cars, yachts and even jets and helicopters are not rare (Soriani, 2015). To be noted in this regard is the use of pipers and other small aircraft as alternative means to transport drugs, persons, and other illicit goods from Morocco, the western Balkans or among EU member states (Europol, 2011; Olimpo, Galli & Santucci, 2014).

Conclusions

The Netherlands is an attractive country for transit crime, in particular drug trafficking and human trafficking. This is due to its geographical location, its historical development as a trade and finance centre and its expertise in logistics, which make it a through-flow country for goods and services. It is attractive for legal business but also vulnerable to illicit business. The country's good infra-structure for trade and transport, including Europe's busiest port and one of the largest European airports, attract legal business. But these very special features are also used by domestic and foreign organised crime groups infiltrating legal businesses. Dutch organised crime is still the most important actor among crimi-nal organisations active in the Netherlands. Foreign OCGs are active in par-ticular types of crime such as drugs, firearms and human trafficking. The most important non-Dutch organised crime groups in the Netherlands are from Turkey and South America, but a total of 27 nationalities could be identified on examin-ing PPO files.

The drug business is the most profitable one, and the transport sector plays an important role in facilitating it. Transportation by land, air and sea is used to transport drugs through the world, using the Netherlands as a hub. Accordingly, it can be concluded that the transport sector in the Netherlands is even more vul-nerable than in most other countries. This vulnerability is further increased by the presence of Schiphol airport (one of the largest in Europe), Rotterdam harbour (the busiest port in Europe), and the truck transportation system for export and import businesses. All these can be misused by organised crime to smuggle drugs and human beings.

The transport sector is difficult to regulate, since it consists of many small com-panies. To limit criminal investments in businesses such as bars and restaurants, the Netherlands has implemented the so-called BIBOB Act that allows administra-tive institutions to revoke or reject licences when there is suspicion of criminal involvement. Since the BIBOB Act came into effect, the Netherlands has become the second European country, after Italy, with administrative regulations against organised crime. An internal evaluation of the BIBOB Act showed that the possib-ility of being screened discouraged several applicants from continuing the applica-tion process for a licence and limited possible effects of displacement (Huisman & Nelen, 2007). Similar creative regulations would be needed for the transport sector and for obscure export and import businesses. Since the location of transport com-panies can be easily moved, cooperation between municipalities or a national register open to all municipalities might be needed. In addition, international cooperation and pre-warning systems to stop criminals at the borders or to trace their individual trafficking routes should be improved.

Notes

1 See Savona & Riccardi (2015) for details on the dataset and the filtering of cases.
2 See Dutch Central Bureau of Statistics (www.statline.cbs.nl).

References

ACB Knowledge Centre. (2011). Factsheet on Chinese.
Anesi, C., & Rubino, G. (2015, 29 September). Fermata la 'Ndrangheta d'élite: droga, tulipani e cioccolata. *CORRECT!V*. Retrieved from https://correctiv.org/it/inchieste/mafia/blog/2015/09/29/fermata-la-ndrangheta-delite-droga-tulipani-e-cioccolata/.

Caulkins, J. P., Kilmer, B., & Graf, M. (2013). Estimating the size of the EU cannabis market. In F. Trautmann, B. Kilmer, & P. Turnbull (Eds.), *Further insights into aspects of the EU illicit drugs market* (pp. 289–323). Luxembourg: Publications Office of the European Union.

de Vries, J., & van der Woude, A. (1997). *The first modern economy success, failure, and perseverance of the Dutch economy, 1500–1815.* Cambridge: Cambridge University Press.

EMCDDA. (2015). *European drug report 2015: Trends and developments.* Lisbon: European Monitoring Centre for Drugs and Drug Addiction.

Europol. (2009). *EU organised crime threat assessment.* The Hague: Europol.

Europol. (2011). *EU organised crime threat assessment.* The Hague: Europol.

Europol. (2013). *EU organised crime threat assessment.* The Hague: Europol.

Ferwerda, J., & Unger, B. (2015a). Organised crime groups in the Netherlands. In E. U. Savona & M. Riccardi (Eds.), *From illegal markets to legitimate businesses: The portfolio of organised crime in Europe* (pp. 120–125). Trento: Transcrime – Università degli Studi di Trento.

Ferwerda, J., & Unger, B. (2015b). Organised crime investments in the Netherlands. In E. U. Savona & M. Riccardi (Eds.), *From illegal markets to legitimate businesses: The portfolio of organised crime in Europe* (pp. 196–201). Trento: Transcrime – Università degli Studi di Trento.

Giommoni, L. (2015). Illicit drugs market. In E. U. Savona & M. Riccardi (Eds.), *From illegal markets to legitimate businesses: The portfolio of organised crime in Europe* (pp. 43–56). Trento: Transcrime – Università degli Studi di Trento.

Huisman, W., & Nelen, H. (2007). Gotham unbound Dutch style. *Crime, Law and Social Change, 48*(3–5), 87–103.

Jansen, F. (2012). *Georganiseerde hennepteelt: Criminaliteitsbeeldanalyse 2012.* Driebergen: KLPD – Dienst Nationale Recherche.

Kilmer, B., & Pacula, R. L. (2009). *Estimating the size of the global drug market: A demand-size approach.* Santa Monica, CA: RAND Corporation. Retrieved from www.rand.org/pubs/technical_reports/TR711.html.

Kleemans, E. R. (2007). Organized crime, transit crime, and racketeering. *Crime and Justice, 35*(1), 163–215.

Kleemans, E. R., De Poot, C. J., Kalidien, S. N., Kouwenberg, R. F., & van Nassou, M. (2007). *Criminele carrières in de georganiseerde misdaad.* Den Haag: Wetenschappelijk Onderzoek- en Documentatiecentrum.

KLPD. (2012). *National threat assessment 2012.* Zoetermeer: Information Service of the National Investigation Service.

KLPD-DNR. (2011). *De 'Ndrangheta in Nederland: aard, criminele activiteiten en werkwijze op Nederlandse bodem.* Driebergen: Korps landelijke politiediensten (KLPD), Dienst Nationale Recherche.

Kruisbergen, E. W., Kleemans, E. R., & Kouwenberg, R. F. (2015). Profitability, power, or proximity? Organized crime offenders investing their money in legal economy. *European Journal on Criminal Policy and Research, 21*(2), 237–256.

Kruisbergen, E. W., van de Bunt, H., Kleemans, E. R., Kouwenberg, R. F., Huisman, K., Meerts, C. A., & de Jong, D. (2012). *Fourth report of the Organized Crime Monitor.* The Hague: Netherlands Ministry of Justice, Research and Documentation Centre.

Olimpo, G., Galli, A., & Santucci, G. (2014). Voli della droga, la flotta dei narcos in Italia. *Corriere Della Sera.* Retrieved from www.corriere.it/reportage/senza-categoria/2014/voli-della-droga-la-flotta-dei-narcos-in-italia/.

Palomo, J., Márquez, J., & Laguna, P. (2015). Organised crime groups in Spain. In E. U. Savona & M. Riccardi (Eds.), *From illegal markets to legitimate businesses: The portfolio of organised crime in Europe* (pp. 126–133). Trento: Transcrime – Università degli Studi di Trento.

Palomo, J., Márquez, J., & Ruiz, N. (2015). Organised crime investments in Spain. In E. U. Savona & M. Riccardi (Eds.), *From illegal markets to legitimate businesses: The portfolio of organised crime in Europe* (pp. 202–209). Trento: Transcrime – Università degli Studi di Trento.

Pasternack, A. (2013). To move drugs, traffickers are hacking shipping containers. Retrieved from http://motherboard.vice.com/blog/how-traffickers-hack-shipping-containers-to-move-drugs.

Petrell, S., & Houtsonen, J. (2015). Organised crime groups in Finland. In E. U. Savona & M. Riccardi (Eds.), *From illegal markets to legitimate businesses: The portfolio of organised crime in Europe* (pp. 95–100). Trento: Transcrime – Università degli Studi di Trento.

Reuter, P., & Truman, E. M. (2004). *Chasing dirty money*. Washington, DC: Institute for International Economics.

Riccardi, M., & Salha, A. (2015). Organised crime groups in France. In E. U. Savona & M. Riccardi (Eds.), *From illegal markets to legitimate businesses: The portfolio of organised crime in Europe* (pp. 101–106). Trento: Transcrime – Università degli Studi di Trento.

Riccardi, M., Soriani, C., & Standridge, P. (2015). Organised crime investments in Europe. In E. U. Savona & M. Riccardi (Eds.), *From illegal markets to legitimate businesses: The portfolio of organised crime in Europe* (pp. 150–165). Trento: Transcrime – Università degli Studi di Trento.

Savona, E. U., & Riccardi, M. (Eds.). (2015). *From illegal markets to legitimate businesses: The portfolio of organised crime in Europe*. Trento: Transcrime – Università degli Studi di Trento.

Soriani, C. (2015). Organised crime investments in Ireland. In E. U. Savona & M. Riccardi (Eds.), *From illegal markets to legitimate businesses: The portfolio of organised crime in Europe* (pp. 178–182). Trento: Transcrime – Università degli Studi di Trento.

Transcrime. (2015). *European outlook on the illicit trade in tobacco products*. Trento: Transcrime – Università degli Studi di Trento.

Unger, B., Siegel, M., Ferwerda, J., de Kruijf, W., Busuioic, M., Wokke, K., & Rawlings, G. (2006). *The amounts and effects of money laundering*. The Hague: Ministry of Finance.

UNICRI. (2011). *Counterfeiting: A global spread, a global threat*. Torino: United Nations Interregional Crime and Justice Research Institute.

UNODC. (2010). *World drug report 2010*. Vienna: United Nations Office on Drugs and Crime.

UNODC. (2015). *World drug report 2015*. Vienna: United Nations Office on Drugs and Crime.

Van der Heijden, A. (2006). *De cannabismarkt in Nederland. Raming van aan voer, productie, consumptie en uitvoer*. Zoetermeer: Korps Landelijke Politiediensten.

Van Koppen, M. V., & De Poot, C. J. (2013). The truck driver who bought a cafe: Offenders on their involvement mechanisms for organized crime. *European Journal of Criminology*, *10*(1), 74–88.

Van Laar, M., Cruts, G., van Gageldonk, A., van Ooyen-Houben, M., Croes, E., Meijer, R., and Ketelaars, T. (2012). *The Netherlands drug situation 2011: Report to the EMCDDA by the Reitox Focal Point*. Utrecht: Trimbos-instituut

Walker, J., & Unger, B. (2009). Measuring global money laundering: 'The Walker Gravity Model'. *Review of Law & Economics*, 5(2), 821–853.

WCO. (2014). *Illicit trade report 2013*. Brussels: World Customs Organization.

Yesilgöz, Y., & Bovenkerk, F. (2004a). The Turkish mafia and the state. In C. Fijnaut & L. Paoli (Eds.), *Organized crime in Europe: Concepts, patterns and control policies in the European Union and beyond* (pp. 585–601). Dordrecht: Springer.

Yesilgöz, Y., & Bovenkerk, F. (2004b). The Turkish mafia and the state. In C. Fijnaut & L. Paoli (Eds.), *Organized crime in Europe: Concepts, patterns and control policies in the European Union and beyond* (pp. 585–601). Dordrecht: Springer.

4 The sex market, bars and nightclubs

Criminal infiltration in Slovenia

Boštjan Slak, Maja Modic, Katja Eman and Branko Ažman

Organised crime in Slovenia

The scope and typology of organised crime in Slovenia are strongly influenced by its geographical characteristics (Maver, 2003) and (economic) history. Before gaining independence, Slovenia was a socialist country where harsh and totalitarian investigative institutions and their extensive powers – though used less strictly than in other socialist countries (Šelih, 2012) – prevented organised crime from developing into a major threat. After the fall of the regime in 1991, Slovenia wanted to distance itself from its legacy of totalitarian governance and began to embrace high standards of human rights, thereby significantly increasing the requirements related to lawfulness of all actions taken in pre-trial and criminal proceedings (Maver, 2000). Combined with re-establishment of the judicial system (Šelih, 2012) and legislative and organisational changes in policing (Gorkič, 2012), these increased requirements had an immense impact on success rates in investigation and prosecution of organised crime.

Simultaneously, the new government sought to open its market to foreign investors by privatising State-owned firms. Privatisation aimed to allow for dispersion of government ownership of the biggest Slovenian companies, thus further spreading political power (Lorenčič, 2009). In order to provide for effective implementation of these ideas, very flexible legislation was adopted, but it failed to adequately regulate both the underlying neoliberal processes and the players involved in the ideological uplift springing from the worldwide fall of socialist regimes (see Felsenreich, 2012). This flexible approach and the damages of economic criminality in the times of privatisation manifested in the years long after gaining independence (see Lorenčič, 2009; Ude, 2008). In this, Slovenia could be a good example of Beetham's (2003) claim that organised crime spreads due to the global development of human rights standards and procedural guarantees, on the one hand, and globalisation and market liberation, on the other.

Slovenia's small size (20,273 km²) and the small number of its metropolitan areas continue to hinder the development of extensive organised crime structures (Logonder, 2013); nevertheless, its location on the Balkan route and the length of its green border make it vulnerable to organised crime's intentions.

The conflicts in the Balkan region fuelled a high demand for weapons, while a low quality of life motivated organised crime structures in these countries to engage in human smuggling (with these countries also being a point of origin) and drug smuggling. Located on the shortest land route between Western Europe, the Balkans and the Middle East, Slovenia is a good place for establishing smuggling networks as well. Its good sea access and a well-developed road infrastructure allow for a lot of cargo to be transported through Slovenia. Organised crime groups

> rely primarily on the fact that at busy border crossings only a small part of the cargo is subject to detailed checks. [...] Organised crime groups usually do not bribe Police or Customs officers, rather, they prefer to use local people for smuggling goods. Human trafficking is usually done by locals, avoiding the official border crossings.
>
> (CSD, 2011, p. 372)

Locals are involved because they are familiar with the topography of the terrain alongside Slovenia's borders; however, according to Slovenian police, the groups engaged in people smuggling have achieved a level of organisation where local 'assistance' is less and less needed (SOJ SGDP GPU, 2014).

The green border issue as such has been in the spotlight lately because of the refugee crisis. In its 2011 Organised Crime Threat Assessment report, Europol highlighted the problems that Greece and Turkey encountered with the substantial volume of organised crime involved in illegal migrations from African and Middle East regions (Europol, 2011). In 2015, the same pathways are daily used by thousands of refugees and immigrants bound for Western Europe, illegally crossing borders without proper documents outside official border crossing points, seriously challenging the Schengen regime and causing problems to which some countries (including Slovenia) now respond by building fences alongside their southern green borders.

Though some authors expressed their concerns about emerging organised crime threats (Dvoršek, 1993; Pečar, 1996) and the police recognised some crimes as related to organised crime even before 1991 (Svetek, 1993), it was not until 1995 that the police started to officially document crimes as organised crime-related (Svetek, 1996). At that time, the relevant criteria for classification of organised crime had not yet been developed. As a result, typical organised crime offences were used as a proxy to estimate the spread of organised crime in general, revealing a relatively high number of criminal acts supposedly perpetrated by organised crime (e.g. Maver, 2003). It was not until after the adoption of Europol guidelines in 2001 (Policija, 2003) that official statistics were calculated and kept in ways similar to other European countries (Figure 4.1). Police statistics from 2002 onwards reveal that organised crime groups are involved in particular in drug-related crimes, illegal trespassing of the state border, and in various types of grand larceny, though the latter two have decreased since 2012 (Meško et al., 2015).

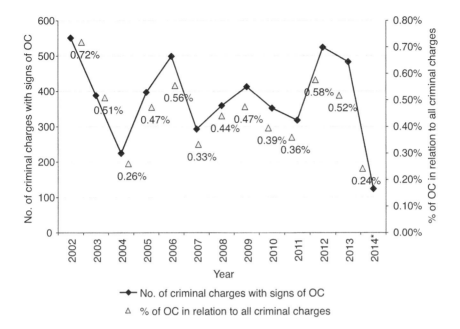

Figure 4.1 Criminal charges with signs of organised crime (OC), 2002–mid-2014 (source: authors' elaboration on Meško et al. (2015)).

Notes

Since Europol's method is perception- and knowledge-based, the figures sometimes differ from those published in annual police reports because additional clarifications of the circumstances reveal that criminal offences were not, in fact, related to organised crime. The calculation of the percentage of organised crime occurrences per year was done by the authors using the data provided, but the results have not been confirmed by the Slovenian police.

* 2014 data refers to the period from January to June 2014.

Generally, Slovenian organised crime groups may be divided into two categories. The first one includes organised white-collar crime groups consisting of members belonging to the top echelons of the Slovenian society. The media and the public usually refer to them as tycoons, especially in pre-election political debate (Ude, 2008). They could be described as the most influential Slovenian businessmen, gaining their fortunes and power by (ab)using the ill-designed economic privatisation legislation (see Lorenčič, 2012). Slovenia is believed to have suffered considerable financial losses because of these legislative decisions (Lorenčič, 2009; Ude, 2008).

The second category includes groups that engage in classic criminal activities (e.g. drug trafficking, human smuggling); these are often small-scale networks based on family or friendship relations (Meško et al., 2015) similar to other organised crime groups in Europe (Fijnaut & Paoli, 2004; Savona & Berlusconi, 2015). These were the focal point of Meško et al.'s (2015) research for the purpose of project ARIEL (Savona & Berlusconi, 2015).[1] White-collar criminality was not included because, first, for the majority of cases trials have not yet ended and, second, as claimed by Fijnaut & Paoli (2004, p. 615), because white-collar criminals engaged in fraud, manipulation of public tenders, and other such practices

> have no need to 'infiltrate' into the legitimate economy as they are already an established part of it, and the revenues of their 'dirty' activities are barely distinguishable from the flows of 'clean' and 'hot' money that are traded incessantly around the world.
>
> (Fijnaut & Paoli, 2004, p. 615)

Organised crime infiltration in the legal economy

Slovenian criminological research suffers from a substantial shortage of research focused on economic issues (Šelih & Meško, 2011), especially in the area of organised crime, where only few studies have proper empirical backing (Slak, Meško & Fank, 2015) despite the fact that the topic is quite popular in academic discourse.[2] This reveals a weak starting point underlying any research on organised crime groups' economic behaviour – a problem also encountered by Meško et al. (2015) in their attempt to research organised crime infiltration in the legitimate Slovenian economy.

The research conducted by Meško et al. (2015) has revealed that only two groups of Slovenian academics have written on the topic. The first one includes authors dealing with criminal investigation strategies that Slovenia and other post-socialist countries have needed to develop to fight post-independence organised crime threats (e.g. Dvoršek, 1993, 1995, 2002). The second one includes those who have researched human trafficking (Pajnik & Kavčič, 2008; Zavratnik, Kavčič, Pajnik & Lesjak-Tušek, 2003). Neither group, however, has paid much attention to the economic and entrepreneurship behaviours of organised crime groups. In non-academic literature (newspapers, mainly), economic behaviour of organised crime is either presented as a threat to the Slovenian economy or, in some cases, as an attempt to somehow tie an organised crime member to a certain location. Nevertheless, media narratives do contain enough information to identify those organised crime groups whose member(s) have had a tie-in with a legitimate business (Meško et al., 2015).[3]

Infiltration across business sectors and criminal groups

Economic sectors with evidence of organised crime infiltration

The evidence gathered in project ARIEL most strongly supports the premise that Slovenian bars, restaurants, and similar businesses are most often infiltrated and owned by members of organised crime groups (Meško et al., 2015). In this regard, the findings support the previous accounts and on-going perception of organised crime as involved in such businesses (Abadinsky, 2010; Devito, 2005;

Fijnaut & Paoli, 2004; Newton, 2011; see also Savona & Berlusconi, 2015). Further, the findings by Meško et al. (2015), as well as those by other research-ers (e.g. Marine, 2006; Riccardi, Soriani & Standridge, 2015; Savona & Ricca-rdi, 2015; Tromp, 2011) reveal that road cargo transportation businesses were infiltrated by members of organised crime groups. In Slovenia, these were usually involved in drug trafficking (Meško et al., 2015). Taxi services were also found to be frequently owned by members of organised crime groups engaged in human smuggling or forced prostitution. Finally, strong evidence of heavy involvement of these groups was found in consulting services, privately owned labour agencies, and, particularly, in amusement and recreation activities (Meško et al., 2015).

Methods of infiltration, control and management

The results from the study conducted by Meško et al. (2015) indicate that members of organised crime groups acquire ownership of a business simply by registering it at an administrative unit. In some cases, they buy an existing busi-ness and re-register it in their names. There have been no indications that former owners have been threatened or forced into the sale or change of ownership. On that note, strong evidence has been found that members of organised crime groups tend to own and/or manage businesses directly and that a business is often registered to one member of the group only, thereby reflecting the fact that, in general, a great number of businesses take on the form of *sole proprietorship*. While family members or life partners often help in managing a business or are employed by it, they are rarely listed as co-owners. In the few cases where they are actually listed as such, it is because the offenders tried to prevent confisca-tion of their assets. This is quite evident when ownership changes occur in the moment the investigation against an owner starts, or when a foreign subject owns a business entity showing strong indications that his/her function is, in fact, that of a straw-man (Meško et al., 2015).

The majority of the infiltrated firms for which Meško et al. (2015) found data in the national business register (AJPES) declared themselves as *micro* firms.[4] Some of these businesses were or still are operational and seem profitable, while others have already been removed from the Slovenian business register. This has hap-pened mainly because, after the owners of companies went to prison or were taken into custody, nobody continued to manage these businesses, while others went bankrupt due to poor business performance. No general rule applies here. Follow-ing the approach adopted by Meško et al. (2015) thanks to a new on-line applica-tion named SUPERVIZOR (Komisija za preprečevanje korupcije, 2014), it was found that some of the companies and businesses managed or owned by the sub-jects arrested for their involvement in classic activities of organised crime had pro-vided services to the Slovenian public sector. Among the 52 business entities analysed, 24 were recipients of funds from the Slovenian budget. The total sum of these funds was almost €300,000. The calculations include the costs of free legal counselling or subsidies for employing disadvantaged categories of people.

Territories with evidence of organised crime infiltration

If we take into account Slovenia's size and the fact that many of the businesses are sole proprietorships (usually registered at home addresses), we should not be surprised by the picture emerging from the analyses of infiltrated territories. The majority of the infiltrated legal businesses are located and/or registered in the Slovenian capital, Ljubljana – a fact contributing greatly to the high frequency of occurrences in the region that includes Ljubljana (Osrednjeslovenska). Moreover, cases of infiltrated businesses have been found in nine out of 12 Slovenian regions (no cases were found in the Koroška, Zasavska and Notranjsko-kraška regions). In 19 cases involving questionable business practices, it was not possible to establish the actual location of registration (Meško et al., 2015).

Motives of organised crime infiltration

Recent research on organised crime infiltration into European legal markets (Savona & Riccardi, 2015) has identified a number of motives for such infiltration: money laundering; concealment and/or facilitating crime perpetration; striving to profit from legitimate entrepreneurship. These were also found to be present in cases of organised crime infiltration in Slovenian legitimate economy (Meško et al., 2015). On the other hand, motives such as control of the territory, influence on the political sphere, or social consensus (Savona & Riccardi, 2015) have been found not to be a driving force in Slovenian cases of organised crime infiltration in legitimate businesses. Of particular note are the cases where an organised crime member already had a legitimate business and engaged in a criminal activity when striving for additional profit (Meško et al., 2015).[5]

Bars and nightclubs to cover prostitution rings

An extensive volume of literature deals with businesses engaged in beverages and food services and their diverse connections to organised crime activities (Abadinsky, 2010; Devito, 2005; Fijnaut & Paoli, 2004; Newton, 2011; Riccardi et al., 2015; Savona & Riccardi, 2015). As in the rest of Europe (Savona & Riccardi, 2015), there is a specific kind of bar that is used as a cover for forced prostitution (Meško et al., 2015). These bars are usually open all night long, and the majority of them provide (erotic) artistic performances. Among the Slovenian population, they are called 'nightclubs'. While this is not an officially recognised or legally stipulated term or category denoting a business entity, it is still used by both visitors and owners of such clubs/bars to show the distinction (Meško et al., 2015). Externally, a nightclub gives an impression of a legitimate business where girls perform various dance routines, but additional sexual services can be purchased (Furlan-Rus, 2009; Lovšin, 2013; Meško et al., 2015; Šori, 2005; Žist, 2006).

One of the few studies on prostitution based on the estimates provided by the Slovenian police, NGOs and other sources (Šori, 2005) found that 'indoor' prostitution is the primary form of prostitution in Slovenia, followed by prostitution in nightclubs, which replaced massage parlour prostitution that used to prevail in the 1990s. A wide literature reveals how the age-old schemes aimed at hiding prostitution behind legitimately operating businesses such as bars, clubs, and massage parlours are still globally used (e.g. Lazaridis, 2001; Savona, Giommoni & Mancuso, 2014; Sawyer, Metz, Hinds & Brucker, 2001). The findings by Meško et al. (2015) provide further evidence. Their analysis of the nightclubs whose owners and/or managers were under investigation for organised crime offences shows that these are low-scale businesses managed by a couple of perpetrators with known connections to a human trafficking network. In relatively few cases, owners themselves manage the recruitment and transportation of their women. While locations and names of nightclubs are more or less constant, their staff and managers often change, and they are often rented and managed by the same person that already managed such nightclubs elsewhere. In some cases, managers are assisted by their family members. Moreover, there are several cases where even the women employed in the bars help run the business, whereby the businesses provide the documents for the female sex workers and bring them into Slovenia legally (Meško et al., 2015).

Labour agencies or business entities providing amusement and recreation activities are also set up and used by organised crime groups to procure proper documentation to foreigners who want to work and live in Slovenia. Also worrying is the fact that once foreigners enter Slovenia legally, they may fall prey to exploiters from other EU countries, as free movement of people inside the EU enables easier migration between countries (Bučar-Ručman & Frangež, 2014). And while Meško et al. (2015) found that foreign women are more often forced into labour (as prostitutes) than men, recent research on human trafficking shows that men are also exploited for physical labour under conditions resembling slavery (Bučar-Ručman, 2014; Bučar-Ručman & Frangež, 2014). These scholars (Bučar-Ručman, 2014; Bučar-Ručman & Frangež, 2014; Meško et al., 2015), together with some reporters (Modic & Kralj, 2014), have discovered that the businesses engaged in these activities are often (re)registered at the same address as other companies, clearly indicating a possibility that they are shell companies. This is something similar to the *modus operandi* in the 'missing trader' fraud.

Receiving offers from Slovenian nightclubs, foreign women often know that prostitution, which is decriminalised in Slovenia, may be a component of their employment; however, the expected earnings are higher than those actually generated, as well as the expected working conditions (Pajnik, 2008; Šori, 2005). In other cases, women are recruited under false promises that they will work as waitresses or hostesses; however, because they need to repay the debt 'accumulated' as a result of their transportation and high 'accommodation' costs, the only way to earn enough money is to prostitute themselves. This *modus operandi* applied in debt coercion schemes is centuries old (Lazaridis, 2001) and well recognised around Europe (see Savona et al., 2014 for a discussion of similar trafficking and prostitution solicitation in Italy). Economic violence as *modus operandi* is becoming increasingly common in corporate criminality and the exploitation of foreign workers (Bučar-Ručman, 2014). Foreigners also lack knowledge of administrative issues and language, and as Lazaridis (2001) observed with regard to human trafficking in Greece, constant movement of women throughout a country prevents the individuals from developing stronger social ties with the local population, isolating and hiding them from those who could help them.

The relative ease with which foreigners could get documents and permits to enter Slovenia lasted until 2009, when some amendments to the existing legislation on employment of foreigners were introduced, particularly those working in such nightclubs: the provisions restrict validity of a work permission to one location, i.e., to one nightclub owned or rented by the employer, making it hard the exchange of women among nightclubs (Cirman, 2010, p. 60). The latest legislative amendments affecting the employment of foreign workers, however, will, again, facilitate exchange of foreign workers among employers because less rigid paperwork shall be required, and foreigners shall enjoy the right to be contracted by several employers (Kamenščak, 2015).

Conclusions

Three conclusions may be derived from what has been presented above. First, infiltration of organised crime in Slovenia occurs in the business sectors traditionally recognised as exposed to organised crime – that is bars, restaurants, and transportation. Due to the fact that in Slovenia privately owned labour agencies or agencies engaged in providing amusement programmes are often established by members of organised crime groups, these businesses are a link in the chain of businesses engaging in or masking human trafficking. Some of them are set up with the sole purpose of providing the documents that foreigners need to enter Slovenia legally, while others are actual employers of these foreigners: females are employed in nightclubs and often forced to provide sexual services, while males are (ab)used for physical labour. Riccardi, Soriani and Standridge (2015) note that organised crime infiltrates labour-intensive sectors; the findings by Meško et al. (2015) and Bučar-Ručman & Frangež (2014) confirm that this is also true in Slovenia.

Second, the analyses of the business entities connected with organised crime groups clearly show that entrepreneurial initiatives are individualistic in nature. This is reflected in the size of the infiltrated businesses: the great majority of them are micro-size businesses. As far as motives are concerned, they range from simple money laundering schemes to masking/hiding/facilitating criminal activities. Taken as a whole, the fact that the number of identified infiltration cases is relatively small indicates that the majority of illegal profits gained by members of classic organised crime groups is used to improve their quality of life and, later, to facilitate otherwise expensive lifestyles, rather than to undertake further business ventures. This goes hand in hand with the research findings of van Duyne (1996) and Savona & Riccardi (2015) that in some cases organised crime members earn enough to afford a lavish lifestyle without having to resort to money laundering.

Third, there are substantial shortages of research on economical behaviours of perpetrators of crime. These shortcomings are partly caused by the fact that, in Slovenia, criminal investigations of economic crimes have no tradition. Because the legislator believed there are extensive illegally gained funds in circulation, the Confiscation of Proceeds of Crime Act (Uradni List RS, 2011) was drafted and adopted to properly prosecute and investigate economic, financial and organised crime (Gorkič, 2012). This act, however, has been severely criticised and portrayed as unconstitutional (e.g. Ščernjavič & Hudej, 2015), which is why it is now being reviewed by the Constitutional Court. In addition, in summer 2015, the National Assembly amended the Companies Act (Uradni List RS, 2006), restricting the provisions regarding company establishment conditions (IUS-INFO, 2015b) to stem the tide of inadequate business practices such as tax avoidance and non-payment of employer's contributions (Kunšek, 2015).[6] Only time will tell whether these legislative changes have been useful. Nonetheless, they will provide some data that might be useful in future academic research undertakings.

Finally, further benefits may spring from the implementation of indirect measures against the informal economy. One of them is a mandated use of certified tax cash registers recently adopted by the Slovenian parliament (IUS-INFO, 2015a).[7] Nevertheless, all the listed measures will not prevent further development of either sophisticated profit-hiding methods or of disputable company establishment schemes because public administration workers continue to be the weak link in the process.[8] Why and how so? Currently, no due consideration has been given to such legislation that would obligate and adequately empower public officials to efficiently conduct basic searches on credit ratings, previous criminal involvement, potential mailbox address schemes, or other considerations prior to issuing certain permits or licences. Public administration needs to recognise and establish itself as a more sentinel player, similar to the one described in Schoot (2006), exercising tight control of administrative screening of business subjects and playing an important role in organised crime prevention.

Notes

1 Project ARIEL – Assessing the Risk of the Infiltration of Organized Crime in EU MSs Legitimate Economies: a Pilot Project in five EU Countries, co-funded by the European Commission, DG Home Affairs.
2 Such shortage of empirical evidence and knowledge was noticed early by Pečar (1996), and subsequently by Karakaš (2004) and Slak et al. (2015). All this indicates a serious lag in research undertaken on organised crime.
3 Meško et al. (2015) used newspapers and other non-academic literature to identify organised crime groups and members that had a connection to a legitimate business. If judicial trials had already ended for those identified groups, then prosecutor files related to their court trials were also accessed. For gaining information on business entities that were found connected to the identified groups, data from the Agency of the Republic of Slovenia for Public Legal Records and Related Services (AJPES) was used. The data on AJPES is freely accessible, but one can receive the data only by

entering a given business entity's name, registration number, or other identifying marker. An owner's or shareholder's name cannot be used in the search, which makes it impossible for outsiders to find out, via AJPES, all business entities connected with one person; however, there are legislative amendments that, if passed, will soften these criteria and facilitate the search of business subjects (IUS-INFO, 2015c). The change is somewhat motivated by economic criminality and to facilitate bankruptcy proceedings.

4   The classification is based on the provisions given in the Companies Act (Uradni List RS, 2006). According to article 55 of this Act,

> a micro company shall be a company meeting two of the following criteria:
>
> • average number of employees in a financial year does not exceed 10,
> • net sales income does not exceed €2,000,000, and
> • value of assets does not exceed €2,000,000.

5   This was most evident in businesses providing taxi services. Furlan-Rus (2014) reports of a trial where a taxi driver confessed he was involved in a human smuggling operation: his role was to drive illegal immigrants across Slovenia, and he even included these earnings in his tax report.

6   These include the provision that a company owner shall prove that the company has settled all its liabilities in connection with employee contributions for the previous year; that a physical person having been fined twice in the last three years by the Labour Inspectorate of the Republic of Slovenia or by the Financial Administration of the Republic of Slovenia may not be an owner or a shareholder of a company; and that a company owner cannot be a person who has been sentenced to prison for economic crimes. In addition, one may start a firm or become a shareholder only once in three months (IUS-INFO, 2015b; Kunšek, 2015).

7   'Certified tax cash registers' are those tax cash registers with on-line internet connections to the Financial Administration of the Republic of Slovenia for the purposes of immediate tax control.

8   For instance, GRETA (2014, p. 19) assessed that in Slovenia human trafficking is further facilitated by the lack of a training programme in which all relevant professionals, including the staff of administrative units in charge of issuing residence permits, labour inspectors, judges, lawyers, would deepen their knowledge of human trafficking and develop the skills needed for early identification of possible human trafficking schemes.

References

Abadinsky, H. (2010). *Organized crime* (9th edn). Belmont, CA: Wadsworth, Cengage Learning.

Beetham, D. (2003). Foreword. In F. Allum & R. Siebert (Eds.), *Organized crime and the challenge to democracy* (pp. xii–xiv). London-New York: Routledge.

Bučar-Ručman, A. (2014). *Migracije in kriminaliteta: Pogled čez meje stereotipov in predsodkov.* Ljubljana: Založba ZRC SAZU.

Bučar-Ručman, A., & Frangež, D. (2014). *Analiza trgovine z ljudmi z namenom izkoriščanja delovne sile, trgovine z otroki, prisilnega beračenja in izvrševanja kaznivih dejanj: Raziskovalno poročilo.* Ljubljana: Fakulteta za varnostne vede za Urad vlade Republike Slovenije za komuniciranje. Retrieved from www.vlada.si/fileadmin/dokumenti/si/THB/ZAKLJUCNO_POROCILO_-_TZL.pdf.

Cirman, T. (2010). *Družbeni vidiki zakonskega urejanja prostitucije: Dekriminalizacija v Sloveniji* (undergraduate thesis). Univerza v Ljubljani, Fakulteta za družbene vede, Ljubljana. Retrieved from http://dk.fdv.uni-lj.si/diplomska/pdfs/cirman-tanja.pdf.

CSD. (2011). *Better management of EU borders through cooperation: Study to identify best practices on the cooperation between border guards and customs administrations working at the external borders of the EU.* Sofia: Center for the Study of Democracy.

Devito, C. (2005). *The encyclopedia of international organized crime.* New York, NY: Facts on File.

Dvoršek, A. (1993). Organizirani kriminal – Problem (pp. 107–115). Presented at the Policija na prehodu v 21. stoletje: Zbornik posvetovanja, Ljubljana: Ministrstvo za notranje zadeve Republike Slovenije.

Dvoršek, A. (1995). Organizirani kriminal v Sloveniji. *Zbornik Strokovno Znanstvenih Razprav, XVIII,* 146–152.

Dvoršek, A. (2002). Strategija omejevanja organiziranega kriminala v Republiki Sloveniji. In M. Pagon (Ed.), *Dnevi varstvoslovja [Elektronski vir]: Zbornik prispevkov.* Ljubljana: Visoka policijsko-varnostna šola.

Europol. (2011). *EU organised crime threat assessment.* The Hague: Europol.

Felsenreich, C. (2012). Human factor analysis: How to build resilience against financial crimes. In M. Edelbacher, P. Kratcoski, & M. Theil (Eds.), *Financial crimes: A threat to global security* (pp. 301–332). Boca Raton, FL: CRC Press.

Fijnaut, C., & Paoli, L. (2004). Comparative synthesis of Part II. In C. Fijnaut & L. Paoli (Eds.), *Organised crime in Europe* (pp. 603–621). Dordrecht: Springer.

Furlan-Rus, M. (2009, 3 May). Prostitutke, a menda samo v prostem času: 100 evrov za uro med rjuhami, 60 evrov za pol ure *Dnevnik.si.* Retrieved from www.dnevnik.si/kronika/ 1042249441.

Furlan-Rus, M. (2014, 20 February). Trije Vozniki že Obsojeni: Dnevnik.si. Retrieved from www.dnevnik.si/1042633499/kronika/trije-vozniki-ze-obsojeni.

Gorkič, P. (2012). Policing organised crime: A paradox of transition? In A. Šelih & A. Završnik (Eds.), *Crime and transition in Central and Eastern Europe* (pp. 97–116). New York: Springer.

GRETA. (2014). *Report concerning the implementation of the Council of Europe Convention on Action against Trafficking in Human Beings by Slovenia: First evaluation round.* Strasbourg: The Group of Experts on Action against Trafficking in Human Beings.

IUS-INFO. (2015a). DZ podprl uvedbo davčnih blagajn. Retrieved from www.iusinfo.si/DnevneVsebine/Novice.aspx?id=147071.

IUS-INFO. (2015b). DZ sprejel novelo zakona o gospodarskih družbah. Retrieved from www.iusinfo.si/DnevneVsebine/Novice.aspx?id=146880.

IUS-INFO. (2015c). V uporabi del novele zakona o sodnem registru. Retrieved from www.iusinfo.si/DnevneVsebine/Novice.aspx?id=147836.

Kamenščak, I. (2015, 29 July). Novi Zakon o zaposlovanju, samozaposlovanju in delu tujcev. Retrieved from www.findinfo.si/DnevneVsebine/Aktualno.aspx?id=147586.

Karakaš, A. (2004). Načini preprečevanje organizirane kriminalitete s poudarkom na ureditvi normativno represivnih ukrepov v Republiki Sloveniji de lata in de lege ferenda. In G. Meško (Ed.), *Preprečevanje kriminalitete: teorija, praksa in dileme* (pp. 486–495). Ljubljana: Inštitut za kriminologijo pri Pravni fakulteti.

Komisija za preprečevanje korupcije. (2014). SUPERVIZOR. Retrieved from http://supervizor.kpk-rs.si/.

Kunšek, M. (2015, 5 June). Z novelo ZGD-1I proti veriženju podjetij. *IUS-INFO.* Retrieved from www.findinfo.si/DnevneVsebine/Aktualno.aspx?id=141687.

Lazaridis, G. (2001). Trafficking and prostitution: The growing exploitation of migrant women in Greece. *European Journal of Women's Studies, 8*(1), 67–102.

Logonder, A. (2013). *Kriminološka analiza notranjih in zunanjih odnosov članov organiziranih kriminalnih skupin iz Srbije* (PhD Thesis). Pravna fakulteta, Ljubljana.

Lorenčič, A. (2009). Pretvorba družbene lastnine v privatno – osrednji problem slovenske gospodarske tranzicije. *Prispevki za Novejšo Zgodovino, 49*(2), 189–206.

Lorenčič, A. (2012). *Prelom s starim in začetek novega: Tranzicija slovenskega gospodarstva iz socializma v kapitalizem (1990–2004)*. Ljubljana: Inštitut za novejšo zgodovino.

Lovšin, P. (2013, 28 October). Tožilstvo terja od zvodniškega para za poldrugi milijon premoženja. *Dnevnik.si*. Retrieved from www.dnevnik.si/kronika/tozilstvo-terja-od-zvodniskega-para-za-poldrugi-milijon-premozenja#.

Marine, F. J. (2006). The effects of organized crime on legitimate businesses. *Journal of Financial Crime, 13*(2), 214–234.

Maver, D. (2000). Tipične obrambne strategije in strategije preiskovanja. *Revija za Kriminalistiko in Kriminologijo, 51*(1), 12–23.

Maver, D. (2003). Organized crime: A perspective from Slovenia. In J. S. Albanese, D. K. Das, & A. Verma (Eds.), *Organized crime: World perspectives* (pp. 165–187). Upper Saddle River, NJ: Prentice Hall.

Meško, G., Sotlar, A., Dobovšek, B., Eman, K., Modic, M., Ažman, B., & Slak, B. (2015). Slovenia. In E. U. Savona & G. Berlusconi (Eds.), *Organised crime infiltration of legitimate businesses in Europe: A pilot project in five European countries*. Trento: Transcrime – Università degli Studi di Trento.

Modic, T., & Kralj, M. (2014, December). Z macolo nad slamnate goljufe, ti še naprej podjetniki. *Dnevnik.si*. Retrieved from www.dnevnik.si/posel/novice/ z-macolo-nad-slamnate-goljufe-ti-se-naprej-podjetniki.

Newton, M. (2011). *Chronology of organized crime worldwide, 6000 B.C.E. to 2010*. Jefferson, NC: McFarland.

Pajnik, M. (2008). *Prostitucija in trgovanje z ljudmi: perspektive spola, dela in migracij* (1st edn). Ljubljana: Mirovni Inštitut.

Pajnik, M., & Kavčič, U. (2008). Sodne prakse, povezane s trgovanjem z ljudmi in prostitucijo v Sloveniji. *Revija za Kriminalistiko in Kriminologijo, 59*(2), 141–154.

Pečar, J. (1996). Podjetniška kriminaliteta in kriminalna politika. *Revija za Kriminalistiko in Kriminologijo, 47*(4), 319–328.

Policija. (2003). *Police annual report 2002*. Ljubljana: Ministrstvo za notranje zadeve. Retrieved from www.policija.si/images/stories/Statistika/LetnaPorocila/PDF/lp2002.pdf.

Riccardi, M., Soriani, C., & Standridge, P. (2015). Organised crime investments in Europe. In E. U. Savona & M. Riccardi (Eds.), *From illegal markets to legitimate businesses: The portfolio of organised crime in Europe* (pp. 150–165). Trento: Transcrime – Università degli Studi di Trento.

Savona, E. U., & Berlusconi, G. (Eds.). (2015). *Organised crime infiltration of legitimate businesses in Europe: A pilot project in five European countries*. Trento: Transcrime – Università degli Studi di Trento.

Savona, E. U., Giommoni, L., & Mancuso, M. (2014). Human trafficking for sexual exploitation in Italy. In B. Leclerc & R. Wortley (Eds.), *Cognition and crime: Offender decision making and script analyses* (pp. 140–163). New York, NY: Routledge.

Savona, E. U., & Riccardi, M. (Eds.). (2015). *From illegal markets to legitimate businesses: The portfolio of organised crime in Europe*. Trento: Transcrime – Università degli Studi di Trento.

Sawyer, S., Metz, M. E., Hinds, J. D., & Brucker, R. A. (2001). Attitudes towards prostitution among males: A 'consumers' report'. *Current Psychology, 20*(4), 363–376.

Ščernjavič, I., & Hudej, N. (2015). Nekatere ustavnopravne dileme glede postopka odvzema premoženja nezakonitega izvora. *Pravna Praksa, 34*(5), I–VII.

Schoot, C. (2006). *Organised crime prevention in the Netherlands.* Den Haag: Boom Juridische Uitgevers.

Šelih, A. (2012). Crime and crime control in transition countries. In A. Šelih & A. Završnik (Eds.), *Crime and transition in Central and Eastern Europe* (pp. 3–34). New York, NY: Springer.

Šelih, A., & Meško, G. (2011). Slovenian criminology – an overview. In G. Meško, A. Sotlar, & J. Winterdyk (Eds.), *Policing in Central and Eastern Europe: Social control of unconventional deviance: conference proceedings* (pp. 13–33). Ljubljana: University of Maribor, Faculty of Criminal Justice and Security.

Slak, B., Meško, G., & Fank, M. (2015). Preučevanje organizirane kriminalitete v Sloveniji. *Revija za Kriminalistiko in Kriminologijo, 66*(2), 105–115.

SOJ SGDP GPU. (2014). Turn back crime. Začetek Interpolove svetovne kampanje o nevarnostih organiziranega kriminala. *Varnost, LXII*(2), 44–46.

Šori, I. (2005). Prostitucija v Sloveniji: Akterji, podoba, problemi in odnosi. *Etnolog: Glasnik Slovenskega Etnografskega Muzeja, 15*(66), 61–80.

Svetek, S. (1993). Kriminaliteta v Sloveniji v letu 1992. *Revija za Kriminalistiko in Kriminologijo, 44*(2), 107–120.

Svetek, S. (1996). Kriminaliteta v letu 1995. *Revija za Kriminalistiko in Kriminologijo, 47*(2), 95–111.

Tromp, S. (2011, 21 July). Recession driving more truckers into organized crime: RCMP. Retrieved from http://thetyee.ca/Blogs/TheHook/Labour-Industry/2011/07/31/RecessionCrime/.

Ude, L. (2008). Politika in pravo v primežu predvolilne propagande. In *Dnevi slovenskih pravnikov 2008* (pp. 1170–1177). Ljubljana: GV Založba.

Uradni List RS. (2006). Companies Act [Zakon o gospodarskih družbah ZGD – 1], Pub. L. No. 42/2006 (2006).

Uradni List RS. (2011). Confiscation of Proceeds of Crime Act [Zakon o odvzemu premoženja nezakonitega izvora (ZOPNI)], Pub. L. No. 91/2011 (2011).

van Duyne, P. C. (1996). *Organized crime in Europe.* Commack, NY: Nova Science Publishers.

Zavratnik, S., Kavčič, U., Pajnik, M., & Lesjak-Tušek, P. (2003). *Where in the puzzle: Trafficking from, to and through Slovenia: Assesment study.* Ljubljana: International Organization for Migration, Peace Institute.

Žist, D. (2006, March 13). Namesto plesa vdajanje prostituciji. *Večer*, 21.

5 From drug trafficking to wholesale trade business

Organised crime infiltration in Spain

Jesús Palomo, Jerónimo Márquez and Pilar Laguna

Organised crime in Spain: from illicit proceeds to investment in legal markets

The presence of organised crime in Spain is not a recent event, since gangs of bandits and organised smugglers have been operating in the country throughout history (Resa, 2013; Conde, 1991 for a detailed review of the history of organised crime in Spain). Although Spain does not seem to be a country of origin for major transnational organised crime groups (hereafter OCGs), Europol has recently included Spain among the five organised crime hubs stabilised in Europe (Europol, 2011).

Several authors have claimed that academic researchers have not yet extensively addressed in general the importance of organised crime. In the case of Spain, the lack of data and the restrictions to access official statistics on organised crime cases could explain the low amount of empirical studies published, which hinders research on infiltration of organised crime in the legal economy (Gomez-Céspedes, 2010; Palomo, Márquez & Laguna, 2015).

The OCGs have been able to find weaknesses in the Spanish systems to seize opportunities and use these channels to obtain higher benefits and gain more power based on high levels of impunity (Ministerio del Interior & CICO, 2013, 2014). The importance and significance of this phenomenon has hit the public debate in recent years (Barras, 2014). Furthermore, there is growing evidence of connections between organised crime and political corruption, denoting a 'higher level' type of infiltration of the legitimate economy, with the involvement of OCGs, entrepreneurs, and representatives of the political and administrative system (CSD, 2010). In the light of these facts, the Spanish government has implemented new laws and measures to fight organised crime more efficiently (Palomo, Márquez & Laguna, 2015).

Organised crime panorama in Spain

Since 2012, the CICO[1] classifies OCGs into three different subtypes of criminal groups – high, medium and low intensity – based on the complexity of their organisational structure and infiltration capabilities (Palomo, Márquez & Laguna, 2015).

A different classification, based on the level of involvement of Spanish criminals in the OCGs, can be found in De la Corte and Giménez-Salinas (2010).

In order to provide a clear snapshot, Table 5.1 presents the characteristics and structure of the OCGs based on the information collected for 2013. Spanish

Table 5.1 Main characteristics of organised crime groups (OCGs) active in Spain in 2013*

	All OCGs		High-intensity groups		Medium-intensity groups	
	N	*%*	*N*	*%*	*N*	*%*
OCGs in 2013	497		29	5.8	383	77.1
OCGs in 2012	482		37	7.7	363	75.3
OCGs active less than 3 years		83		62		81
Single nationality						
Foreign		*9*		*0*		*10[e]*
Spanish		*18*		*3.5[a]*		*17[d]*
Multinationality		73		93[b]		73[c]
Single-activity		NA		48[f]		79
International activity		67[g]		100[h]		72[i]
Main activities						
Cocaine trafficking		*31[j]*		*38*		*29*
Hashish trafficking		*21*		*24*		*19*
Theft with force		*17*		*14*		*15*
Money laundering		*6*		*14*		*6[k]*
Human trafficking for sexual purposes		*8*		*14*		
Fraud		*7*		*10*		
Theft with violence or intimidation		*12*				*13*
Tax fraud				*10*		
Extortion				*10*		
Estimated wealth	€1,250 million		€525 million		NA	

Source: authors' elaboration on CICO (2014).

Notes

* All the percentages and data in the table correspond to 2013, unless it is indicated explicitly that the reference year is 2012.

a It corresponds to one group with only Spaniards mainly focused on hashish trafficking.

b Main nationalities: Spanish (≈100%), Colombian (38%), Moroccan (34%), Italian (34%). See Table 5.2 for details on the illicit activities of these groups. 3.5% mixed foreign members that corresponds to one group focused on human trafficking for sexual exploitation purposes and forging documents with the following nationalities: Chinese, Japanese, North Korean, Taiwanese, Malaysian, Russian.

c Main nationalities: Romanian, Moroccan, Chinese, Colombian.

d It corresponds to OCGs with only Spanish members focused on cocaine and hashish trafficking, and theft with violence.

e Main nationalities: Spanish (88%), Colombian (29%), Moroccan (31%), Romanian (26%). An increase of Spanish members has been experienced since the 64% observed in 2012.

f However, in 2012 the majority of these groups was characterised by a single main illegal activity.

g Countries: Morocco, France, Colombia, the Netherlands, Romania, UK, Italia, Portugal, Germany, Dominican Republic.

h Countries: France, Morocco, The Netherlands, UK. Emerging countries: Russia, Italy, Venezuela.

i Countries: Morocco (17%), France (11%), Colombia (10%).

j In 2014, a total of 458 OCGs were detected. Involvement in drug trafficking activities and fraud increased to reach 57% and 5% of the OCGs, respectively; involvement in human trafficking and money laundering both reduced to 5%.

k As linked activity it reached 37%.

OCGs seem to be capable of creating alliances with foreign criminal groups, allowing them to increase their activities in several illegal markets (Jaime-Jiménez & Castro, 2010) and to adopt their *modus operandi* and organisational patterns (Sands, 2007). Mainly, they participate jointly in international illegal activities with Colombian, Italian, Moroccan and Romanian criminals.

In terms of activity, it is noteworthy that 67 per cent of the groups present some kind of international activity, 73 per cent are composed of a variety of nationalities and 83 per cent remain active less than the three-year threshold. The transnational profile affects the investment allocation and infiltration activity; this will be further stressed in the following sections.

In 2013, the estimated value of the total amount of seized assets to *intense economic crime and corruption* groups, not included in Table 5.1, reached €130 million; these groups mainly focused on tax avoidance and tax fraud (62 per cent), money laundering (52 per cent), fraud (29 per cent), forging documents (29 per cent), bribery (14 per cent), and misappropriation of public funds (14 per cent).[2] The most common *modus operandi* is the use of fake companies with no commercial activity to conceal illegal immigration, social benefits and tax fraud. The main nationalities in these groups are Spanish (51 per cent), Moroccan (24 per cent), Chinese (11 per cent), Argentinian (4 per cent) and Romanian (3 per cent) (Ministerio del Interior & CICO, 2014).

Main organised crime groups: activity and location

When looking at major OCGs, Table 5.2 presents their most frequent illicit activities and business sectors with evidence of infiltration in Spain. For example, Russian and Ukrainian groups are focused on cybercrime, French and Russian criminals concentrate on money laundering, and Spanish, Moroccan and Chinese groups seem to be mainly active on hashish trafficking and counterfeiting. In terms of leadership, there is evidence of OCGs having Spanish individuals as key members attributing leadership to the group; more than half of the Colombian OCGs have Colombian individual leaders; 20 per cent of the Italian OCGs are led by Italians; and 50 per cent of the OCGs involve Moroccans as principal members. Chinese criminals always lead and become the main members of Chinese criminal groups (Ministerio del Interior & CICO, 2013, 2014).

The geographical distribution of OCGs' activity is shown in Figure 5.1, where the number of detected high-intensity groups are presented both in 2013 (left) and 2014 (right). At a regional level (NUTS3), the areas showing a higher concentration of OCGs are Madrid and Barcelona, followed by Cadiz, Malaga, Alicante, Valencia and Murcia. The high correlation between illegal activity (Figure 5.1) and investments (Figure 5.2) is clear when comparing both figures (see the section 'Infiltration of organised crime in the legal economy' for details).

One of the main characteristics of the medium-intensity groups is specialisation; 75 per cent of the medium-intensity groups tend to concentrate on one to three regions and, typically, on a single illicit activity. The lack of a 'predominant' group and the limited episodes of violence among competing OCGs within

Table 5.2 Main organised crime groups' (OCGs) illicit activities and business sectors with evidence of infiltration in Spain*

Main OCGs	Illicit activities	Business sectors with evidence
Italian mafias	Money laundering (97%)	Real estate
	Cocaine trafficking (64%)	Agriculture and fishing
	Human trafficking	Construction
	Extortion	Bars and restaurants
	Counterfeiting	Transportation
		Renting of motor vehicles
Russian OCGs	Money laundering	Real estate
	Drug trafficking	Bars and restaurants
	Human trafficking	Construction
	Fraud	
	ITTP[a]	
	Extortion	
Chinese OCGs	Money laundering	Real estate
	Counterfeiting	Wholesale and retail trade
	Human smuggling	
	ITTP[a]	
Western European	Money laundering	Real estate
	Drug trafficking	Bars and restaurants
	Human trafficking	
	Extortion	
	Counterfeiting	
Moroccan OCGs	Money laundering	Real estate
	Counterfeiting (43%)	Wholesale and retail trade
	Human smuggling	
	Hashish trafficking (70%)	
	Fraud (43%)	
Colombian OCGs	Cocaine trafficking (95%)	Wire transferring services
	Money laundering	Bars and restaurants
	Extortion/racketeering (61%)	
	Illegal abduction (60%)	
Spanish OCGs	Cocaine trafficking (48%)	
	Hashish trafficking (31%)	
	Theft with force (16%)	

Source: authors' elaboration on CICO (2014).

Notes
* Percentages in brackets refer to the fraction of high-intensity OCGs dedicated to the illegal activity. If no figures in brackets are reported, then there is low evidence of high-intensity OCGs involvement and, mostly, small and medium-intensity groups.
a Illicit trafficking in tobacco products.

the same illicit market might suggest a certain level of collaboration among OCGs (Jiménez, 2005) denoting that Spain still offers a wide array of opportunities for criminal groups to seize.

Illicit proceeds are the base for organised crime investments. Table 5.3 provides the available estimates of the annual revenues attributed to OCGs in Spain for the main illicit markets. Thanks to the proceeds from drug trafficking,

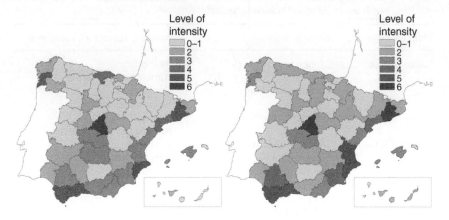

Figure 5.1 Organised crime groups by region in 2013 (left) and 2014 (right) (source: authors' elaboration on Ministerio del Interior & CICO (2013; 2014)).

especially cannabis and cocaine, Spain has ranked among the top European countries in terms of proceeds seized and confiscated from these two illegal markets (Caulkins, Kilmer & Graf, 2013; EMCDDA, 2014; UNODC, 2014). These estimates should be considered as proxies of the actual gross revenue available for investments. An attempt to estimate the net profit of the main illicit markets in Spain is provided in Giommoni (2015) where, based on costs at wholesale, trade and retail level of the supply chain, the estimated net profit from the supply of heroin is €67.4–157.2 million.

The international dimension of organised crime in Spain offers the chance to seize investment opportunities and profits across borders. Spain is considered a recipient country of inward criminal investments and, being a transit country, a base for foreign and non-local OCGs' investments in search for financial return and money laundering.

Infiltration of organised crime in the legal economy

The wide array of criminal groups active in Spain may imply a significant level of investments and money laundering activities, based on the high levels of illicit financial inflows and outflows (Almoguera, Morcillo & Muñoz, 2012). In Palomo, Márquez and Ruiz (2015) it is presented that the OCGs' investments are mostly related to their illicit activities. Hence, we use seized data as a proxy of the investments in the legal economy by OCGs (Thomas et al., 2009). Table 5.4, presents the amount of seized assets.

Real estate assets seem to be higher in high-intensity groups than in medium-intensity. Italian mafias, Moroccan and Colombian OCGs tend to invest in immovable and registered assets both in Spain and their country of origin. It is also worth mentioning that registered assets are acquired as instruments for: the

Table 5.3 Estimated annual revenues attributed to organised crime groups (OCGs) in Spain

Illicit market	OCGs' annual revenue (2013) million euro*	Average revenue per OCG million euro*	Number of OCGs and percentage of the total involved	
			2013	2014
Heroin trafficking	134.2	4.5	30 (6%)[a]	26 (6%)
Cocaine trafficking	767.7	5.0	154 (31%)	138 (30%)
Hashish trafficking	571.7	5.5	104 (21%)[a]	94 (21%)
Ecstasy (MDMA) trafficking	48.6	1.9	25 (5%)[a]	24 (5%)

Source: authors' elaboration on Palomo, Márquez and Laguna (2015).

Notes

* Estimates based on seizures. The fact that Spain is a transit country may affect these estimates.

a Approximated percentage based on the percentage of OCGs observed active in 2014 for a particular illicit market.

Table 5.4 Assets seized from organised crime groups (OCGs) in Spain

Seized assets	Total 2012	Total 2013	High-intensity OCGs (2013)		Medium-intensity OCGs (2013)	
			N	%	N	%
Vehicles	1,670	2,102	376	17.9	1,395	66.4
Vessels	118	119	25	21.0	81	68.1
Aircrafts	2	6	2	33.3	1	16.7
Firearms	549	558	64	11.5	479	85.8
Sharp weapons	201	630	15	2.4	582	92.4
Computers	615	909	123	13.5	706	77.7
Electronic appliances	6,455	4,498	800	17.8	3,119	69.3
Real estate	–	94	51	54.2	35	37.2
Jewels	–	13,000kg and US$10,500	1,513	14.1	–	
Cash	€44 million	€29.6 million	€3.1 million	10.5%	€25 million	84.5%
Fake cash	–	30,000	–		13,890	

Source: authors' elaboration on CICO (2014).

commission of the criminal activity itself (e.g. cars or watercraft are widely used to transport drugs between North Africa and Southern Spain); personal use and recreation; investment purposes. Cocaine trafficking is conducted mainly by maritime transportation (Barcelona and Pontevedra) and the use of containers (Madrid). Hashish trafficking is mainly conducted in small trucks, typically among groceries (Madrid), and with recreational crafts and water-powered bikes (Cadiz and Malaga) (CICO, 2014). A significant number of registered assets were recovered in Spain by operation *Laurel VII* against the Camorra (Polverino clan). A total of 117 vehicles were confiscated, including 62 trucks and 23 motorcycles (Fernandez, 2013; Guardia Civil, 2012; Muñoz, 2013; Tobella, 2013).

Movable assets represent an important part in an OCG's portfolio since the criminal enterprise does not have access to financial credit. In this sense, it is important to notice that the availability and management of cash or highly liquid financial instruments is crucial for OCGs' activity. These types of assets have historically drawn the attention of organised crime as investment instruments (PNSD, 2014). Most common assets in this category include jewellery and other luxury goods, cell phones and electronics (20 minutos, 2014; Aragón Digital, 2014; El País, 2012). Recently, electronic appliances (e.g. mobile phones, laptops, tablets) have become an essential part for the development of the illicit activities, mainly based on ICT.

The fast-paced growth of the real estate market, especially in the coastal areas and big urban areas, has collected a great part of the organised crime investments. The housing boom experienced by Spain since the second half of the 1990s has increased real estate prices to levels never seen before (European Commission, 2014b; Palomo, Márquez & Ruiz, 2015). It is not surprising that southern Spain, and in particular Andalusia, also comprises most of the real estate confiscated in relation to illicit drug trafficking. Due to the lack of information about the type of real estate, it is difficult to establish comparisons or to rank the different types of properties (Palomo, Márquez & Ruiz, 2015). However, houses and apartments appear more frequently than other categories (EFE, 2013; Europa Sur, 2013; Moltó, 2013).

Although real estate does not represent an important part of the assets confiscated and managed by the PNSD, there is evidence of cases where a large part of the benefits coming from illegal activities are invested in real estate properties (Agencia Tributaria, 2013; An Garda Síochána, 2011). In particular, it is important to mention that in the cases related to drug trafficking, 63 per cent involved investments in real estate, and, in those related to money laundering, 79 per cent involved investments in real estate (Palomo, Márquez & Ruiz, 2015).

Drivers and facilitators of investments: Spain as a preferred destination for organised crime investments

Among the different European countries where organised crime is present, Spain ranks among the first in the level of incidence of organised crime in terms of both criminal investments and infiltration in the legal economy (Diez, 2013). When analysing the drivers of criminal investments in Spain, although no official data is available, Palomo, Márquez and Ruiz (2015) indicate a variety of purposes, including money laundering, profit, control of territory, building social consensus, concealment of illicit activities and economies of scale with illegal markets. Macro opportunities such as economic conditions, government regulation and the demand of illegal products, among others, seem to be important factors that draw the attention of OCGs. In addition, micro opportunity factors, such as the criminal environment conditions (e.g. corruption), increase the attractiveness of the country in terms of criminal investments (Palomo, 2015).

The strategic location of Spain seems to attract different types and forms of illicit activities and, hence, the investment of the proceeds in the country. Along with this geographical factor, the Spanish tourism sector has been used by criminals as a multicultural environment that facilitates anonymity (EFE, 2014a). Also, high luxury living standards in certain areas, especially on coastal areas such as Andalusia, act as a perfect cover for criminals trying to invest their illicit benefits. In terms of illicit financial flows and money laundering practices, the proximity to nearby tax havens (Gibraltar and Andorra) seems to be a facilitator to create screen companies (Presidencia del Gobierno, 2013; Rodríguez, 2013). The growth of the Spanish economy and the rise of house prices until 2007 boosted investments in real estate, mainly for money laundering purposes (Fundación Seguridad Ciudadana, 2012; Global Property Guide, 2015).

Recently, the use of information technology among OCGs is becoming more critical for their illegal activities. According to official reports, the Spanish national communication network could contribute to the attractiveness of Spain for OCGs focused on cybercrime, online fraud and money laundering (CICO, 2014). Also, the use of freelance experts and ICT companies by OCGs is becoming common. In 2013, high-intensity criminal groups frequently used experts in different fields for money laundering purposes through complex business structures (CICO, 2014). The medium-intensity groups used experts in more than 90 per cent of their activities along with the progressive use of ICT companies for communications and logistics. The use of legal business structures to conceal illicit activities and money laundering has increased to 79 per cent in 2013 from 65 per cent in the previous year.

As already mentioned, the close relationship between economic crime, corruption and organised crime is evident in Spain. Although political corruption and fraud (in its various modalities) cannot be attributed directly to organised crime, it has been proven that these two factors feedback criminal activities. There is evidence that when transnational OCGs establish themselves in Spain, they seek to influence institutions and society as they do in their country of origin. In this regard, corruption, which can be found at political and business levels in Spain (Diez & Gomez-Céspedes, 2008), is perceived by the Spanish population as rampant in the country (European Commission, 2014a). These illegal practices may play a crucial role for OCGs looking to choose a destination for their illicit proceeds.

Geographical location of organised crime investments

Evidence of organised crime investments can be found in every Autonomous Community (*Comunidad Autónoma*). However, as displayed in Figure 5.2, based on the results of project OCP (Palomo, Márquez & Ruiz, 2015),[3] the intensity varies, with higher evidence in the coastal region areas.

The geographical distribution of criminal investments is characterised by the following factors: historical (or well-rooted) presence of OCGs (e.g. Andalusia); border regions and regions with important ports or proximity to tax havens (e.g. Andalusia, Valencia and Catalonia); large urban areas (e.g. Barcelona and Madrid), and tourist or coastal areas (e.g. Andalusia, Valencia and Murcia). Among the different regions, the autonomous community of Andalusia presents the highest level of organised crime investments. Due to its strategic geographical position, it serves as 'entry point' for a variety of illicit drugs (mainly cannabis and, to a lesser extent, cocaine), illicit tobacco products, and human trafficking (CICO, 2014).

The massive flows of tourism arriving to Andalusia and the Canary Islands create the perfect scenario for foreign OCGs to start investing without drawing

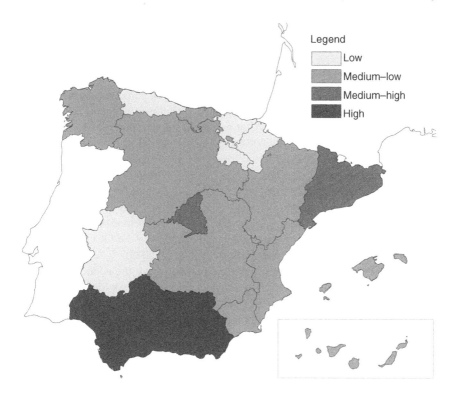

Figure 5.2 Autonomous communities with evidence of organised crime investments in Spain (source: authors' elaboration on Palomo, Márquez & Ruiz (2015)).

Note
Classes are identified using Jenks natural breaks optimisation.

the attention of immigration authorities (Instituto de Turismo de España, 2012). In addition, recent statistics on tourism show that Russian tourists have increased their average spending in Spain, which might be related to the notorious presence of Russian OCGs (see Table 5.1; TURESPAÑA, 2014).

Madrid also presents evidence of criminal investments. In this area, there is a notorious presence of OCGs investing in movable assets and companies related to real estate activities. Along with Madrid, Catalonia also shows evidence of organised crime investments, probably because of the different opportunities of investment that capital cities offer in Spain.

Finally, a wide range of regions appear to have less evidence of OCGs' investments. The autonomous community of Valencia also receives high flows of tourism, showing the same tendency as Andalusia. Malaga has seen a reduction in OCGs' activity since 2013; however, the broad range of real estate investment opportunities in the Costa del Sol and its privileged coast facilitates drug trafficking and money laundering activities.

Based on Palomo, Márquez and Ruiz (2015), the main regions with OCG investments were (in decreasing order) Andalusia, Madrid, Catalonia and the Balearic Islands. In terms of the variety of OCGs investing in the legitimate economy, evidence was recorded for 28 out of 35 defined categories of OCGs.

Business sectors: evidence of investments

From an economic point of view, every investment in a particular business sector contributes to a goal. For example: cash-intensive sectors (e.g. hotels, bars and restaurants, retail trade) could be used for money laundering purposes (see Ferentzy & Turner, 2009; Fijnaut & Paoli, 2004); territorial-specific sectors (e.g. real estate, construction) could be used for territory control purposes (Standridge, 2012; Unger, 2007). Also, low-tech and labour-intensive businesses (e.g. bars and restaurants, construction, retail trade) could be used to employ low-skilled criminals and to build social consensus, conceal illicit activities, and for irregular work exploitation and forced labour (Calderoni, 2014; Caneppele & Calderoni, 2014; Gambetta & Reuter, 1997). For more detailed analysis on the OCGs' investment sectors in Europe see Riccardi, Soriani and Standridge (2015).

Table 5.5 presents the main illicit purposes that drive the economic infiltration of organised crime in Spain. Investments are made in a wide array of business sectors (Kegö & Molcean, 2011; Transcrime, 2013). However, there is not enough information to rank all the different types of businesses, although some patterns can be highlighted. Table 5.6 presents the higher and lower level of evidence according to Palomo, Márquez and Ruiz (2015). In terms of attractiveness to criminal groups, emerging sectors are also presented. The amount of groups in a particular sector, e.g. real estate or bars and restaurants, could be seen as a signal of the level of investment opportunities that are still available for organised crime.

Based on the evidence in Table 5.6, it cannot be concluded whether infiltrated business sectors are those that are most profitable. However, from an economic

Table 5.5 Drivers behind criminal investments in legitimate businesses in Spain

Illicit purpose	Business sector
Concealment of illicit traffics	Real estate, business premises and industrial building. Typically for drugs loads, arms, counterfeited products
Money laundering and tax evasion	Screen companies. Typically bars, restaurants, real estate, construction, financial services, hotel and tourist accommodations, petrol and gas supply
Fraud	Companies to generate false documents (e.g. invoices, statements)
Shelter	Real estate
Human trafficking for sexual purposes	Nightclubs and bars
Distribution of counterfeits and illegal drugs	Wholesale, retail companies, and fitness clubs

Source: authors' elaboration on Palomo, Márquez and Ruiz (2015).

Table 5.6 Business sectors with evidence of criminal investments in Spain

Level of evidence	Business sectors	Number of identified criminal groups involved in the sector
High (>8%)	Real estate activities (28.0%)	High
	Bars and restaurants (15.0%)	High
	Wholesale and retail trade (19.6%)	High
Medium (4–8%)	Agriculture and fishing (5.6%)	High
	Hotels and other tourist accommodations (4.7%)	Medium–High
	Construction (4.7%)	Medium–Low
	Transportation (4.7%)	Medium–Low
Emerging sectors	Sports and gaming	Medium–Low
	Repair and retail of vehicles	Medium–Low
	Waste and scrap management	Medium–Low
	Renewable energy	Medium–Low
	IT and other services	Medium–Low
	Petrol and gas supply	Medium–Low
	Money wire transfer	Low

Source: authors' elaboration on Palomo, Márquez and Ruiz (2015).

viewpoint, most of them are mainly cash- and unskilled labour-based. The main investment criteria could be driven by low risk, concealment power or living standards of the criminals (see Kruisbergen, Kleemans & Kouwenberg, 2015; Riccardi, 2014; Standridge, 2012 for more details on the uncorrelated relationship between profitability and OCGs' investments).

The real estate sector has been traditionally chosen by organised crime as an outlet for their illicit benefits (Sands, 2007). Some of the main motivations behind the decision to invest in this sector include: the general thought that real estate is a safe haven asset; high expected returns in the short term (especially during the speculative bubble); the facilitation of illicit activities to conceal criminals, labs or warehouses; and its perception as a status symbol to gain prestige and a luxury lifestyle. Closely related to this sector, there is also evidence of OCGs investing in the construction sector in the Costa del Sol and the Canary Islands (Palomo, Márquez & Laguna, 2015).

Bars and restaurants seem to also draw the attention of organised crime. The evidence reveals a notorious presence of Russian, Italian and Spanish OCGs infiltrating this business sector for money laundering purposes, mainly of proceeds coming from drug trafficking (Diario Jurídico, 2011; Garcia, Castedo & Carranco, 2013; Kegö & Molcean, 2011). In addition, there is also evidence of bars and restaurants in south-west Spain being used by North African and other western European groups, including British and Irish OCGs, as screen companies to justify their illicit benefits and sustain their high living standards (Europa Sur, 2013; Olles & Peris, 2013).

In terms of infiltration strategies, the use of complex financial and business structures seems to be commonly extended among organised groups. During 2013, 79 per cent of the high-intensity groups (65 per cent in 2012) used some kind of business structure, in most cases, as a way to conceal illegal activities from the authorities (Ministerio del Interior & CICO, 2013). The identification of companies related to criminal groups has become a difficult task, mainly due to lack of accessible data (Diez & Gomez-Céspedes, 2008) and to the wide use of fake societies, screen companies and tax haven-registered companies. There is evidence of OCGs investing in legitimate companies (Eurojust, 2012; Giménez-Salinas, 2010). As an example, in 2005 the anti-money laundering operation *Ballena Blanca* started in Spain. It helped discover a complex money laundering network operated through a law firm in Marbella (Andalusia) that managed more than 500 different companies distributed among various countries (EFE, 2014b; El País, 2011; Pagola & Muñoz, 2013).

Wholesale trade, food import-export and money transfers: laundering the proceeds of crime

As mentioned in the previous section, it is worth analysing why there are some business sectors that seem to attract a wider array of criminal groups than others (see Table 5.6 for more details). We now describe various infiltration cases in some selected business sectors as an example of the laundering process conducted by different OCGs in Spain. The lack of data on the dynamics of the infiltrations in the legal economy limits the analysis of the degree of collaboration among OCGs.

First, wholesale and retail trade businesses have been commonly chosen by organised crime to invest illicit benefits (An Garda Síochána, 2011; Kegö &

Molcean, 2011). There is evidence of different criminal groups infiltrating this sector (i.e. Chinese, Russian and Georgian, British, Irish and Spanish OCGs) but none of them seems to control it. Chinese OCGs appear to be particularly involved in this sector. Most drivers behind these investments are related to the use of these businesses as shelters for illegal immigrants or to hide the trade of counterfeit products and money laundering activities. In 2012, a major Chinese OCG involved in a complex network of screen companies, most of them involved in the wholesale and retail trade business, was dismantled in operation *Emperador*; the operation seized around 130 real estate properties, 202 vehicles, jewellery, art, firearms, bank accounts and 235 companies. The criminal group was able to launder between €200 and €300 million per year, and the companies, mainly bazaars, were also used as a main distribution channel for counterfeit products, including clothes and illegal rolling of pipe tobacco (EFE, 2013; Policía Nacional, 2012). Operation *Aguijón* in 2012 dismantled a Chinese OCG that used wholesale logistics and retail trade businesses to import illegal tobacco to Spain in order to distribute it across Europe afterwards (Agencia Tributaria, 2012).

The Spanish food import-export sector has also attracted criminal groups. There is evidence of Italian mafias, mainly Camorra and Cosa Nostra, operating in the agriculture and fishing sector. The Spanish fishing sector occupies a distinctive place in the world, since Galicia is one of the most important regions in terms of fish and shellfish canning (Amigo & Gil, 2008). In 2008, authorities dismantled a network of companies controlled by Camorra and Cosa Nostra dedicated to the export of shellfish and fish, but with the main purpose to launder illicit proceeds from drugs, and human and firearms trafficking (El Faro de Vigo, 2008; La Opinión de Galicia, 2008; Tojo, 2008). Since 2006, the companies, most of them based in Vigo (Galicia), laundered illicit proceeds locally and then diverted them to Italy through money transfers in small amounts, below the legal threshold, in order not to arouse any suspicions (La Voz de Galicia, 2008). As for the agriculture sector, there is also evidence of Italian mafias investing in the olive oil business, particularly in the Andalusia region (Transcrime, 2013). In this case, the mafia groups carried out frauds and thefts of products from legitimate local competitors.

Finally, the financial services sector also presents evidence of infiltration by organised crime for money laundering-related purposes, although this particular sector does not seem to show a high level of infiltration when compared to others (see Table 5.6). Alternative financial services are emerging as a common way of transferring illicit proceeds, e.g. the use of crypto-currency, money wire transfers and prepaid cards. The use of the so-called *smurfing* technique, i.e. money transfers below the legal threshold, has been performed through money business services to send money abroad (Prieto, Garcia & Martín, 2010). According to the latest evidence (see Álvarez, 2011; El Economista, 2011; Muñoz, 2013; Sepblac, 2008) criminal groups have started investing directly and/or setting up money transfer agencies with the main purpose of laundering and transferring their proceeds abroad. These wire transfer services can be found in non-bank outlets such as call centres and small communication centres that offer money transfer services. It is also worth mentioning that the final destination of an important number of these money transfers with origins in Spain is usually in Latin American countries, especially Colombia (US Department of State, 2013). In 2013, operation *Ransomware* dismantled an Eastern European OCG (with members from Ukraine, Russia and Georgia) that used crypto-currency transfers and prepaid cards, such as Ukash, PaySafeCard and Moneypak, to transfer money to Russia while reducing the likelihood of being traced. The illicit origin of the proceeds came from *phishing* email campaigns. As scam *modus operandi*, they asked internet users for money in order to remove a fake police virus from their computers; separately, they also sold the illegal access to and control of 21,000 corporate private servers that were previously compromised in 80 countries. In Spain, 1,500 companies' computer servers were compromised. The amount laundered by the criminal group in two months has been estimated at €600,000 (Policía Nacional, 2013).

Conclusions

Several factors have driven organised crime towards Spain. The presence of a wide array of OCGs seems to be an indicator of the investing opportunities that criminal groups are able to seize. However, the efforts that law enforcement has taken towards controlling high- and medium-intensity criminal groups have had a deterrent impact, with numerous successful international operations. In this sense, it is important to note that there is no evidence of a dominant OCG either present in a particular illicit market or infiltrated in a particular business sector.

Although it is difficult to directly measure the impact of organised crime activity and infiltration into the legitimate economy, there is evidence that highlights the importance of this phenomenon in several business sectors. In this chapter we have reviewed the investments of the proceeds of crime in Spain and highlighted the correlation between the geographic location of organised crime investments and the areas where illegal activities take place. The main investment criteria could be driven by low risk, concealment power or living standard of the criminals. In this sense, the most common investments are registered and movable assets (e.g. cars, watercrafts, jewellery, weapons).

In terms of infiltration, the preferred business sectors are mainly related to the illegal activity of the group or money laundering enablers. Infiltrated business sectors are mainly cash intensive and based on unskilled labour. The use of screen companies, and infiltration in the real estate sector, along with the wholesale and retail trade businesses, seem to be the more recurrent options. Emerging infiltration cases in business sectors such as food import-export, agriculture and wire money transfer agencies indicate opportunities that are attracting OCGs with the main purpose of money laundering.

Finally, the lack of previous research on infiltration and investments of organised crime in Spain and the difficulty of access to official data both limit the analysis and show the necessity for future publically accessible data. In this sense, future studies should be devoted to analysing the dynamics of the different

OCGs participating in a business sector, in order to better understand, for example, whether or not criminal groups challenge each other or, instead, find agreements and set up rules that govern joint ventures.

Notes

1 Law 991/2006 of 8 September 2006 created the Centre of Intelligence against Organised Crime (CICO), whose mission is the development of strategic intelligence in the fight against all forms of organised crime, as well as the establishment of criteria for the operational coordination of services in cases of coincidence or concurrence in investigations. The general tasks of the CICO include gathering and analysing information related to organised crime in order to develop strategic intelligence against organised crime groups. It also determines the criteria for coordination of the operational units of Law Enforcement Agencies. Moreover, the CICO issues annual reports with relevant statistics on the situation of organised crime in Spain. Note that CICO has recently been renamed CITCO (Centre of Intelligence against Terrorism and Organised Crime).
2 Note that percentages do not sum 100 per cent because the same group can commit more than one felony.
3 Project OCP – Organised Crime Portfolio (www.ocportfolio.eu), co-funded by the European Commission, DG Home Affairs.

References

20 minutos. (2014, 17 January). Detenidos 54 miembros de una red dedicada al narcotráfico y el blanqueo de capitales. *20minutos.es – Últimas Noticias*. Retrieved from www.20minutos.es/noticia/2031764/0/detenidos-54-miembros/red-dedicada-narcotrafico/blanqueo-de-capitales/.

Agencia Tributaria. (2012, 16 June). La Agencia Tributaria refuerza sus actuaciones contra el tabaco de contrabando. Retrieved from www.agenciatributaria.es/AEAT.internet/en_gb/Inicio/La_Agencia_Tributaria/Sala_de_prensa/Notas_de_prensa/La_Agencia_Tributaria_refuerza_sus_actuaciones_contra_el_tabaco_de_contrabando.shtml.

Agencia Tributaria. (2013, 6 May). La Agencia Tributaria desmantela en Pontevedra una trama de blanqueo de capitales procedentes del narcotráfico. Retrieved from www.agenciatributaria.es/AEAT.internet/Inicio/La_Agencia_Tributaria/Sala_de_prensa/Notas_de_prensa/La_Agencia_Tributaria_desmantela_en_Pontevedra_una_trama_de_blanqueo_de_capitales_procedentes_del_narcotrafico.shtml.

Almoguera, P., Morcillo, C., & Muñoz, P. (2012, 15 May). La mafia rusa sobornó a un alcalde de IU para blanquear dinero del crimen organizado. *ABC*. Retrieved from http://sevilla.abc.es/20120515/andalucia/sevi-mafia-rusa-soborno-alcalde-201205142251.html.

Álvarez, M. J. (2011, 25 August). El 80 por ciento del dinero de los «narcos» se «lava» en locutorios. *ABC*. Retrieved from www.abc.es/20110825/madrid/abcp-ciento-dinero-narcos-lava-20110825.html.

Amigo, D. L., & Gil, M. D. G. (2008). La pesca en Galicia: Dimensión económica de las empresas transformadoras. *Universidad, Sociedad Y Mercados Globales*, 556–562.

An Garda Síochána. (2011). *Annual report of An Garda Síochána 2010*. Dublin: An Garda Síochána – Ireland's National Police Service.

Aragón Digital. (2014, July 2). Detenidas 16 personas por tráfico de hachís en la provincia de Zaragoza. *Aragondigital.es – Sociedad*. Retrieved from www.aragondigital.es/noticia.asp?notid=116899.

Barras, R. (2014). El crimen organizado transnacional. Mecanismos de lucha previstos en la Estrategia de Seguridad Nacional 2013. *UNISCI Discussion Papers, N. 35.*

Calderoni, F. (2014). Measuring the presence of the mafias in Italy. In S. Caneppele & F. Calderoni (Eds.), *Organized crime, corruption and crime prevention* (pp. 239–249). New York, NY: Springer.

Caneppele, S., & Calderoni, F. (Eds.). (2014). *Organized crime, corruption and crime prevention: Essays in honor of Ernesto U. Savona.* New York, NY: Springer.

Caulkins, J. P., Kilmer, B., & Graf, M. (2013). Estimating the size of the EU cannabis market. In F. Trautmann, B. Kilmer, & P. Turnbull (Eds.), *Further insights into aspects of the EU illicit drugs market* (pp. 289–323). Luxembourg: Publications Office of the European Union.

CICO. (2014). *Informe de situación del Crimen Organizado en España 2013.* Madrid: Ministerio del Interior.

Conde, P. (1991). *La conexión gallega: Del tabaco a la cocaína.* Barcelona: Ediciones B.

CSD. (2010). *Examining the links between organised crime and corruption.* Sofia: Center for the Study of Democracy. Retrieved from www.csd.bg/artShow.php?id=15192.

De la Corte, L., & Giménez-Salinas, A. (2010). *Crimen.org: Evolución y claves de la delincuencia organizada.* Barcelona: Planeta.

Diario Jurídico. (2011, October 19). Fiscalía impulsa la Operación Pozzaro con éxito contra el blanqueo de capitales en Tenerife. *Diario Jurídico.* Retrieved from www.diariojuridico.com/fiscalia-impulsa-la-operacion-pozzaro-con-exito-contra-el-blanqueo-de-capitales-en-tenerife/.

Diez, J. L. (2013). *Estrategia de Seguridad Nacional: Un proyecto compartido.* Madrid: Instituto Español de Estudios Estratégicos.

Diez, J. L., & Gomez-Céspedes, A. (2008). La corrupción urbanística: Estrategias de análisis. *Revista Española de Investigación Criminológica, 5*(6).

EFE. (2013, 6 May). La Camorra tenía 136 inmuebles en España fruto del blanqueo. *El Mundo.* Retrieved from www.elmundo.es/elmundo/2013/06/05/espana/1370422807.html.

EFE. (2014a, 21 January). España recibió 60,6 millones de turistas en 2013, un 5,6% más, y marcó un nuevo récord. *ABC.* Retrieved from www.abc.es/economia/20140121/abci-turistas-record-201401211049.html.

EFE. (2014b, 17 February). En prisión el abogado Del Valle por el caso 'Ballena Blanca', la mayor causa de blanqueo en España. *El Diario.* Retrieved from www.eldiario.es/politica/Valle-Ballena-Blanca-blanqueo-Espana_0_229927731.html.

El Economista. (2011, 25 August). Los locutorios blanquean el 80% del dinero procedente del tráfico de droga en España. Retrieved from www.eleconomista.es/espana/noticias/3327571/08/11/Los-locutorios-blanquean-el-80-del-dinero-procendete-del-trafico-de-droga-en-Espana.html.

El Faro de Vigo. (2008, 28 December). El jefe de la camorra detenido puso sus negocios a nombre de su pareja de Vigo. *El Faro de Vigo.* Retrieved from www.farodevigo.es/sucesos/2008/12/24/jefe-camorra-detenido-puso-negocios-nombre-pareja-vigo/283817.html.

El País. (2011, 31 March). Claves de la Operación Ballena Blanca. *El País.* Retrieved from http://elpais.com/elpais/2011/03/31/actualidad/1301559423_850215.html.

El País. (2012, 7 December). La red de Gao Ping tiene unos 130 inmuebles y 120 vehículos en toda España. *El País.* Retrieved from http://politica.elpais.com/politica/2012/12/07/actualidad/1354887113_958747.html.

EMCDDA. (2014). *European drug report 2014: Trends and developments.* Lisbon: European Monitoring Centre for Drugs and Drug Addiction.

Eurojust. (2012). *Annual report 2011*. The Hague: Eurojust.

Europa Sur. (2013, 7 July). La Policía de Algeciras coordina la caída de una banda criminal en Marbella. *Europa Sur*. Retrieved from www.europasur.es/article/algeciras/1559775/la/policia/algeciras/coordina/la/caida/una/banda/criminal/marbella.html.

European Commission. (2014a). *European anti-corruption report 2014*. Brussels: European Commission.

European Commission. (2014b). *International capital flows and the boom-bust cycle in Spain* (Economic Papers). Brussels: European Commission.

Europol. (2011). *EU organised crime threat assessment*. The Hague: Europol.

Ferentzy, P., & Turner, N. (2009). Gambling and organized crime — A review of the literature. *Journal of Gambling Issues*, *23*, 111–155.

Fernandez, A. (2013). *Informe de situación del Crimen Organizado en España 2013*. Madrid: Universidad Computense de Madrid.

Fijnaut, C., & Paoli, L. (Eds.). (2004). *Organised crime in Europe: Concepts, patterns and control policies in the European Union and beyond* (Vol. 4). Dordrecht: Springer.

Fundación Seguridad Ciudadana. (2012). Las mafias eligen España por su ubicación, el turismo y el ladrillo. *Revista Policía Y Criminalidad*, *18*. Retrieved from www.fundacionseguridadciudadana.es/publicaciones/REVISTA_POLICIA_Y_CRIMINALIDAD_N_18.pdf.

Gambetta, D., & Reuter, P. (1997). *Conspiracy among the many: The mafia in legitimate industries*. Cambridge: Cambridge University Press.

Garcia, J., Castedo, A., & Carranco, R. (2013, 25 January). Operación contra la mafia rusa en el Ayuntamiento de Lloret de Mar. *El País*. Retrieved from http://ccaa.elpais.com/ccaa/2013/01/25/catalunya/1359105749_210239.html.

Giménez-Salinas, A. (2010). Drug trafficking and money laundering in Spain: Evidence and political response. Presented at the 3rd Research Conference on Organised Crime, Frankfurt. Retrieved from www.bka.de/nn_230638/SharedDocs/Downloads/DE/ThemenABisZ/Forschung/OK-Forschungskonferenz/2010/vortragGimenezSalinasFramis,templateId=raw,property=publicationFile.pdf/vortragGimenezSalinasFramis.pdf.

Giommoni, L. (2015). Illicit drugs market. In E. U. Savona & M. Riccardi (Eds.), *From illegal markets to legitimate businesses: The portfolio of organised crime in Europe* (pp. 43–56). Trento: Transcrime – Università degli Studi di Trento.

Global Property Guide. (2015, 12 August). Property in Spain | Spanish Real Estate Investment. Retrieved from www.globalpropertyguide.com%2FEurope%2FSpain.

Gomez-Céspedes, A. (2010). Conducting organised crime research in Spain: An appraisal of the pros and cons. Presented at the 3rd Research conference on Organised Crime, Frankfurt. Retrieved from www.bka.de/nn%20_192960%20/EN/%20SubjectsAZ/%20Research/.

Guardia Civil. (2012). Con las detenciones llevadas a cabo por la Guardia Civil se descabeza el 'clan Polverino', único de la camorra napolitana relacionado con 'Cosa Nostra'. Retrieved from www.guardiacivil.es/es/prensa/noticias/4030.html.

Instituto de Turismo de España. (2012). *Informe anual 2012: Informe de Movimientos Turísticos en Frontera (Frontur) y Encuesta de Gasto Turístico (Egatur)*. Madrid: Instituto de Turismo de España.

Jaime-Jiménez, Ó., & Castro, L. (2010). La criminalidad organizada en la Unión Europea: Estado de la cuestión y respuestas institucionales. *Revista CIDOB d'Afers Internacionals*, *91*, 173–194.

Jiménez, Ó. J. (2005). Transborder organized crime in the new Europe: A vision from Spain. Presented at the EU Prospects and Security in South Eastern Europe: Hidden Economy, Transborder Crime and Development, Sofia.

Kegö, W., & Molcean, A. (2011). *Russian speaking organized crime groups in the EU*. Stockholm: Institute for Security and Development Policy.

Kruisbergen, E. W., Kleemans, E. R., & Kouwenberg, R. F. (2015). Profitability, power, or proximity? Organized crime offenders investing their money in legal economy. *European Journal on Criminal Policy and Research, 21*(2), 237–256.

La Opinión de Galicia. (2008, 23 December). Los negocios de la Camorra en Galicia. *La Opinión de Galicia*. Retrieved from www.laopinioncoruna.es/galicia/2008/12/24/negocios-camorra-galicia/246712.html.

La Voz de Galicia. (2008, 17 November). Desmontan en Vigo una organización delictiva vinculada a la Mafia italiana. *La Voz de Galicia*. Retrieved from www.lavozdegalicia.es/galicia/2008/11/17/0003_7320334.htm.

Ministerio del Interior & CICO. (2013). *El crimen organizado: Balance situación 2012 y avance Enero-Mayo 2013*. Madrid: Ministerio del Interior. Retrieved from www.interior.gob.es/web/interior/prensa/balances-e-informes/2013.

Ministerio del Interior & CICO. (2014). *Balance de la Lucha contra el Crimen Organizado en España*. Madrid: Ministerio del Interior. Retrieved from www.interior.gob.es/web/interior/prensa/balances-e-informes/2013.

Moltó, E. (2013, 4 July). Desarticulada una banda que robaba droga a otras redes de narcotráfico. *El País*. Retrieved from http://ccaa.elpais.com/ccaa/2013/07/04/valencia/1372929317_597297.html.

Muñoz, P. (2013, 22 January). Una red de narcos utilizó locutorios para blanquear 4 millones de euros. Retrieved from www.latribunadeciudadreal.es/noticia/ZB458D723-DACB-25A2-3E894C9BC9E80DAC/20130122/red/narcos/utilizo/locutorios/blanquear/4/millones/euros.

Olles, M., & Peris, X. (2013, 9 July). Desarticulada una banda que copaba el tráfico de drogas en la comarca de Inca. *Diario de Mallorca*. Retrieved from www.diariodemallorca.es/sucesos/2013/09/07/desarticulada-banda-copaba-trafico-drogas/873000.html.

Pagola, J., & Muñoz, P. (2013, 28 September). Más de 200 operaciones de blanqueo de la Policía han llevado hasta Gibraltar. *ABC*. Retrieved from www.abc.es/espana/20130929/abci-gibraltar-operacion-policial-201309282028.html.

Palomo, J. (2015). *Tackling illegal economy*. Madrid: TIE Project. Retrieved from www.tieproject.eu/?page_id=8.

Palomo, J., Márquez, J., & Laguna, P. (2015). Organised crime groups in Spain. In E. U. Savona & M. Riccardi (Eds.), *From illegal markets to legitimate businesses: The portfolio of organised crime in Europe* (pp. 126–133). Trento: Transcrime – Università degli Studi di Trento.

Palomo, J., Márquez, J., & Ruiz, N. (2015). Organised crime investments in Spain. In E. U. Savona & M. Riccardi (Eds.), *From illegal markets to legitimate businesses: The portfolio of organised crime in Europe* (pp. 202–209). Trento: Transcrime – Università degli Studi di Trento.

PNSD. (2014). *Informe sobre la actividad del fondo procedente de los bienes decomisados por tráfico ilícito de drogas y otros delitos relacionados durante el año 2013*. Madrid: Plan Nacional Sobre Drogas.

Policía Nacional. (2012, 17 October). Operación Emperador: 83 detenidos, 108 registros y más de 11.600.000€ en efectivo intervenidos. Retrieved from www.policia.es/prensa/20121017_1.html.

Policía Nacional. (2013, 27 September). Desarticulada la rama económica responsable del 'virus de la Policía' y que había comprometido la seguridad de 1.500 empresas en España. Retrieved from www.policia.es/prensa/20130927_1.html.

Presidencia del Gobierno. (2013). *Estrategia de Seguridad Nacional: Un proyecto compartido*. Madrid: Gobierno de España. Retrieved from www.lamoncloa.gob.es/documents/EstrategiaSeguridad_3105.pdf.

Prieto, A. M., Garcia, D. I., & Martín, A. (2010). La deconstrucción del concepto de blanqueo de capitales. *Revista Para El Análisis Del Derecho*, (3).

Resa, C. (2013, 16 August). Transnational organised crime in Spain: Structural factors explaining its penetration. Universidad Autónoma de Madrid. Retrieved from https://www.uam.es/personal_pdi/economicas/cresa/text9.html.

Riccardi, M. (2014). When criminals invest in businesses: Are we looking in the right direction? An exploratory analysis of companies controlled by mafias. In S. Caneppele & F. Calderoni (Eds.), *Organized crime, corruption and crime prevention* (pp. 197–206). New York, NY: Springer.

Riccardi, M., Soriani, C., & Standridge, P. (2015). Organised crime investments in Europe. In E. U. Savona & M. Riccardi (Eds.), *From illegal markets to legitimate businesses: The portfolio of organised crime in Europe* (pp. 150–165). Trento: Transcrime – Università degli Studi di Trento.

Rodríguez, J. (2013, 16 August). El misterio de las empresas de Gibraltar. *El País*. Retrieved from http://politica.elpais.com/politica/2013/08/16/actualidad/1376681836_768780.html.

Sands, J. (2007). Organized crime and illicit activities in Spain: Causes and facilitating factors. *School of Politics and International Studies*, *12*(2), 211–223.

Sepblac. (2008). *Tipologías de blanqueo de capitales*. Madrid: Servicio Ejecutivo de la Comisión de Prevención del Blanqueo de Capitales e Infracciones Monetarias.

Standridge, P. (2012). *Gli investimenti delle organizzazioni criminali. Un'analisi di casi studio di aziende mafiose in Italia*. Università Cattolica del Sacro Cuore, Milano.

Thomas, J., Wilson, D., Vettori, B., Cordero, I. B., Palomo, J., Vico, A. V., Rosendo Ríos, V., Geysen, N., Wozniak, R., Matuszewska-Ceglarek, M. M., Árvait, J., Tabernero Alonso, R., Colodrás Lozano, J. M., González-Novo, Á. R., García Fresno, M., MacDonald, L., Everest, G. (2009). *CEART project: White paper on best practices in asset recovery*. Madrid: Ministerio del Interior. Retrieved from http://eciencia.urjc.es/bitstream/10115/11993/1/white%20paper.pdf.

Tobella, A. (2013, 5 June). El clan Polverino tenía 136 inmuebles en España fruto del blanqueo de dinero. *El País*. Retrieved from http://politica.elpais.com/politica/2013/06/05/actualidad/1370432150_325444.html.

Tojo, A. (2008, 11 April). Los mafiosos de Vigo 'lavaban' su dinero en una empresa de Alipio. *El Correo Gallego – Diario de La Capital de Galicia*. Retrieved from www.elcorreogallego.es/terras-desantiago?idEdicion=1077&idNoticia=368118.

Transcrime. (2013). *Progetto PON Sicurezza 2007–2013. Gli investimenti delle mafie*. Milano: Transcrime – Joint Research Centre on Transnational Crime.

TURESPAÑA. (2014). *Egatur. Encuesta de gasto turístico*. Madrid: Instituto de Turismo de España – Ministerio de Industria, Energía y Turismo. Retrieved from www.iet.tourspain.es/es-es/estadisticas/egatur/paginas/default.aspx.

Unger, B. (2007). *The scale and impacts of money laundering*. Cheltenham: Edward Elgar Publishing.

UNODC. (2014). *World drug report 2014*. Vienna: United Nations Office on Drugs and Crime.

US Department of State. (2013). *International narcotics control strategy report*. Washington, DC: US Department of State, Bureau for International Narcotics and Law Enforcement Affairs.

Part II
Infiltrating legitimate businesses to develop fraud schemes

6 Welfare fraud and criminal infiltration in Sweden

Johanna Skinnari, Lars Korsell and Helena Rönnblom

Organised crime and its infiltration in Sweden

Organised crime and its use of companies

Organised crime in Sweden consists of gangs, groups and networks. The number of stable, organised crime groups seems to be low (Brå, 2005; Korsell, Skinnari & Vesterhav, 2009). The networks are the most important actors on this scene. Besides traditional crimes, organised crime members also commit economic crimes – and sometimes with the help of experts as they lack knowledge of the financial systems (Brå, 2014b; Malm & Bichler, 2013). As a possible consequence of this, notorious white-collar criminals are said to be teaming up with organised crime in joint criminal projects (NBI, 2012). Companies are used by organised crime as a crime tool. Interest in using companies in crime is also increasing, according to law enforcement and regulatory agencies (Brå, forthcoming; NBI, 2012; NUC, 2015).

While infiltration in the legal economy is an unfamiliar concept in Sweden, organised crime has always shown an interest in legal businesses for a variety of reasons. One reason will be explored in this chapter – the use of companies (as employers) to obtain benefits from the welfare system. Other common reasons are to use the company as a front for criminal activities.

Traditionally, it is relatively easy to set up a company in Sweden – something that organised crime takes advantage of (EBM, 2012). Relatively few sectors require permits to operate, and few business owners are subjected to screening by the authorities. A few important exceptions are taxis, haulage, financial services and restaurants that serve alcohol. Lately the use of permits has also increased in the welfare sector. Permits are required for companies that provide personal care assistance to the disabled, and this is expected to extend to a wider range of actors in this sector (Brå, 2015a, 2015b). All of these factors are likely to affect the process of infiltration.

As Swedish organised crime in general is small scale, short term and moderate in terms of profits, most perpetrators just make ends meet. Previous research shows that profits are often *consumed* in Sweden and elsewhere (Brå, 2007b, 2014a). One can talk of conspicuous consumption where thousands of

Swedish crowns are spent in restaurants, bars, on travelling and entertainment. Some consume profits in the legal economy, but very few have funds or are interested in investing in bonds or shares.

The volume of investments is hard to assess but, compared to consumption levels, investments are rare (Brå, 2007b, 2011b, 2014a; Hall, Winlow & Ancrum, 2008). Actors often choose familiar and low-key technological sectors such as restaurants, bars, shops, transport and construction businesses (Brå, 2014a; Kruisbergen, Kleemans & Kouwenberg, 2015; van de Bunt & van der Schoot, 2003). The sectors are either cash- or labour-intensive, and are therefore affected by illicit work and tax fraud. Perpetrators who have been interviewed in earlier studies talked about investments in legal businesses as an exit strategy or 'early retirement' from organised crime (Brå, 2007b; Junninen, 2006). In reality 'retirement' can be difficult, and these companies are often later used as fronts or crime tools. Some investments take place abroad – usually in places where the offender has family, friends or other ties.

Available studies suggest that organised crime infiltration in Sweden mainly takes place in the three metropolitan regions: the counties of Stockholm, Skåne (Malmö) and Västra Götaland (Gothenburg) (Rönnblom, Skinnari & Korsell, 2015). As Sweden is highly urbanised, most economic activities take place in these regions. Suspicious transaction reports (signs of money laundering) are also highly concentrated in these three city regions. Eighty-four per cent of the reports are from the counties of Stockholm (61 per cent), Skåne and Västra Götaland (Brå, 2011a). Finally, another concept related to infiltration, extortion of businesses, is also over-represented in Stockholm: more than 50 per cent of reported extortion cases concern businesses in Stockholm while only 24 per cent of all jobs are located in the city (Brå, 2012c).

The concept of infiltration

The concept of infiltration is not used in research and hardly ever in the media or in general debate (see Chapter 2 of this book for a broader discussion). This meant that a lot of creativity was needed to find relevant research that in some way described how organised crime groups take over and use legitimate businesses. Since there is no penal code using the term infiltration, law enforcement agencies combat this phenomenon through investigations into crimes that are a consequence of infiltration. They are likely to include various types of forgery, fraud, tax evasion, accounting offences and extortion.

One possible reason for the lack of the term infiltration is that Swedish law does not penalise legal entities such as businesses and associations (corporate criminal liability does not exist). Rather, the law targets *individuals* and their actions. However, legal developments in Sweden have meant an increasing use of corporate fines (not penalties in the formal sense) and administrative sanctions against legal entities. This chapter is based on research and literature studies conducted for project ARIEL (Savona & Berlusconi, 2015).[1]

Economic sectors at risk

Infiltration takes place in a variety of economic sectors. Organised crime is very interested in cash-intensive businesses such as hairdressing, beauty salons, cafés and restaurants (Brå, 2011b, 2012b; EBM, 2010, 2012; Kruisbergen et al., 2015; NBI, 2012, 2013). In cash-intensive sectors, it is easier to avoid registration of payments and tax on services and goods. With large sums of unaccounted cash, untaxed salaries can be paid to employees. For these reasons and for the purpose of money laundering, cash-intensive businesses attract organised crime (Brå, 2007b, 2011b; NBI, 2013).

Most sectors are in some sense at risk of infiltration: transportation and logistics, online gaming and regular betting, travel agencies, marketing/tele-marketing, recycling, retail and wholesale gold, haulage firms, import of alcohol and cigarettes are some examples (Kruisbergen et al., 2015; Rönnblom et al., 2015; van de Bunt & van der Schoot, 2003). There are also risks from infiltration in parts of the property sector where estate agents overvalue property (EBM, 2012; NBI, 2013). Some sectors, however, are more exposed to infiltration than others. The risk seems to increase when a sector is subject to rapid change, such as deregulation or privatisation, and control mechanisms are absent or not well developed. The main sectors at risk are discussed below. Residential care and other welfare financed sectors are also at risk, but will be described in more detail later.

The financial sector and currency exchange

The financial sector is subject to a number of regulations, some of which are aimed at curbing money laundering but at the same time can prevent infiltration (Rönn-blom et al., 2015). For example, a permit from the Financial Supervisory Authority is needed in order to start a business in cash-in-transit and currency exchange. In this process the leading persons in the company are subject to screening and register checks against crime registers. Often there are requirements in terms of experience and knowledge of the sector. Once the permit is issued, there seems to be little control over business activities (Rönnblom et al., 2015).

There are examples of persons involved in organised crime setting up companies in currency exchange and money transfer. These can be used to wire or exchange currency used to pay for drug consignments bought from international distributors, or for individuals to wire home income from prostitution. They are also used to transform money in a company account into cash – money derived from fraud or tax crimes. The main problem seems to be related to currency exchange and money transfer. However, a few cases have been identified regarding banks (Rönnblom et al., 2015). In those cases bank officials have assisted members of organised crime by granting loans despite insufficient cred-itworthiness and even agreeing to lend money on the same property several times at different banks. In one case the multiple bank loans were in turn invested in a restaurant, run by the same criminal group.

Another financial service at risk of infiltration is factoring, i.e. the purchase of invoices (debts) (Rönnblom et al., 2015). There are different types of factoring services, all of which may be combined with debt collection. According to the Economic Crime Authority, factoring companies are often at the centre of complex criminal enterprises involving several actors and businesses (Brå, 2011b; EBM, 2013). Factoring may also be essential for certain crime plans, since it enables rapid cash flow to the infiltrated company when buying invoices before the payment due date. Sometimes, owners of factoring businesses are unaware of their participation in criminal activities. However, they can also take an active role by offering a package solution including consulting, debt collection, factoring, fabricated invoices and cash supply. As with currency exchange, organised crime may also start up their own factoring companies (Brå, 2011b; EBM, 2013).

The construction industry

The construction industry is at recurring risk of infiltration (Rönnblom et al., 2015). The construction sector no longer consists of contractors involved in all stages of the project. Instead, they frequently use subcontractors for different tasks. A subcontractor can use their own subcontractors. This, in combination with large contracts, can facilitate the use of illicit workers. Another aspect is that the work is often carried out as projects, in which different companies carry out different tasks. In addition, reported and unreported labour is often combined, making it harder for authorities to identify irregularities (Brå, 2007a, 2011b, 2012b; van Duyne & Houtzager, 2005). Studies also show that the construction industry attracts people from, for example, outlaw motorcycle gangs (Brå, 2011b, 2012b; Rönnblom et al., 2015).

In the construction sector, widespread tax evasion is said to have affected market pricing. This means that criminal individuals and organisations not only make a profit, but some also argue that their actions may cause other 'honest' entrepreneurs to start evading taxes to keep their bids at a low and 'competitive' level (Brå, 2011b). The honest entrepreneurs thereby become vulnerable to infiltration, as they are involved with organisers and facilitators within the illicit part of the construction sector. Also, as will be explained later, welfare fraud is used to lower labour costs.

Restaurants, bars and related business

The fact that restaurants and bars attract criminal individuals is well established in organised crime research (Brå, 2007b, 2011a, 2012b; EBM, 2010; Korsell et al., 2009; Kruisbergen et al., 2015; NBI, 2012). The reasons are manifold: first, frequent visits to restaurants and bars are part of the criminal identity; and owning or controlling a restaurant gives you high status within organised crime (Brå, 2007b). Restaurant owners are also over-represented in victims of extortion (Brå, 2012b). It is a known risk sector for tax fraud (Brå, 2011b). Sometimes infiltrated businesses are also used to provide restaurants and small shops with smuggled or untaxed alcohol and cigarettes (EBM, 2010).

The cleaning and maintenance sector

For decades, the cleaning and maintenance sector has been known as a risk sector for economic and organised crime (Brå, 2011b). The sector shares two risk factors with construction, namely, subcontracting and labour-intensive work (Brå, 2011b; National Tax Agency, 2009). Other reasons that make the cleaning and maintenance industry interesting for organised crime are first that the work is unqualified; one does not need to understand the language and there is little need for training. Therefore illicit workers and illegal immigrants can be hired on low salaries. Second, the work is mostly carried out during evenings, nights and early mornings, when control is low. There are also reports from the sector that some companies are involved in welfare fraud (employer benefits), to cut costs and compete for tenders (Brå, 2015b).

Methods of infiltration and control

Infiltration is characterised by different levels of voluntariness, ranging from mutually beneficial to coercion, threats and extortion. Depending on the methods used, companies may be more or less aware of infiltration taking place. One general strategy is to use straw men, especially in formal and visible positions (Brå, 2011b; Rönnblom et al., 2015). Sometimes it is the former business owner, other times it is someone recruited for the position. Their key role is to be responsible for taxes and other claims against the company. In some regulated sectors the straw man needs a clean record and adequate finances if the business is to receive necessary permits. In some sectors, research indicates that the infiltrated business is kept within the family. This is perhaps not surprising since this reduces the risks of leaks, disloyalty and cheating (Korsell et al., 2009).

Easy to start up new businesses

While the concept of infiltration suggests that an actor takes control of an organisation step by step from the outside, research shows that it is not uncommon for persons in organised crime to start up their own businesses (Brå, forthcoming; Rönnblom et al., 2015). However, the benefits of newly started companies are disputed. Research shows that some criminals avoid start-ups since they draw the attention of both authorities and possible business partners (Brå, forthcoming, 2011b). However, to acquire established companies with good creditworthiness may take time and financial resources so this is likely to be limited to actors with high capacity (Brå, 2011b).

Legal acquisition

While infiltration involves irregularities at best and illegal actions at worst, methods for taking over and taking control of companies may be perfectly legal. In some cases, a company with good creditworthiness is purchased and used for fraud. Sometimes, the former owners, knowingly or unknowingly, are used as straw men.

Another advantage of acquiring an existing business rather than starting up a new one is the company's good reputation. Depending on the sector, a good reputation may be more or less crucial for future business and criminal set-ups. Research indicates that companies with good creditworthiness and spotless records are highly sought after in criminal circles (Brå, forthcoming, 2011b; Rönnblom et al., 2015). Perpetrators also seem to be willing to pay accordingly, since these companies attract better clients and delay suspicion from the authorities (Brå, 2011b). It is sometimes in the interest of retiring company owners (and their consultants) to sell their company quickly to avoid tax claims. Therefore, there is a market where infiltrators can buy this kind of trustworthy company with a long history. As previously mentioned, in sectors that require permits it may be more attractive to take over existing businesses with associated permits or licences.

Threats and extortion

In general, threats and extortion seem like unusual methods of infiltration. Even if the business owner feels threatened the threats are not always explicit. Members of organised crime have different levels of intimidation capital that they can use to achieve their objectives; actual threats are seldom necessary to scare the victim. Studies on extortion of entrepreneurs also indicate that the actual use of violence is rare (Brå, 2012b). Some perpetrators with high levels of intimidation capital offer 'insurance' or protection to business owners. It is not a real insurance but rather a regular payment to the perpetrator to keep his friends from vandalising the business or setting it on fire (racketeering) (Brå, 2012b; Skinnari & Stenström, 2012). It is a form of infiltration process: the insurance premium is constantly increased to the point where the business owner assumes the role of straw man for his or her own company. Interviews with perpetrators suggest that extortion sometimes leads to demand for ownership of the company (Brå, 2012b).

Bribery and collaborations

Another method of infiltration involves offering financial compensation. In a few cases perpetrators have convinced employees at currency exchange offices to collaborate for a share of the profit from the crime. These arrangements can be seen as win–win concepts. There are also examples of financial advisors and consultants whose business idea was to design crime plans for organised crime, and these collaborations are voluntary (Brå, 2011b; National Tax Agency, 2008).

Instead of a lengthy infiltration process, organised crime probably prefers to simply buy services, i.e. bribing officials or business owners. As long as the cooperation runs smoothly, both parties gain and organised crime has no reason to embark on a deeper infiltration. Should the business owner hesitate or stop cooperating, organised crime can use more forceful methods (Brå, 2012b, 2014b; Rönnblom et al., 2015). Besides being easy, one advantage of buying services is the flexibility of working with many businesses instead of focusing on infiltrating just a few.

Hijacking

One method for infiltration is to temporarily take control of a business, a form of 'hijacking'. In these cases, control over decision-making processes may be limited and short term, but still sufficient to complete fraud, for example (Brå, 2011b; Rönnblom et al., 2015).

One method of hijacking a business is to create false documents and submit these to the Companies Registration Office and subsequently change the board of directors. If the registration office has no reason to suspect irregularities, the change goes through with no questions asked (Brå, 2015a; Rönnblom et al., 2015).

Management strategies vary

The management strategies of infiltrated companies are perhaps the least studied aspect of organised crime infiltration. The depth of infiltration (i.e. the influence of management) depends on the offenders' capacity, their opportunity to infiltrate and the crime plan. The amount of time that the perpetrator plans to spend on the infiltrated business is of importance, i.e. different strategies require different time horizons. Bankruptcy alone may be profitable enough, although profit further increases if the company is also cleared of all its resources. As we shall see, the management strategies chosen often mirror the methods of infiltration discussed above.

Short-term business strategies seem most common

Both research and reports from authorities suggest that when organised crime groups infiltrate legitimate businesses, their involvement is often short-lived. This is often the case in long-firm fraud cases and when the goal is to plunder a company of its assets (Brå, forthcoming; Rönnblom et al., 2015). A typical fraud set-up involves acquiring a company, taking up credits and loans followed by emptying it of all its assets and eventually bankruptcy (Brå, 2011b, 2012a; NBI, 2012). In these cases, 'the faster the better' is probably an adequate description of the business strategy. In one case, the process and cash flow was accelerated by the use of a factoring company before the business was closed and the organisers disappeared with the proceeds of the crime (Rönnblom et al., 2015). In cases where a company is hijacked, time is even more crucial since the fraud needs to be completed before the real owners suspect they have been victimised.

Some set-ups require longer time horizons

Sometimes members of organised crime groups are interested in running the infiltrated business long term. This is particularly crucial in crime set-ups where the illicit profit cannot be retrieved at once, but is spread out over a longer time period. Typical examples include restaurants, hairdressers and other small businesses that generate profit over time by using illicit labour while also failing to register cash payments (Rönnblom et al., 2015). Another example is welfare fraud that is based on monthly payments that amass over time.

Infiltration to commit welfare fraud

The welfare system in Sweden

The Swedish social welfare system is relatively comprehensive by international standards. For decades there has been a political consensus on the establishment and maintaining of a form of welfare state. High taxes have guaranteed relatively generous benefits. This welfare system offers a basic security from birth to retirement, and the benefits are managed by five agencies, seven county administrative boards, 290 municipalities and 28 unemployment funds. The benefits are (in general) based on an individual's registered income for taxation purposes. Because of this, employers play an important role: they declare the employee's income. A high prior income generates a higher benefit. As a result of infiltration, employers can hire individuals 'on paper', and declare false salaries. In other cases salaries are exaggerated. In these cases the infiltrated company generates individual benefit frauds regarding, for example, parental insurance, sickness benefits and unemployment benefits. All of these benefits generate future pensions (as the pension is based on prior income) (Brå, 2015b).

Organised crime has realised that an employer can both declare high salaries, and avoid actually paying the taxes and fees, which has led such actors to include welfare fraud in their portfolios (Brå, 2011b, 2015b). The company 'owner' files for bankruptcy or sells the business to a straw man to avoid demands from the Tax Agency. In other cases the period of employment is short, and the employee reimburses the employer for the taxes and fees to qualify for a longer period with benefits (Brå, 2011b, 2015b).

For organised crime running a business, the welfare system also offers opportunities for employers to keep the illicit wages low. This is possible as employees can survive on small wages and at the same time claim unemployment and sickness benefits (Brå, 2011b; ISF, 2011; NBI, 2012). They do not demand more from the employer, especially not the employer helping them into the welfare system by providing the necessary fake documentation. The frauds that are committed by organised crime are mainly directed at employers' subsidies, salary guarantee and personal assistance care compensation.

Legal businesses that commit welfare fraud

Compared to benefits for individuals, employers receive the largest payments. The Unemployment Agency administers several subsidies aimed at stimulating employers to hire persons in a 'weak labour market position'. This often means hiring the long-term unemployed, the disabled, immigrants or even individuals with a criminal record. Because of high salaries, even for unskilled workers, and high payroll taxes, frauds are directed at the part of the benefit system that compensates employers for hiring workers.

In cases of benefit fraud against the Unemployment Agency, organised crime members act in the role of employers and hire staff, at least on paper. These individuals are sometimes aware of the frauds; in other instances they are cheated by the employer. They work, but at a lower cost than is declared to the Unemployment Agency (Brå, 2015b). There are also examples of 'no show jobs', where the 'salary' is returned to the employer. A previous study included an interview with an organiser of large-scale tax fraud (Brå, 2011b). This organiser had people hired using subsidies, but as they were not qualified to do the work, they were paid smaller sums to stay away (as the workers did not qualify for unemployment benefits, this was also a perfect solution for them). Instead the organiser used their identities for his illicit workers.

Residential care

This study has discovered two kinds of fraud connected to residential care. The first involves home care services for the elderly, where the work is either not carried out, or is carried out to a much lower extent than the municipality pays for. Whereas the first large-scale frauds involving infiltration were only recently discovered regarding home care services, the second type has been known about for a long time (Brå, 2015b; ISF, 2011). This is called personal assistance care compensation fraud and involves much larger payments from the Social Insurance Agency. By carrying out less care than is reported to the authorities, or keeping costs very low, the company can make a lot of money illegally (welfare fraud). In one identified case, the fraud had been going on since 2007. The prosecutor in the case argued that more than 30 million SEK (more than €3.2 million at current exchange rates) had been wrongly paid to the company by the Social Insurance Agency.

Residential care for the disabled, carried out by personal care assistants, is sometimes highlighted as especially vulnerable to irregularities (ISF, 2011; SOU, 2012). While some approaches only require one person to completely fabricate or exaggerate his or her disability and a couple of care assistants to take part in the fraud, large-scale and organised arrangements require a legitimate company. The latter approach requires higher levels of organisation involving a company and multiple employees. The basis for the fraud is that the care assistants do not perform the work tasks that are reported to the Social Insurance Agency. The company still reports the work and is compensated by the Agency (ISF, 2011; SOU, 2012).

There are also examples of beneficiaries that are unaware of the fraud. In these cases, they are often unaware of their right to receive care. If so, relatives, friends or others are orchestrating the fraud. In some cases family members are employed as assistants. In these instances, the income of the entire family may be dependent on preserving the image of a disabled family member (ISF, 2011; SOU, 2012).

In other cases, the company organising the care is the instigator, often taking advantage of the fact that the disabled person and his or her relatives are unaware of the legal framework and their right to care assistance. Sometimes, relatives of the disabled person carry out the work with very low salary, unaware of the size of the lump sum for each hour of care granted. The lower the wages, the larger the profit. In some of these cases there are also suspicions that instead of using human smuggling, some foreigners have been 'imported' (using working permits based on their employment as assistants) to play a part in these organised benefit fraud set-ups (Brå, 2015b; ISF, 2011).

Some seminar participants argue that deregulation of the care sector is part of the reason for the emergence of organised crime in this sector. Deregulation has resulted in several private, profit-driven actors (SOU, 2012, 2014). Residential care for the disabled and elderly is publicly financed but may be carried out by private enterprises. A lump sum (280 SEK, about €30) for each hour of granted care for the beneficiary is given to the company, and the company is responsible for ensuring that the care is being carried out. The sector is characterised by little transparency since it takes place in private homes. Therefore, regulators such as the Social Insurance Agency or the municipalities' social administration have limited ability to verify that rules are complied with and reported work is actually carried out.

Until 1 January 2011, personal care assistance was characterised by a lack of control mechanisms: no permits were needed in order to start a business in this sector (SOU, 2012, 2014). At present, a permit from the National Board of Health and Welfare is needed. Some argue that prior to the reform there were few incentives for organised crime to infiltrate existing companies since starting new ones was relatively easy (Rönnblom et al., 2015). Concerns have since been raised that following the reform it is more appealing to infiltrate a business with a licence to carry out personal care assistance. However, research suggests that neither the screening process nor the supervision by the National Board of Health and Welfare is prioritised or well developed (Brå, 2015b).

Salary guarantee fraud

In the event of bankruptcy, salary guarantee is paid by the County Administrative Board to employees to cover the first three months of unemployment. This has given some perpetrators with ties to organised crime an incentive to start businesses, pretend to create job opportunities, and then lead the company into bankruptcy.

It is the Salary Guarantee Act that compensates the employee for the loss of salary during notice. In 2015, the maximum sum per employee amounts to

178,000 SEK (about €20,000).[2] The strategy behind the fraud is to falsely indicate that one has been employed in a bankrupted company and is entitled to this benefit (Brå, 2011b, 2015b; SAMEB, 2011; The Swedish Enforcement Authority, 2010). The benefit is often paid to several employees who share the profit with the organiser. Some perpetrators have registered false identities and later claimed salary guarantees in their names.

Different strategies exist, ranging from 'all-fake set-ups' in which all documentation is false (including court decisions and certificates from liquidators) to strategies involving real, legitimate companies acquired solely for the purpose of salary guarantee fraud (Brå, 2015b; The Swedish Enforcement Authority, 2010). In one case, people have unknowingly been 'employed' in an infiltrated company, and been paid salary guarantees which have been 'collected' by members of organised crime groups (The Swedish Enforcement Authority, 2010). Other studies include cases where the payroll list has been enlarged, and real employees are mixed with new 'members of staff'.

Conclusions

To summarise, although the term infiltration is not used in the Swedish context, the phenomenon of organised crime establishing or taking over legal businesses is a reality in Sweden and, according to law enforcement agencies, a problem on the rise. Because of the network structure and entrepreneurial orientation of Swedish organised crime, companies are used primarily as a tool for committing crime, and seldom with the sole purpose of investing in legal markets. The use of businesses for the purpose of tax crime has a long history in the construction and cleaning sectors. What is new is the use of companies for large-scale frauds and the abuse of the welfare system.

The most basic use of an infiltrated company is for tax crimes in order to conduct illicit work. Large-scale tax crimes require other companies to create false paper trails by producing fabricated invoices. The invoices are used to transform legal money in accounts into cash that can vanish without a trace. In these cases actual work is carried out, but without paying taxes. A similar use of an infiltrated company is found in excise fraud. In these cases goods such as tobacco, alcohol or oil are imported and through a system with licences the companies can postpone paying excise. In reality the companies distribute the goods without paying excise or taxes. In both cases profit is increased by avoiding payments to the state. Two more parasitic ways of using an infiltrated company is via VAT fraud and welfare fraud. In VAT fraud no real import/export needs to take place, the 'trade' only exists on paper. The idea behind both types of fraud is to get payments from the state. In other words the main source of profit is the state.

At first glance, long-term infiltration strategies are directed at generating profits from running a legal business and mixing legal income with illicit work and other irregularities. In fact, that is a strategy that characterises economic crime, and not necessarily organised crime. This study found that organised

crime prefers to use the companies for scams and frauds, where, through fabricated invoices, employer's certificates, time-sheets and other false documentation,
they convince other actors – in this case the welfare state or legal businesses – to
pay out substantial amounts of money. The duration of the infiltration is affected
by the characteristics of the scams. Often, when the money comes from other
legal businesses, for example invoice frauds, the infiltrated company only sur-
vives a few months, and therefore a large number of legal businesses are
deceived from the start. In welfare frauds it is sometimes possible to use the
same infiltrated company for several years before it is identified by the authorities (Brå, 2015b).

As for methods of infiltration, this study suggests that the choice of starting a
new business or infiltrating an existing company may depend on the crime plan
and business sector infiltrated. Licenses, permits, the importance of creditworthiness and an existing customer base are some factors that indicate that taking over
an established business is preferable to starting a new one. Quick credit or tele-
marketing frauds, on the other hand, may be more suitable for new businesses.
Some seminar participants even argue that constantly starting up new businesses
has become a strategy for organised crime. Even brand new companies can be
granted the subsidies and benefits described here.

Management strategies of infiltrated businesses are perhaps the least
researched aspect of infiltration. This may have to do with the fact that some
infiltrated companies are often used to conduct credit fraud and, when this is
achieved, they simply go bankrupt. Also, management strategies may be of
limited relevance in the legal process. Research, however, suggests that the
longer the time frame of the criminal group, the more careful they are to keep
the company in general, and the records in particular, orderly (see Brå, 2011b).
In scams with a short time frame, the accounting is not as important.

A hypothesis is that business controls are underdeveloped in terms of combating infiltration. In a formal sense Sweden has a control system. It consists of
licences, tax controls and inspections of regulatory agencies. However, there is a
tendency to rely on register checks, where only known criminality, debts and
irregularities are found. Members in organised crime with infiltrated companies
are able to answer questions from authorities, find credible straw men and make
the company appear legitimate on the surface. It takes more thorough checks to
move beyond the credible surface and instead discover infiltration and organised
crime. Law enforcement and regulatory agencies are focusing on crimes and not
the infiltration processes behind these crimes. This is hardly surprising, as their
role is to identify and tie suspects to specific crimes. A problem with this situation is that the agencies fail to see early warnings and signs of infiltration. The
crimes only occur later – by then, organised crime has often managed to create a
credible facade, which makes detection harder.

Another aspect is that it may be more efficient to target preventive measures
at infiltration rather than the later crimes. First of all, there is a wider group of
actors who can prevent infiltration. Alongside the law enforcement agencies
Sweden has a wide range of regulatory agencies. Added to this list are, in some

cases, owners of legal businesses, creditors and distributors of services and goods. With a more in-depth knowledge of the infiltration process they could detect problems before an infiltration has been successful, and long before the actual crimes are committed.

Previous studies have revealed that racketeering (part of infiltration) through criminal damage is highly visible to customers, competitors, insurance companies and agencies undertaking field inspections (Brå, 2012b). This gives them an opportunity to act and help the targeted business owner. There are surely many indicators of different types of infiltration processes that could be used by similar actors.

In this first study on infiltration in the Swedish context, the concept is introduced and a first analysis is made. A future step would be to study this phenomenon from a preventive perspective. Our study suggests that preventive measures against infiltration are the way forward.

Notes

1 Project ARIEL – Assessing the Risk of the Infiltration of Organized Crime in EU MSs Legitimate Economies: a Pilot Project in five EU Countries, co-funded by the European Commission, DG Home Affairs. For more information on the Swedish data collection see Rönnblom, Skinnari, & Korsell (2015).
2 The average salary in Sweden is 32,200 SEK (around €3,500) per month, for private sector employees in 2014 (see www.mi.se/files/PDF-er/att_bestalla/loneskillnader/ Kvinnors%20och%20m%c3%a4ns%20l%c3%b6ner%202014.pdf).

References

Brå. (2005). *Narkotikabrottslighetens organisationsmönster* (No. 2005:11). Stockholm: Brottsförebyggande rådet.
Brå. (2007a). *Organiserat svartarbete i byggbranschen* (No. 2007:27). Stockholm: Brottsförebyggande rådet.
Brå. (2007b). *Vart tog alla pengarna vägen? En studie av narkotikabrottslighetens ekonomihantering* (No. 2007:4). Stockholm: Brottsförebyggande rådet.
Brå. (2011a). *Penningtvätt. Rapportering och hantering av misstänkta transaktioner* (No. 2011:4). Stockholm: Brottsförebyggande rådet.
Brå. (2011b). *Storskaliga skattebrott. En kartläggning av skattebrottslingens kostnader* (No. 2011:7). Stockholm: Brottsförebyggande rådet.
Brå. (2012a). *Brottslighet och trygghet i Malmö, Stockholm och Göteborg.* Stockholm: Brottsförebyggande rådet.
Brå. (2012b). *Otillåten påverkan mot företag. En undersökning om utpressning* (No. 2012:12). Stockholm: Brottsförebyggande rådet.
Brå. (2012c). *Utpressning i Sverige. Tvistelösning, bestraffning och affärsidé* (No. 2012:6). Stockholm: Brottsförebyggande rådet.
Brå. (2014a). *Gå på pengarna. Antologi om tillgångsinriktad brottsbekämpning* (No. 2014:10). Stockholm: Brottsförebyggande rådet.
Brå. (2014b). *Korruption i Myndighetssverige. Otillåten påverkan mot insider* (No. 2014:4). Stockholm: Brottsförebyggande rådet.
Brå. (2015a). *Administrativa åtgärder mot ekonomisk och organiserad brottslighet. Del*

1. *Tillstånd att bedriva verksamhet* (No. 2015:15). Stockholm: Brottsförebyggande rådet.

Brå. (2015b). *Intyget som dörröppnare till välfärdssystemet. En rapport om välfärdsbrott med felaktiga intyg* (No. 2015:8). Stockholm: Brottsförebyggande rådet.

Brå. (forthcoming). *Kriminell infiltration av företag.* Stockholm: Brottsförebyggande rådet.

EBM. (2010). *Rapport om den ekonomiska brottsligheten.* Stockholm: Ekobrottsmyndigheten.

EBM. (2012). *Underrättelsebild 2012.* Stockholm: Ekobrottsmyndigheten.

EBM. (2013). *Factoring – Rapport om en servicefunktion – öppen version* (No. 2013:2). Stockholm: Ekobrottsmyndigheten.

Hall, S., Winlow, S., & Ancrum, C. (2008). *Criminal identities and consumer culture: Culture: Crime, exclusion and the new culture of narcissm.* London: Routledge.

ISF. (2011). *Bidragsbrott och skattebrott. Välfärdens dubbla kriminalitet* (No. 2011:12). Stockholm: Inspektionen för socialförsäkringen & Brottsförebyggande rådet.

Junninen, M. (2006). *Adventures and risk-takers: Finnish professional criminals and their organisations in the 1990s cross-border criminality.* Helsinki: European Institute for Crime Prevention and Control, affiliated with the United Nations (HEUNI).

Korsell, L., Skinnari, J., & Vesterhav, D. (2009). *Organiserad brottslighet i Sverige.* Stockholm: Liber.

Kruisbergen, E. W., Kleemans, E. R., & Kouwenberg, R. F. (2015). Profitability, power, or proximity? Organized crime offenders investing their money in legal economy. *European Journal on Criminal Policy and Research, 21*(2), 237–256.

Malm, A., & Bichler, G. (2013). Using friends for money: The positional importance of money-launderers in organized crime. *Trends in Organized Crime, 16*(4), 365–381.

National Tax Agency. (2008). *Slutrapport: RPE Servicefunktioner – ett kontroll- och kartläggningsprojekt.* Solna: National Tax Agency.

National Tax Agency. (2009). *Utvärdering av städutredningar* (No. 2009:1). Solna: National Tax Agency.

NBI. (2012). *Polisens lägesbild av organiserad brottslighet 2012* (No. 2012:2). Stockholm: National Bureau of Investigation.

NBI. (2013). *Finanspolisens årsrapport 2012.* Stockholm: National Bureau of Investigation.

NUC. (2015). *Lägesbild av den grova organiserade brottsligheten 2016–2017.* Stockholm: Nationella underrättelsecentret.

Rönnblom, H., Skinnari, J., & Korsell, L. (2015). Sweden. In E. U. Savona & G. Berlusconi (Eds.), *Organised crime infiltration of legitimate businesses in Europe: A pilot project in five European countries* (pp. 57–67). Trento: Transcrime – Università degli Studi di Trento.

SAMEB. (2011). *Missbruk av statlig lönegaranti. Slutrapport.* Stockholm: SAMEB (Collaboration against economic crime).

Savona, E. U., & Berlusconi, G. (Eds.). (2015). *Organised crime infiltration of legitimate businesses in Europe: A pilot project in five European countries.* Trento: Transcrime – Università degli Studi di Trento.

Skinnari, J., & Stenström, A. (2012). Extortion from organised crime in Sweden. Presented at the GLODERS Conference on Extortion Racket Systems, Vienna: University of Vienna.

SOU. (2012). *Åtgärder mot fusk och felaktigheter med assistansersättning* (No. 2012:6). Stockholm: Governmental committee of inquiry (SOU).

SOU. (2014). *Förändrad assistansersättning – en översyn av ersättningssystemet* (No. 2014:9). Stockholm: Governmental committee of inquiry (SOU).

The Swedish Enforcement Authority. (2010). *Temagranskning avseende brottsanmälningar i konkurs 2010*. Stockholm: The Swedish Enforcement Authority, Tillsynsmyndigheten i konkurser.

van de Bunt, H., & van der Schoot, C. (2003). *Prevention of organised crime: A situational approach*. The Hague: Boom Juridische Uitgevers.

van Duyne, P. C., & Houtzager, M. (2005). Criminal sub-contracting in the Netherlands: The Dutch 'koppelbaas'. In P. van Duyne, K. von Lampe, M. van Dijck, & J. Newell (Eds.), *The organised crime economy. Managing markets in Europe* (pp. 163–188). Nijmegen: Wolf Legal Publishers.

7 Organised crime infiltration in the UK

Crash-for-cash and VAT carousel fraud

David Wall and Yulia Chistyakova

Introduction

Far removed from the cinematic drama of organised crime is a much more subtle and under-researched development: the increasing manipulation of the business sector to achieve criminal goals once achieved by more brutal methods. Frauds such as the 'crash-for-cash' car insurance fraud and 'VAT carousel' tax frauds fall under the contemporary rubric of 'organised crime', but what specifically characterises these particular offences is that a legitimate business has been infiltrated by criminals in order to commit the frauds. It is the nature of infiltration in specific UK-based cases that will be focused upon in this chapter. In so doing, the chapter will show the involvement of traditional career criminals which typify UK organised crime groups, but it will also indicate the involvement of professional white-collar criminals in some of the more complex cases of infiltration. The presence of this latter group in the 'higher end' (more sophisticated and complex) infiltration frauds raises some important questions about current thinking about organised crime policy and policing practice in the UK.

The first part of this chapter will outline the structure of organised crime in the UK. The second part will look at which parts of the business sector are infiltrated by organised crime groups. The third part will examine how the sectors are infiltrated and will describe the different forms of criminal infiltration and fraud schemes found in the UK. It will then focus upon two distinctive case studies relating to 'crash-for-cash' (car insurance fraud) and VAT carousel (tax) frauds found to operate in the UK. This chapter reflects the contribution of the UK team working on the EU co-funded project OCP[1] (Savona & Riccardi, 2015) and project ARIEL[2] (Savona & Berlusconi, 2015) that were conducted between 2013 and 2015.

The characteristics of organised crime groups in the UK

Although there are many 'ifs and buts' regarding the meaning of organised crime, no matter how one looks at it, the bottom line is that it is very costly to society both financially and also more broadly. Project OCP estimated the general cost of organised crime to European countries to be about €100 billion (Savona & Riccardi, 2015). In the UK, specifically, the National Security

Strategy (HMG, 2013) and the Serious and Organised Crime Strategy have also identified the activities of organised crime groups as a significant risk to the UK's national security. Drug supply, organised fraud and organised immigration crime are all thought to have major impacts on the UK's economic infrastructure; but also society more broadly. Child sexual exploitation and abuse, criminal use of firearms, cyber-crime, economic crime and organised acquisitive crime are all identified as key threats by national authorities (HMG, 2013). In terms of geographical impact, organised criminal activity seems to be mainly concentrated in London and the South East, the North West and West Midlands, but other areas of the country are affected to a lesser extent (HMG, 2013).

As of December 2014, the number of organised crime groups (hereafter OCGs) operating in the UK was estimated by the National Crime Agency (NCA) to be about 5,800, comprising approximately 40,600 organised criminals (HMG, 2015). A Home Office study on the criminal profiles of organised criminals in the UK by Francis, Humphreys, Kirby and Soothill (2013) has also shown that the vast majority (87 per cent) were UK nationals. Whilst the majority had been convicted for drug-related offences (73 per cent), only 12 per cent of them specialised in a particular crime type – most were generalists in crime.

One of the key concerns for UK policy makers, practitioners and academics is the structure of the country's organised crime groups and the extent to which they reflect or differ from the socio-geographically based mafia groups found in Italy and elsewhere. The reality of organised crime in the UK is very different from the traditional mafia model, or Sergi's (2014) 'Italian Structure Model' which is fixed in the public imagination. Instead, the reality of UK organised crime groups leans towards an 'English Activity Model' (Sergi, 2014) comprising conglomerations of career criminals who temporarily join with others to commit crimes until they are completed and then re-form with others to commit new crimes. However, it will also be shown in this chapter that some of the more complex infiltrations can involve professional white-collar criminals and, as stated earlier, raise some questions about current organised crime policing practice, which tends to focus upon individual criminal actions and often misses the complexities of infiltration.

Perhaps the most interesting finding of the OCP and ARIEL projects (Savona & Berlusconi, 2015; Savona & Riccardi, 2015) is that if the large Italian mafia groups such as Cosa Nostra, 'Ndrangheta, Camorra and Sacra Corona Unita are taken out of the equation, the pattern of organised crime groupings is roughly similar in character to the rest to Europe, including the UK. Most studies characterise UK organised crime groups as polymorphous, adaptable, and fluid multi-commodity criminal networks (Hobbs, 1998; Hornsby & Hobbs, 2007; Levi, 2014). Whilst kinship and ethnicity remain important factors for group cohesion, multiple cross-ethnic linkages also play an important role in group formation (Akhtar & South, 2000; Kirby & Nailer, 2013; Pearson & Hobbs, 2001) and such mixed networks may be more viable, successful, continuous, and reputed (Ruggiero & Khan, 2006). While most evidence points to domestic groups and networks, there is some indication of activity by foreign-based organised groups operating legal businesses in the UK (Campana, 2011).

Dynamic illicit markets

By constantly reflexing and adapting, organised crime groups are shifting towards less risky and less violent, but lucrative market niches where detection of organised crime activities is more difficult (Edwards & Jeffray, 2014). Frauds, drugs trafficking, counterfeiting and tobacco smuggling are currently the largest organised illicit markets in the UK (Mills, Skodbo & Blyth, 2013). Other profitable markets are trafficking for sexual exploitation and organised vehicle crime (Mills et al., 2013). Alongside traditional markets of organised crime such as drugs and human trafficking, there is growing evidence of its presence in the financial sector, renewable energy, and waste and recycling.

Revenues and investments

Estimations of the profits of organised criminal enterprise offences in the UK vary from tens of thousands to hundreds of millions of pounds (Chistyakova & Wall, 2015). Contrary to popular belief, not all organised crime is associated with vast profits; many offenders make just enough to cover living expenses: they 'offend and spend' (Levi, 2014). This is arguably one of the demonstrable effects of the Proceeds of Crime Act 2002, which empowers various agencies to seize the profits of crime and presumably forces offenders to spend their money immediately. When criminals do invest, their main motivation is to satisfy personal and family consumption needs and lifestyle preferences. But they may also use the proceeds of crime to facilitate further crime.

The first type of investment behaviour, lifestyle and symbolic investments, is in high-value assets and consumer goods and includes properties, cars, motorbikes, number plates, boats, and in some situations even private jets and helicopters (Dubourg & Prichard, 2008; Hobbs, 1998; L'Hoiry, 2013; Ruggiero & Khan, 2006). They are important as symbols of success (Hobbs, 2013) and enablers of luxury lifestyle. High-value antiques, art and jewellery are particularly favoured investments and a way to launder money (Thompson, 2003). The second type of investment behaviour is functional investments – investments in businesses used as fronts for illicit activities, to launder illicit proceeds (Annison, 2013; Silverstone, 2011), or to perform criminal activities (Hobbs, 1998; Jackson, Jeffrey & Adamson, 2010; Silverstone & Savage, 2010). Both types of investment are mainly tactical and what appear to be absent, according to project OCP (Chistyakova & Wall, 2015), are strategic investments in share portfolios and businesses: investments that would increase wealth and power.

Business sectors vulnerable to organised crime infiltration

If organised crime groups are using businesses, then which of them are the most vulnerable to infiltration? The OCP research found that the most frequently mentioned business sectors with evidence of tactical illicit investments were wholesale and retail, bars and restaurants, transportation and renting of motor vehicles

(Chistyakova & Wall, 2015). Bars and restaurants were regarded as investments, but often used as fronts for criminal activities (Fellstrom, 2014; Hobbs, 1998; Leask, 2010; Silverstone & Savage, 2010). Convenience stores and off-licences are typically fronts for illicit activities (Silverstone & Savage, 2010), or used to sell illicit goods such as alcohol, tobacco or fake designer goods (Kington, 2009). Small retailers may be tempted by cheap illicit goods offered by organised crime groups (Tilley & Hopkins, 2008); in one case, foodstuffs imported by an Italian criminal group were used in restaurants in Scotland (Campana, 2011).

Transportation companies are often used for criminal activities: for example, taxi firms are used as fronts for money laundering and drug-trafficking activities. But they can also be part of larger criminal activities: for example, haulage businesses can be used for the transportation of illicit goods (drugs, illicit or counterfeit cigarettes, alcohol and other counterfeit goods), and warehouses used to store illicit goods or as venues for 'cutting up' lorry loads or distributing stolen goods (Hobbs, 1998, p. 413). Another sector in which OCGs typically invest is the renting of motor vehicles, perhaps because of the ways in which these businesses can be used to facilitate or conceal different criminal activities at no extra cost (Antonopoulos & Hall, 2015). Auto-recovery companies, for example, can be used as part of a criminal business, as in the 'crash-for-cash' scams described later (Durham Constabulary, 2013; Hobbs, 1998; Leask, 2010).

Construction companies are another favoured type of investment. Money from drugs trafficking, cigarette smuggling, arms sales, money laundering and other crimes is typically invested in construction, renovation or decoration businesses or infrastructure (Hobbs, 1998; Surinenglish, 2010). This observation is also based on the records collected by Chistyakova and Wall (2015).

Sports and gaming clubs (e.g. football and other sports) are among the sectors most often used for money laundering purposes (Fellstrom, 2014). Investments in sports clubs have been found, for example, in several areas of the UK including Southern Scotland, Essex, Outer London and Berkshire, Buckinghamshire and Oxfordshire (Chistyakova & Wall, 2015). Similarly, cash-rich money service businesses such as foreign currency exchange, money transfer, and cheque cashing services are typically used for money laundering (Thompson, 2003). Yet another way to launder money is through the purchase of financial products such as mortgages and investments (National Crime Agency, 2014). Mortgage fraud is often used to buy real estate. Payday loan companies offer a good legal cover for laundering income from drugs, prostitution and racketeering (Leask, 2010).

Personal services such as nail bars, tanning salons, hair salons, massage parlours, sunbed parlours and escort companies are also used as fronts for criminal activities. For example, nail bars have been used by Vietnamese communities as fronts for human and drugs trafficking (Silverstone & Savage, 2010).

UK OCGs have also been found to own hotels in several locations in the UK and overseas. Typically purchased as investments, hotels are also used as fronts for criminal activities and to launder money. This includes investments in holiday villages and tourist complexes in tourist/beach resort areas of southern UK, but also in Italy, Spain and Turkey (Surinenglish, 2010; Thompson, 2003).

Other sectors with some evidence of criminal investments include casinos, video lottery terminals (slot machines) and other betting activities; IT and other services; real estate activities; and repair and retail of second-hand vehicles. Investment in companies outside the UK is also growing. For example, a Northern Irish criminal group was reported to have invested proceeds from the illegal drug trade in several tourist complexes in Spain and Brazil, as well as in the sectors of renewable energy, infrastructure, recycling, telecommunications and recreational activities (Surinenglish, 2010).

To conclude, there are various drivers behind investments in companies. Some are functional and directly linked to the performance of an illegal activity because they conceal, enable or assist illegal activity. Others are used to 'save and legitimise' (and launder) illegal proceeds.

Criminal infiltration and fraud schemes

The patterns of interaction between legal and illegal markets are more complex than those described by the term 'infiltration', which implies a one-way flow of influence. Examples of infiltration indicate the presence of a more dynamic relationship between the infiltrator and infiltrated. For example, Antonopoulos and Hall (2015) refer to 'systemic synergy' between tobacco manufacturers and tobacco smuggling in the late 1980s to the beginning of the 2000s when tobacco companies created an illegal market for their own products (cigarettes) in the UK and facilitated exportation and then re-importation of these products. Similarly, Naylor (1999) characterises the relationship between legitimate and illegitimate sectors of the economy as a symbiotic free-market relationship: 'enterprise crimes [...] involve a symbiosis between the legitimate and the illegitimate sectors of society, the first providing the demand and the second the supply in a free-market relationship' (Naylor, 1999, p. 9). These synergic characteristics are also illustrated in the later case studies.

Where legal and illegal businesses are owned or managed by the same individual or a group and are part of a business portfolio, then capital can more easily be moved between the legal and illegal sectors. For example, a legal business may be used to fund an illegal business, or illegal proceeds may be invested in a legal business. A legal business may be an integral part of an illegal business (e.g. regularly used for transportation, storage etc.) while also continuing to operate as a legal business. Or, a legal business, such as a pub, club or restaurant, may be a convenient setting within which illegal business links are formed (Antonopoulos & Hall, 2015; Chistyakova & Wall, 2015; Hall & Antonopoulos, 2015).

To facilitate the infiltration of legal businesses, a third party, often a professional facilitator or broker (Morselli, 2009) may be used to bring together the various parties, especially in the complex 'higher end' frauds. Accountants or legal professionals, for example, may be illicitly recruited to assist with the business side of a fraud (Middleton & Levi, 2015). However, until recently, such professional groups have traditionally not been targeted by law enforcement agencies as enablers of organised crime because these links are difficult to prove. S.45 of The Serious Crime Act 2015, however, aims to address the gap by introducing a new offence of 'participation in an organised crime group' (see Travis, 2014). In addition to the use of facilitators or brokers, some researchers have suggested that the bribery of law enforcement officials, such as customs officers, often takes place to encourage their use of discretion with regard to the smuggling of illicit goods (Hall & Antonopoulos, 2015; L'Hoiry, 2013; Matrix Knowledge Group, 2007).

The various literature sources suggest that infiltration takes place in the following ways:

- *A legal business is sold illicit goods.* The criminal group offers businesses illicit (counterfeit, stolen or smuggled) goods, usually at cheaper than normal prices. In one study, these businesses included a wide range of types, but retailers, bars or restaurants were most at risk (Tilley & Hopkins, 2008). Related to this is the situation where the legal supply chain is infiltrated by criminals, as was found in the 'horsemeat' scandal in the UK (Daneshkhu & Rashid, 2013). By knowingly accepting the illicit goods, the act of not questioning why prices are much cheaper than normal makes businesses immediately complicit in the crime; though they continue to run their legitimate business model.

- *A legal business is invited to invest in an illegal business.* A legal business (UK-based or foreign) is invited to invest in an illegal activity such as, for example, cigarette smuggling (Antonopoulos & Hall, 2015). This activity takes the previous example one step further.

- *A legal business issues fake invoices for an organised crime group.* The criminal group becomes a customer of a struggling legal business and lures or threatens the owner into issuing fake invoices for goods and services (Armitage & Clarke, 2014). Such invoices are often for small amounts, which are less likely to be challenged and more likely to be paid.

- *Employees of a legal business are recruited into an illegal business.* Employees of a legal business such as truck drivers may be recruited to transport illicit tobacco or alcohol, or they may even transport it without knowing about it (Antonopoulos & Hall, 2015; L'Hoiry, 2013); or the owner of a transportation company may be involved in the smuggling of illicit products, sometimes unaware of what is going on (Antonopoulos & Hall, 2015; L'Hoiry, 2013).

- *Smuggling through duty-free shops.* Duty-free shops can facilitate tobacco and alcohol smuggling into the UK (Antonopoulos & Hall, 2015).

- *Illegal-legal business portfolio.* The owners of illegal businesses also own a legal business or hold a business portfolio and use their illicit proceeds to create a legal business or to launder money. They can also use their legal business to facilitate his illegal business, for example, to transport illicit goods such as for example drugs, tobacco, alcohol, or other counterfeit goods, store them in a warehouse or sell illicit goods via shops, cafes and pubs; or use money from the legal business to purchase illicit merchandise (Antonopoulos & Hall, 2015; Chistyakova & Wall, 2015; Hall & Antonopoulos, 2015; L'Hoiry, 2013). For example, in one case a drug dealer owned a portfolio of businesses including a pub chain, a beer distribution firm, several hundred private hire taxis and an accountancy business (Findlay, 2013).

Case studies of criminal infiltration: crash-for-cash and VAT carousel fraud

The following infiltration case studies explore two distinctive types of organised fraud found in the UK and illustrate the ways that infiltration takes place. Both case studies are drawn from open media sources, police investigation files and judicial documents. They are 'crash-for-cash' and VAT carousel frauds, and both are explained below.

Crash-for-cash car insurance fraud

The first infiltration case study is the 'crash-for-cash' car insurance fraud, which typically involves criminals staging car accidents and then fabricating and manipulating the circumstances. The criminals work with legitimate companies to defraud the insurance companies. 'Crash-for-cash' was a phase of criminal activity in the UK that emerged in the mid-2000s and peaked during the early to mid-2010s. A retrospective data mining initiative brought a number of fraudsters to justice (Grant, 2007).

The *County Durham Crash-for-Cash case*. This case is believed to be the largest 'crash-for-cash' fraud in the UK. A group of career criminals scammed insurance companies for hundreds of thousands of GB pounds between 2008 and 2010 (BBC, 2015). The owner of a car recovery, storage and hire company formed a partnership with the owner of a claims management and taxi hire/replacement company. Together with the employees, family members and friends of the two businesses, the group defrauded insurance companies as part of a scam that involved staging and voluntarily causing car accidents and fabricating and/or manipulating circumstances. The claims management company could actually operate legally without any criminal activity, and frauds were simply a way to accelerate business and increase profit. However, the car recovery, storage and hire company collapsed once the criminal activities were eliminated. The two companies merged their activities in order to place, layer, and integrate cash through personal and business bank accounts and they obtained assets with the aim of legitimising cash gained from fraudulent insurance claims. Economic profit was the main reason for the infiltration, and the targeted sector was the insurance industry, which appears to suffer from structural fragmentation and to be exploitable by criminals. Some members of the group had been active as local criminals in the area for years before this case.

The *Double Decker Crash-for-Cash case*. In this (smaller) case an accident was staged between a bus and a car. The bus inspector withheld information about his previous convictions in order to obtain a job as a night inspector for a bus firm. After infiltrating the firm, the inspector conspired with a friend to drive his car in front of the bus, causing the bus to crash into the back of it. The bus inspector apparently arrived at the scene of the crash within minutes to interview the driver, who was unaware of the conspiracy, and also take the passengers' names. Although none of the 30 passengers were hurt, the insurers became suspicious after 29 claims for whiplash were made against them and employed private investigators who subsequently found that all the claims were bogus (Camber, 2014). Only a few individuals were involved in this case; but it nevertheless illustrates infiltration and also a high level of organisation.

VAT carousel fraud

The second infiltration case study is 'VAT carousel fraud', which typically involves a relationship that mixes good and bad trading to exploit 'VAT-free' trading in multi-jurisdictional economies. At the heart of the fraud, false paper trails are created to reclaim VAT on transactions which do not exist. Very often the activity also reduces apparent earnings in order to avoid corporation tax as well as VAT. The fraud attracts the description 'carousel' because of the way that goods, and the VAT that is related to them, are passed across companies and jurisdictions in order to evade tax liability, as if they were horses on a carousel.

The *London mobile phones related VAT fraud case*. In this first VAT fraud example the fraudster was a London 'business celebrity' who orchestrated a missing trader intra-community (MTIC) fraud involving 200 companies importing/ exporting mobile phones in the UK, Spain and the Netherlands between 2001 and 2008. He used his own firm ('company A') as an umbrella for firms under similar names, but he also infiltrated other companies. One such company was an import-export business ('company B') which had an estimated turnover in excess of £100,000 and did not expect to receive regular VAT repayments. In mid-2005, company B was lured by an advertisement placed by company A stating it was looking for partners to act as brokers in the export of mobile telephones to overseas customers. Company B was assured that there would be no risk of MTIC fraud as company A would be importing the goods itself (although it did not) or sourcing them directly from the manufacturers. The reputation of company A and its famous owner lulled company B into a false sense of security that the deals were legitimate. Company A expected its brokers (e.g. company B) to purchase the goods on credit and transfer them pending payment from the customer. Company B started trading with company A and, shortly afterwards, requested that HMRC (HM Revenue and Customs) allow it to change from quarterly to monthly VAT returns as it was a repayment trader. HMRC refused this request because they were concerned about MTIC frauds in the wholesale mobile phone trade sector. To overcome this obstacle, one of the two shareholders of company B acquired a company exporting mobile phones ('company C') which already submitted monthly VAT returns and would enable repayments to be received quickly. Company C started acting as a broker by purchasing goods from company A which provided it with a European customer and dictated the profit margin for the sale. Between April and May 2006 company C purchased over 36,000 mobile phones from company A (which itself was supplied by a chain of buffer companies) and resold them to a company based in Spain ('company D'). In some of these deals, despite the customer being based in Spain, the goods were transported to an address in the Netherlands (a fictitious company which was a house with no storage facilities in a residential part of the city) on a 'ship on hold' basis until payment was received by company C. Payments for these deals were processed through a secretive offshore bank in Curacao which offered anonymous and fast transfers, so that fraudsters could create immediate false paper trails of trades and reclaim VAT on transactions which did not exist (see Edwards, 2008).

The *Metal traders in London, VAT fraud case.* The second VAT fraud infiltration case study, like the previous case study mixed good trading with bad. It involved a metal trader who persuaded a lending company to advance large sums of money for metal trading transactions to company A and its sister company B in the USA. By falsifying documents relating to the purchase and sale of metal – which never took place – the fraudster made it appear that the amount of the purchase price was far greater than the true amount and showed losses, thus avoiding paying VAT. The fraudsters were a gang of criminals who used a metal trading firm ('company A') based in London to defraud banks and creditors all over the world between 1996 and 2002. The owner of the company, with the help of accomplices and three of his brothers living in the USA, the UAE and Singapore, coordinated over 300 bogus customers and companies based in the USA, Singapore, India, Dubai, Hong Kong, Italy and France to create false trades that could give credibility to company A and allow it to ask for advance money from banks and creditors which believed they were giving money to an important metal trading firm. The company was so lucrative that its owner ended up in the *Sunday Times* Rich List. It also managed to dupe a number of politicians to act as advisers and give the company further credibility. The fake customers and companies were accomplices with addresses in different countries; they used false documents to present themselves as independent traders and win the confidence of auditors and banks. The fraud was to persuade lending institutions to advance large sums of money for metal trading transactions to company A and its sister company in the USA ('company B'), which was controlled by the owner of company A with the involvement of his brother. Lending institutions were deceived into believing that the transactions involved genuine purchase and sale of metal with customers independent of company A and company B. While there was some honest trading, the majority was fraudulent and related to the purported purchase or sale of metal which never took place or the falsification of documents so as to make it appear that the amount of the purchase price was far greater than the true amount, typically by the documentary substitution of a more valuable metal for what was a less valuable metal. The money advanced by the banks had been of benefit to the group either by way of the sale of receivables or by way of funding the purchase of metal (see Edwards, 2008). This case, like its predecessor, is a 'higher end' fraud – sophisticated and involving professional white-collar criminals.

'The Day of the Jackal' internet identities VAT fraud case. This third example of VAT fraud is internet-related. It is often referred to as the 'Day of the Jackal' Case because the fraudsters copied the tactics of Frederick Forsyth's assassin in his 1971 novel *The Day of The Jackal* by appropriating the identities of 200 dead babies and using the identities to infiltrate the tax system and set up bogus HMRC accounts. The fraudsters also set up accounts using the names of sports celebrities and members of the public from whom they had gathered personal information. Once the HMRC accounts were set up, the fraudsters bombarded HMRC with tax repayment applications (see Cockroft, 2015). What this case illustrates is the way that the internet can be used to further reduce the number of participants and also increase the volume of the frauds.

The *Del-Boy VAT fraud case.* In the final example, two fraudsters conspired to commit VAT fraud. One fraudster owned a series of firms including rail maintenance, construction, and car fleet hire companies which had legitimate business models. This person would pay the other, who owned a shell company, for fake consultancy work. The cash would be handed back, but the activity reduced the on-the-book earnings and therefore tax liabilities (Pleasance, 2014). This case is an interesting twist on the VAT fraud because of the relationship between the business owner and fraudster. The business owner was, in effect, performing an act of self-infiltration.

Both the 'crash-for-cash' and 'VAT carousel fraud' case studies demonstrate how infiltration can vary and also take place at different points in the business model. They also show that the organised crime groups involved can often be comparatively small in size and sometimes comprise only a few career criminals working together – much in line with the UK organised crime model described earlier. However, more importantly, some of the 'higher end' fraud examples also show that the infiltration can be sophisticated, international and involve an entirely different group of professional white-collar criminals. This group of criminals would normally fall outside the traditional UK organised crime policing model.

What is also striking about the above cases is that they lack the cinematic drama normally associated with organised crime narratives. They all seem to begin on the right side of the law and creep over to the criminal side, and no one notices until something happens. Usually one of the fraudsters makes a mistake or becomes greedy and makes a duplicate or nonsensical claim which brings the activity to the attention of authorities, and an investigation ensues which brings it to public attention. What the cases reveal is that the relationships between legitimate and illegitimate business practices are dynamic and flexible and are only just being understood in the UK.

The traditional pattern of criminal investigation tends to focus upon the criminal world, but clearly many of the activities described above and found in our ARIEL research indicate a more nuanced relationship between the legal and illegal. In the case of crash-for-cash, for example, one of the fraudsters in the County Durham case had a viable business model in claims, but made multiple claims to increase his profit which led to the fraud being exposed. In the second crash-for-cash case the fraudster infiltrated the legitimate company into a trusted position and exploited that trust. However, he aroused the suspicions of the insurers when he engineered claims for the same complaint by all of the passengers. These modes of discovery were similar to those in the VAT carousel frauds, although the subsequent investigations were more lengthy and complex. In case one, a suspicious transaction was exposed by a VAT claim for a product that was not yet on sale because of a manufacturing delay. In the second VAT fraud example, suspicions were aroused by a careless mistake by an employee who pressed the wrong button on a fax machine. In case three, the fraudsters used internet cafes thinking that they were anonymous, but the data trail pointed to the deceased individuals. In case four, the main fraudster brought attention to himself via his public persona (Facebook profile) as his earnings and claims to wealth did not match his tax profile.

Conclusions: the infiltration of legitimate economies in the UK

The true extent of criminality for these insurance and VAT frauds may be underestimated because we only know about the perpetrators who are caught. It is also likely that those who work closely to a legitimate business model are less likely to be found out and investigated. Our analysis also raises some interesting questions about whether or not current investigative practice is locked into an outdated paradigm. Are the right questions about organised crime being asked? Are investigators still tending to focus upon the organised crime groups rather than exploring the actual offence or its outcome? In other words, should an 'enterprise approach' be taken that looks at the viability of the business, rather than looking for criminals. This, in turn, raises some interesting questions about the costs of investigating these cases. It is a more expensive approach, and it raises questions about granularity. For example, on what should the lens of the justice process be focused, especially in terms of the outcomes of the investigation? Should the end game be a punitive quest to close down the business, which usually involves the redundancy of innocent staff? Or would an alternative solution be to wrest control from criminals and make the business work legally and develop the successful part of its business model? Whilst the latter solution seems the more rational, it may be the more impractical in this age of heightened political sensibility of the organised crime agenda.

The picture of organised crime that emerges from the UK contribution to project ARIEL (and also project OCP) is that of opportunistic, evolving, adaptable (and on occasions) transnational business models which clearly point to the need for a fundamental change in the general approach towards policing organised crime. Policing twentieth-century organised crime requires more innovative responses that must in some ways resemble organised crime itself in terms of its flexibility, networked organisation and information sharing across a range of sectors. It must be based on novel conceptualisations of the threat of organised crime and of approaches to harm reduction, and be supported by a stronger evidence base. Both the OCP and ARIEL pilot projects are steps towards developing such a knowledge base.

Notes

1 Project Organised Crime Portfolio, co-funded by the European Commission, DG Home Affairs (Grant No HOME/2011/ISEC/AG/FINEC/400000222). Thanks to the Chief Constable and members of Durham Constabulary for their help and support with this research.
2 Project ARIEL – Assessing the Risk of the Infiltration of Organized Crime in EU MSs Legitimate Economies: a Pilot Project in five EU Countries, funded by the European Commission, DG Home Affairs (Grant No. HOME/2012/ISEC/FP/C1/4000003801).

Acknowledgements

We would like to thank Dr Stefano Bonino for his contribution to the ARIEL project and his analysis of the Durham 'Crash-for-crash' case and the first two VAT fraud cases mentioned in this chapter (see further Savona & Berlusconi, 2015); also for his comments on an earlier draft of this chapter.

References

Akhtar, S., & South, N. (2000). Hidden from heroin's history: Heroin use and dealing within an English Asian community. In N. Natarajan & M. Hough (Eds.), *Illegal drug markets* (pp. 153–178). New York: Criminal Justice Press.

Annison, R. (2013). *In the dock: Examining the UK's criminal justice response to trafficking*. London: Anti-Slavery International.

Antonopoulos, G. A., & Hall, A. (2015). United Kingdom: The low entry threshold. In CSD (Ed.), *Financing of organised crime* (pp. 242–264). Sofia: Center for Study of Democracy.

Armitage, J., & Clarke, D. (2014). Villains choose 'safe' London to launder their dirty money. *Independent*. Retrieved from www.independent.co.uk/news/people/profiles/david-clarke-villains-choose-safe-london-to-launder-their-dirty-money-9155974.html.

BBC. (2015, May 30). Insurance fraud at record high, says ABI. *BBC News*. Retrieved from www.bbc.co.uk/news/business-27608316.

Camber, R. (2014, 11 December). Bus inspector jailed for 16 months after he risked passengers' lives in £500,000 double decker crash-for-cash fraud. *Daily Mail*. Retrieved from www.dailymail.co.uk/news/article-2832304/Bus-inspector-jailed-oragnised-500-000-crash-cash-fraud.html.

Campana, P. (2011). Eavesdropping on the mob: The functional diversification of mafia activities across territories. *European Journal of Criminology, 8*(3), 213–228.

Chistyakova, Y., & Wall, J. (2015). United Kingdom. In E. U. Savona & M. Riccardi, (Eds.), *From illegal markets to legitimate businesses: The portfolio of organised crime in Europe* (pp. 134–143). Trento: Transcrime – Università degli Studi di Trento.

Cockroft, S. (2015, March 3). Fraudsters who used the names of more than 200 dead children to launder profits from attempted £1m VAT fraud jailed for more than 16 years. *Daily Mail*. Retrieved from www.dailymail.co.uk/news/article-2981497/Fraudsters-used-names-200-dead-children-launder-profits-attempted-1m-VAT-fraud-jailed-16-years.html.

Daneshkhu, S., & Rashid, T. (2013, 12 December). UK food industry 'vulnerable' to criminal infiltration. *Independent*. Retrieved from http://search.ft.com/search?queryText=UK+food+industry+%E2%80%98vulnerable%E2%80%99+to+criminal+infiltration.

Dubourg, R., & Prichard, S. (2008). *The impact of organised crime in the UK: Revenues and economic and social costs*. London: Home Office.

Durham Constabulary. (2013). Crash for cash. *Press Release*. Durham: Durham Constabulary.

Edwards, C., & Jeffray, C. (2014). *Organised crime and the illicit trade in tobacco, alcohol and pharmaceuticals in the UK*. London: Royal United Services Institute.

Edwards, R. (2008, 6 May). Rich list businessman Virendra Rastogi jailed for £350m fraud. *Telegraph*. Retrieved from www.telegraph.co.uk/news/uknews/2080288/Rich-List-businessman-Virendra-Rastogi-jailed-for-350m-fraud.html.

Fellstrom, C. (2014, 5 April). West Ham owner's £1m loan to crime boss. *Independent*. Retrieved from www.independent.co.uk/news/uk/crime/west-ham-owners-1m-loan-to-crime-boss-9321418.html.

Findlay, R. (2013, 11 October). Scots drug baron Willie O'Neil could face up to five years in prison for £1.5 million money laundering racket. *Daily Record*. Retrieved from www.dailyrecord.co.uk/news/crime/scots-drug-baron-willie-oneil-2714522.

Francis, B., Humphreys, L., Kirby, S., & Soothill, K. (2013). *Understanding criminal careers in organised crime*. London: Home Office. Retrieved from www.gov.uk/government/publications/understanding-criminal-careers-in-organised-crime.

Grant, I. (2007, 8 September). Insurance fraud bureau's data mining initiatives net fraudsters. *Computer Weekly*. Retrieved from www.computerweekly.com/news/2240082446/Insurance-Fraud-Bureaus-data-mining-initiatives-net-fraudsters.

Hall, A., & Antonopoulos, G. A. (2015). United Kingdom: The shifting structures of a market with high demand. In CSD (Ed.), *Financing of organised crime* (pp. 242–266). Sofia: Center for Study of Democracy.

HMG. (2013). *Serious and organised crime strategy*. London: HMSO.

HMG. (2015). *The serious and organised crime strategy: Annual report for 2014*. London: HM Government.

Hobbs, D. (1998). Going down the glocal: The local context of organised crime. *The Howard Journal of Criminal Justice, 37*(4), 407–422.

Hobbs, D. (2013). *Lush life: Constructing organized crime in the UK*. Oxford: University Press.

Hornsby, R., & Hobbs, D. (2007). A zone of ambiguity: The political economy of cigarette bootlegging. *British Journal of Criminology, 47*(4), 551–571.

Jackson, K., Jeffrey, J., & Adamson, G. (2010). *Setting the record: The trafficking of migrant women in the England and Wales off-street prostitution sector*. London: ACPO.

Kington, T. (2009, 27 December). The British connection: Italian mafia finds UK good for doing business. *Guardian*. Retrieved from www.theguardian.com/world/2009/dec/27/mafia-crime-italy-gangs-camorra.

Kirby, S., & Nailer, L. (2013). *Using a prevention and disruption model to tackle a UK organised crime group*. Lancaster: Lancaster University.

Leask, D. (2010). Criminal gangs linked to 300 Glasgow firms. *Evening Times*. Retrieved from www.lexisnexis.com/uk/nexis/docview/getDocForCuiReq?lni=7YTY-0DR0-YBK0-5538&csi=239558&oc=00240&perma=true.

Levi, M. (2014). Thinking about organised crime. *The RUSI Journal, 159*(1), 6–14.

L'Hoiry, X. D. (2013). 'Shifting the stuff wasn't any bother': Illicit enterprise, tobacco bootlegging and deconstructing the British government's cigarette smuggling discourse. *Trends in Organized Crime, 16*(4), 413–434.

Matrix Knowledge Group. (2007). *The illicit drug trade in the United Kingdom online*. London: Home Office.

Middleton, D., & Levi, M. (2015). Let sleeping lawyers lie: Organised crime, lawyers and the regulation of legal services. *British Journal of Criminology, 55*, 647–668.

Mills, H., Skodbo, S., & Blyth, P. (2013). *Understanding organised crime: Estimating the scale and the social and economic costs.* London: Home Office.

Morselli, C. (2009). *Inside criminal networks.* New York, NY: Springer.

National Crime Agency. (2014, 5 January). National strategic assessment of serious and organised crime 2014. Retrieved from www.nationalcrimeagency.gov.uk/publications/207-nca-strategic-assessment-of-serious-and-organised-crime/file.

Naylor, T. (1999). Wash-out: A critique of the follow-the-money methods in crime control policy. *Crime, Law and Social Change, 32*(1), 1–57.

Pearson, G., & Hobbs, D. (2001). *Middle market drug distribution* (Home Office Research Study 227). London: Home Office Research, Development and Statistics Directorate.

Pleasance, C. (2014, 10 August). Self-styled Del Boy who applied to be on TOWIE and listed Bentley and Maserati as company expenses jailed for £5.8 million VAT fraud. *Daily Mail.* Retrieved from www.dailymail.co.uk/news/article-2785511/Self-styled-Del-Boy-applied-TOWIE-listed-Bentley-Maserati-company-expenses-jailed-5-8million-VAT-fraud.html.

Ruggiero, V., & Khan, K. (2006). British South Asian communities and drug supply networks in the UK: A qualitative study. *International Journal of Drug Policy, 17*(6), 473–483.

Savona, E. U., & Berlusconi, G. (Eds.). (2015). *Organised crime infiltration of legitimate businesses in Europe: A pilot project in five European countries.* Trento: Transcrime – Università degli Studi di Trento.

Savona, E. U., & Riccardi, M. (Eds.). (2015). *From illegal markets to legitimate businesses: The portfolio of organised crime in Europe.* Trento: Transcrime – Università degli Studi di Trento.

Sergi, A. (2014). Structure versus activity. Policing organized crime in Italy and in the UK, distance and convergence. *Policing: A Journal of Policy and Practice, 8*(1), 69–78.

Silverstone, D. (2011). From Triads to snakeheads: Organised crime and illegal migration within Britain's Chinese community. *Global Crime, 12*(2), 93–111.

Silverstone, D., & Savage, S. (2010). Farmers, factories and funds: Organised crime and illicit drugs cultivation within the British Vietnamese community. *Global Crime, 11*(1), 16–33.

Surinenglish. (2010, 6 April). Irish mafia on the Costa del Sol linked to 20 murders across Europe. *Surinenglish.com.* Retrieved from www.surinenglish.com/20100526/news/costasol-malaga/irish-mafia-costa-linked-201005261221.html.

Thompson, T. (2003, 3 September). Drug gangs go to London's diamond dealers for cash. *Guardian.* Retrieved from www.theguardian.com/uk/2003/mar/09/drugsandalcohol.ukcrime/print.

Tilley, N., & Hopkins, M. (2008). *Business views of organised crime* (Research Report No. 10). London: Home Office.

Travis, A. (2014, 6 March). Home Office to unveil fresh powers to track down organised crime associates. *Guardian.* Retrieved from www.theguardian.com/world/2014/jun/03/theresa-may-fresh-powers-organised-crime-associates.

Part III

Infiltrating legitimate businesses to control the territory and influence policy makers

8 Mafia infiltration in legitimate companies in Italy

From traditional sectors to emerging businesses

Michele Riccardi, Cristina Soriani and Valentina Giampietri

Introduction

Infiltration by mafias in the legitimate economy has been widely acknowledged by public and private institutions as a key threat to the Italian social, economic and political system.[1] Since the 1980s a wide range of measures – at investigative, administrative and judicial levels – have been introduced to tackle this phenomenon; in particular, to improve the tracing and confiscation of the businesses controlled by organised crime (see Florio, Bosco & D'amore, 2014 for a review). The Italian asset recovery regime has proved to be a powerful instrument with which to interrupt the mafia business cycle, and it has become an international model to combat the infiltration of the legitimate economy by organised crime (European Commission, 2012; Forsaith, Irving, Nanopoulos & Fazekas, 2012).

To some extent, regulators have gone beyond what researchers have produced in this field. Studies on the infiltration of organised crime (OC hereafter) in the Italian economy are not lacking, but they often have, with some exceptions, a qualitative nature (Savona & Riccardi, 2015, p. 183). To date, empirical studies have more often focused on the involvement of criminal groups in illicit markets than in legitimate ones; and on estimating the quantity of criminal proceeds generated rather than on analysing how and where they are laundered (see Calderoni, 2014b for a review). Overall, research on the financial aspects of criminal organisations is limited to Italian mafias, while studies on foreign OC are almost absent.

This chapter provides an analysis of the infiltration of legitimate businesses in Italy by both Italian and foreign organised crime groups (OCGs hereafter). Based on police and judicial evidence, and on the latest academic research studies, it discusses the drivers, geographical patterns, and business sectors of infiltration, also considering the ownership and management strategies of infiltrated businesses. Finally, it discusses some research and policy implications.

Methodological issues

Until recently, most of the studies on criminal infiltration have aimed at profiling, from a qualitative and sociological perspective, the characteristics of the 'ideal mafia company' and of the entrepreneur victims but also facilitators of criminal infiltration (Arlacchi, 1983; Catanzaro, 1988; Santino & La Fiura, 1990).

The first attempts to conduct empirical analysis of the phenomenon used confiscated companies in Italy as a proxy for infiltrated businesses (Transcrime, 2013; Riccardi, 2014b). Data on about 2,000 businesses definitively confiscated from OC between 1983 and 2012 at national level were retrieved from the national agency for the management of seized and confiscated assets (ANBSC) (see Transcrime, 2013 for details). By using this data, researchers were able to study the geographical and sectorial distribution of infiltrated businesses, also measuring their correlation with contextual variables – e.g. industry profitability, level of tax evasion in the territory (Riccardi, 2014b), their accounting and management strategies (Di Bono, Cincimino, Riccardi & Berlusconi, 2015; Donato, Saporito & Scognamiglio, 2013; Transcrime, 2013), their ownership structure (Riccardi, Soriani & Standridge, 2015b; Sarno, 2015), and their interactions with competitors and suppliers (Gurciullo, 2014).

At present, confiscated assets represent the best proxy available to study companies belonging to criminal organisations, but they have some limitations. First, they mainly concern Italian mafias, because to date almost no businesses have been definitively confiscated from foreign criminals. Second, they may provide an out-of-date picture of the phenomenon which omits territories and business sectors of emerging infiltration. Third, they may overestimate regions, sectors and business types for which confiscation is easier or is more intense (e.g. companies with simple ownership structures or areas with more effective anti-mafia prosecution offices) (Soriani & Riccardi, 2015; Transcrime, 2013).

In order to address these biases, more recent studies (Savona & Berlusconi, 2015; Savona & Riccardi, 2015) have extended the analysis to a wider variety of sources, including evidence taken from police investigations, judicial files and institutional reports – for example annual Direzione Investigativa Antimafia (DIA), Direzione Nazionale Antimafia (DNA) and Financial Intelligence Unit (FIU) reports. These studies have also adopted a wider definition of infiltration which takes into account not only companies traced to organised criminals and confiscated from them, but also cases of more indirect OC involvement intended to influence the decision-making process of the business (Savona & Berlusconi, 2015). Although these studies have provided a more updated picture of the phenomenon, they may have lost in terms of details and methodological soundness.

The infiltration of legitimate businesses by Italian mafias

The drivers of mafia infiltration

According to some scholars, since the 1960s mafias have gradually converted from racketeering-based organisations to 'entrepreneurial' ones: traditional activities (such as extortion) were no longer sufficient to guarantee profits and control of the territory (e.g. Arlacchi, 1983; Santino & La Fiura, 1990). This inter- pretation is rejected by other authors, who suggest that mafias invested in the legal economy long before the 1950s (Catanzaro, 1988; Fijnaut & Paoli, 2004).

Despite these diverse interpretations, empirical evidence shows that mafias no longer discriminate between illicit and legitimate markets, but see them as a con- tinuum along which to grasp profit opportunities and expand their influence (DIA, 2014b; Savona & Riccardi, 2015). Infiltration in legitimate businesses plays a crucial role in this respect: companies are used not only to launder money but also as tools to expand mafias' power and influence and to exploit economies of scale with the criminal activities in which mafias are involved. It is not sur- prising that mafias invest in the same sectors, such as construction or the retail trade, where they are also most active in terms of extortion racketeering (Lis- ciandra, 2014; Mugellini & Caneppele, 2012). In particular the infiltration of legitimate businesses responds to a range of goals, or drivers (Giampietri & Sarno, 2015; Riccardi, 2014b; Savona & Berlusconi, 2015; Transcrime, 2013).

The first is money laundering: businesses are widely used by mafias as layers for converting criminal proceeds and concealing illicit flows. In particular, some scholars have explained the shift to mafia-entrepreneurship by the need to launder the monetary surplus, generated in the 1980s by drug trafficking, in assets other than real estate properties and movable goods (Riccardi & Savona, 2011). Not surprisingly, the business sectors preferred by mafias (and by OC in general) are often cash intensive in nature because this makes it easier to place dirty money and more difficult to trace illicit transactions (Europol, 2015).

Second, businesses are often instrumental to mafias' illicit activities: for example, they are used to commit tax and excise fraud, conceal illicit trade (e.g. wholesale companies as fronts for drug trafficking, see below) and to sell counter- feits (CNEL, 2011; DIA, 2014b) or stolen goods (for example pharmaceuticals – Riccardi, Dugato, Polizzotti & Pecile, 2015c – or even stolen chocolate – Marangon, 2015).

The third driver is economic profit. Infiltration in businesses provides mafias with an additional source of proceeds besides illicit markets. However, accord- ing to empirical evidence, the profitability of 'mafia companies' and of the sectors in which mafias invest is not higher than the average (Di Bono et al., 2015; Riccardi, 2014b; Transcrime, 2013). But mafia companies are rent-seeking rather than profit-maximising organisations: instead of improving their competit- iveness, they endeavour to obtain monopolistic rents in protected sectors (e.g. public procurements) through criminal methods such as corruption or market abuse infractions.

Moreover, in the fourth place, infiltration in businesses also plays a crucial role in terms of increasing social consensus. Investing in companies allows mafias to distribute jobs, share subcontracts with friendly enterprises, provide strategic goods and services (e.g. healthcare or education) to the local popula- tion, and promote a respectable image of themselves (Fantò, 1999; Giampietri & Sarno, 2015; Riccardi, 2014b).

Fifth, the infiltration of industries with high territorial specificity (e.g. hotels and restaurants, gas and water supply, construction), as well as public protected sectors, enables mafias to monitor pervasively the territory in which they are active, and to maximise their physical and strategic control (Riccardi, 2014b; Transcrime, 2013). By connecting with representatives of the local public administration and business elite, mafias are able to influence politicians and other policy-makers.

According to some authors, infiltration in businesses may also depend on cultural or personal reasons (Riccardi, 2014b; Transcrime, 2013). Mafias will prefer sectors and/or territories close to their cultural and family traditions (e.g. agri-food, construction or restaurants) and to their members' background, which is generally low skilled.

Infiltrated business sectors

Mafias prefer those business sectors which best respond to the drivers described above. Inspection of the figures on companies confiscated from mafia organisations since 1983 to 2012 shows that almost half of them were active in the construction and wholesale and retail trade sectors, followed by hotels and restaurants (Figure 8.1). Lower percentages, but higher ratios with respect to registered companies, are recorded also by mining/extraction and health and social services. Most of these are low-tech, cash-intensive, labour-intensive and protected sectors, with high involvement of public resources (e.g. public procurements) (Riccardi, 2014b; Transcrime, 2013). Moreover, they are often the sectors most victimised by extortion racketeering (Lisciandra, 2014). However, there are sectorial differences among territories, among different mafia organisations (and within the same organisations) and over time (Riccardi, 2014b; Transcrime, 2013).

Construction and public procurements

The construction industry is a traditional sector of criminal infiltration in Italy, and the one where mafias can better exploit their power of intimidation, corruption and market abuse to obtain procurements and other public resources (Caneppele, 2014; Savona, 2010; Sciarrone, 2011; Transcrime, 2013). Other characteristics facilitate infiltration – high cash-intensiveness, low technological level, high labour intensity, abundance of small firms and of subcontracts – as well as the possibility to commit fraud (e.g. the use of low-cost and low-quality materials), employ irregular workers, and maintain control over other activities in the area (Riccardi, 2014b; Sacco, 2010; Sciarrone, 2011).

Infiltration occurs at any stage of the cement supply chain: from extraction to the production and supply of concrete, from building to renovation services. It is widespread throughout Italy, including northern regions, where in recent years important public works (*grandi cantieri*) have provided numerous opportunities for infiltration (see below). Mining in particular (the sector with the highest ratio between confiscated and registered companies) plays a strategic role in the

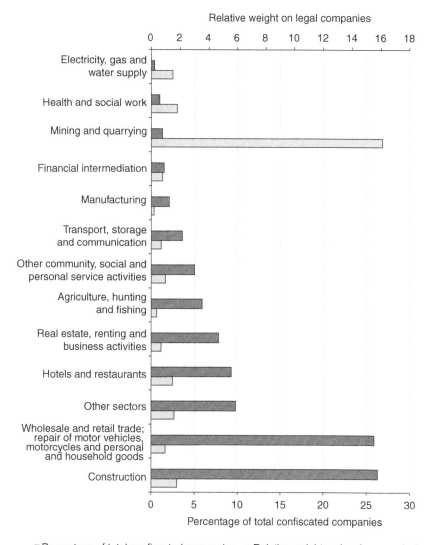

Figure 8.1 Business sectors of confiscated companies in Italy (1983–2012) (source: authors' elaboration on Soriani & Riccardi (2015)).

* Calculated as the relative weight of the business sector I comparing confiscated companies and registered companies, i.e. $Wi = \dfrac{C_i}{\Sigma i C_i} : \dfrac{R_i}{\Sigma i R_i}$, where C = confiscated companies; R = registered companies and i = business sector. If Wi > 1, then the weight of sector i among confiscated companies is higher than among registered companies, i.e. in the legal economy. If Wi < 1, then business sector i weighs more on the legal economy than among confiscated assets. If Wi ~ 1, then the business sector has the same weight between confiscated and registered companies.

economy of all the main mafia organisations. It is the first link in the cement cycle and also a useful front for illicit waste trafficking: abandoned quarries become ideal places to stock illicit waste, as documented by numerous investigations (Anselmo & Braucci, 2008; Commissione parlamentare d'inchiesta, 2000).

Waste management is another traditional source of public procurements and a target of infiltration by Italian mafias, both in Italy and abroad: in Romania, the companies managing the largest dumpsite in Europe, near Bucharest, have been seized by Italian authorities on mafia and money laundering charges (Riccardi, Soriani & Standridge, 2015a, p. 161); in Canada, an investigation conducted by the Italian and Canadian police in 2010 revealed a connection between a waste management company operating in Montreal, Toronto, and Ottawa and an 'Ndrangheta group (Transcrime, 2013, p. 250).

Wholesale and retail trade

The wholesale and retail trade has a large weight in the mafia economy. It accounts for about 30 per cent of all confiscated businesses in the past 30 years, with an even higher percentage for Camorra groups (Riccardi, 2014b; Transcrime, 2013). Wholesale and retail clothing businesses are often related to the trade in counterfeit clothes and apparel (in particular by Camorra groups). Trade in food products is widely used by all mafia organisations as a front to conceal illicit drug trafficking, both in Italy and abroad (Savona & Riccardi, 2015). It is also driven by mafia culture and geographical proximity to food clusters in Southern Italy, like dairy products in Campania or agri-food in Sicily (Brunello, 2011). Links with food fraud have also been proven (EURISPES, 2015).

Emerging cases of investments in department stores (*GDO – Grande Distribuzione Organizzata)* can be identified, especially by Cosa Nostra and Camorra groups in Sicily, Campania and Lazio (DIA, 2014b). These businesses enable intense money laundering because of the high volume of cash transactions. The same applies to retail trade shops in gold and jewellery (*compro oro*), which may also be used to 'launder' stolen jewels (DIA, 2013).

Transportation and logistics

Due to the high number of individual enterprises, subcontractors and regulatory loopholes, transportation has proved highly vulnerable to mafia investments. Infiltration is often associated with a variety of illicit activities: drug trafficking, corruption, extortion and intimidation (as in the *Decollo Ter* investigation targeting the 'Ndrangheta – Soriani & Riccardi, 2015), exploitation of irregular workers (Di Vico, 2014), and cargo theft, especially in pharmaceutical transportation (Riccardi et al., 2015c). In regard to the transportation of agricultural and food products, there is proven evidence of cooperation among 'Ndrangheta, Camorra and Cosa Nostra groups, which set up joint ventures to control logistic services in the main agri-food markets in Northern, Central and Southern Italy, such as Fondi, Milan and Piacenza (Soriani & Riccardi, 2015).

Emerging sectors

Besides the traditional sectors described above, others have been identified by recent police investigations, although they have not yet recorded high numbers of confiscations. The first is renewable energy, in particular wind power: according to Caneppele, Riccardi and Standridge (2013), approximately 10 per cent of the installed wind-power plants in Italy are under investigation for corruption, fraud, criminal and mafia association. The sector is attracting the interest of mafias for various reasons: copious public subsidies, strong territorial specificity, and vulnerabilities in their regulation, especially at the regional and local level (Caneppele et al., 2013).

Infiltration in petrol and gas supply, which concerns Camorra and Cosa Nostra groups in particular, enables mafias to maintain close control over the territory (Cantone & Di Feo, 2010) and also to carry out a wide range of fraud schemes: VAT fraud, excise fraud, manipulation of fuel counters (DIA, 2013; Transcrime, 2013).

Betting agencies and distributors of slot-machines and video lottery terminals (VLTs) are increasingly targeted by mafia infiltration: they serve for a range of criminal activities including money laundering (due to the high cash turnover), extortion (in certain areas bars and clubs are obliged to rely on certain VLT distributors appointed by mafia groups), and usury (mafia groups act as last resort creditors for 'video-lottery victims' short of cash) (DIA, 2014b; Savona & Riccardi, 2015).

Infiltrated territories

Although attempts to map and measure the presence of Italian mafias are common in the literature (see Calderoni, 2014a for a review), atlases of mafia investments are much rarer. Recent studies in Italy have used data on confiscated companies at provincial level (Riccardi, 2014b; Transcrime, 2013) or evidence taken from police reports and judicial files at regional level (Savona & Berlusconi, 2015; Savona & Riccardi, 2015). They are reported in Figures 8.2 and 8.3.

The vulnerability of Southern Italy to mafia infiltration in legitimate businesses has been acknowledged by a large body of literature (Sciarrone, 2011; Transcrime, 2013 for a review). Previous studies have shown that the distribution of criminal investments concentrates in areas with high mafia presence, low levels of openness towards international trade and foreign investments, low levels of R&D and of infrastructural development, high levels of tax evasion and of money laundering suspicious transaction reporting (e.g. Daniele & Marani, 2011; Riccardi, 2014b). The analyses suggest that Italian mafias prefer to invest in 'traditional' territories under their close control (Dugato, Giommoni & Favarin, 2015; Riccardi, 2014b; Transcrime, 2013) or where the social, economic and financial environment is weaker and more vulnerable (Polo, 2011; Sciarrone, 1998). It is difficult to determine the extent to which mafia infiltration is a cause or a consequence of the underdevelopment of these economies, but, as

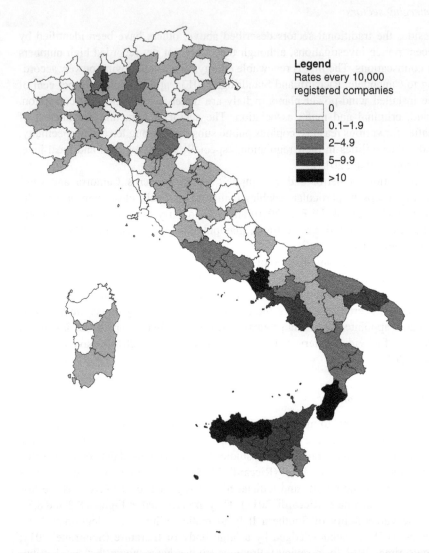

Figure 8.2 Geographical distribution of confiscated companies in Italy (1983–2012) (source: authors' elaboration on Riccardi (2014b)).

pointed out by some scholars, it is more likely that the causality goes in both directions (Pinotti, 2015).

The importance of Northern Italy and 'non-traditional regions' increases if consideration is made of not only confiscated companies but also more recent judicial and police evidence (Figure 8.3). The transplantation of mafia companies to central and northern regions has been widely recognised by both public authorities (DIA, 2014a, 2014b; Presidenza del Consiglio dei Ministri, 2014) and

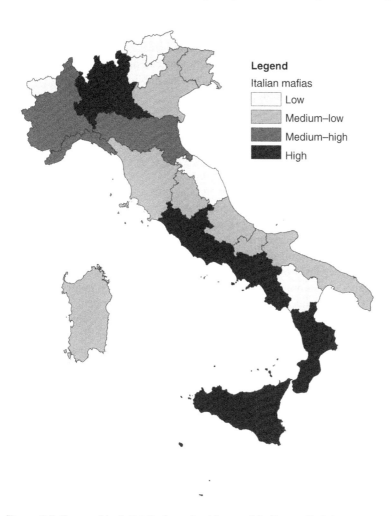

Figure 8.3 Geographical distribution of evidence of Italian mafias' investments in Italy (source: authors' elaboration on Soriani & Riccardi (2015)).

scholars (Campana, 2011; Riccardi, 2014b; Sciarrone & Storti, 2014; Trans-crime, 2013; Varese, 2011).

The expansion follows business opportunities, in particular large-scale public works such as construction of the high-speed railway (*TAV – Treni Alta Velocità*) in Piedmont, the new metro line in Rome, the post-earthquake reconstruction in Emilia Romagna and Abruzzo, or the international Milan 2015 EXPO fair (DIA, 2014a, p. 217). It benefits also from the support of local entrepreneurs, professionals and politicians of the so-called 'grey area', who act as bridges between criminal groups and the local legal economy and public administration.[2]

In this regard, recent studies have highlighted that mafias, especially 'Ndrangheta groups, may have shifted their infiltration strategy from large urban conurbations to smaller municipalities and peripheral areas (e.g. small towns in the provinces of Milan, Turin or Imperia), where they can hide better, are less monitored, and can more easily infiltrate or corrupt the public administration (Caneppele et al., 2013; CROSS, 2014, p. 10).

Infiltration, ownership and management strategies

Infiltration and ownership strategies

In order to infiltrate companies, mafia groups use a wide array of strategies ranging from direct to more indirect forms of ownership. These are chosen by balancing typical mafia needs (e.g. keeping control of the business 'in-house') with money laundering strategies (e.g. concealing the beneficial ownership) (Riccardi et al., 2015b; Transcrime, 2013).

The most direct form of control implies the personal involvement of mafia group members, as administrators and/or shareholders, in the company's management. Empirical evidence shows that, on average, 45 per cent of the shareholders of companies confiscated in Italy from 1983 to 2012 were members of the organisation, although this percentage has diminished over the years (Riccardi et al., 2015b). The opposite scenario is also possible, i.e. legal entrepreneurs who decide to enter into contact with, and then participate in, a criminal organisation (Giampietri & Sarno, 2015; Santino & La Fiura, 1990).

Indirect forms of control are related first of all to the use of strawmen. Figureheads are more often selected by mafias among relatives in order to maintain in-house and family control over the company (Fantò, 1999; Graebner Anderson, 1979; Sarno, 2015; Transcrime, 2013). In this respect, women (e.g. wives or daughters of mafia mobsters) play a crucial role: the percentage of female shareholders within confiscated businesses in 2006–2012 is almost two times higher than that among Italian legitimate companies (Riccardi et al., 2015b).

An alternative to strawmen is the use of complex cross-shareholdings and 'Chinese boxes' schemes, especially when mother companies are registered in tax havens or in off-shore jurisdictions. Nevertheless, empirical evidence suggests a limited use of these types of schemes while mafia companies have more direct 'ownership trees', with some exceptions (Steinko, 2012; Transcrime, 2013).

Other, even more indirect, ownership strategies relate to the ability of mafia members to influence the decision-making process of a company without being formally involved themselves or through the use of figureheads. For example, entrepreneurs can be persuaded to cooperate with the mafia organisation by intimidation, extortion, threats or violence (Sciarrone, 1998). In some cases, the same entrepreneurs resort to mafia groups in order to obtain benefits (e.g. the exclusivity of a product on the market) or extra funding (in the forms of usury), but are then taken over by the same criminal organisation (CENSIS, 2009; Lo Bello, 2011; Scaglione, 2014).

To be monitored in this regard are the cases of 'mafia banks' lending to legal companies at usurious interest rates and conditioning, in practice, their management: recent investigations have highlighted the growing use of these systems in northern Italian regions by both the 'Ndrangheta (Marangon, 2015) and the Camorra (Soriani & Riccardi, 2015).

When discussing ownership strategy, it is also important to consider the type of entity used by mafias. Empirical evidence suggests that limited liability companies (*srl – società a responsabilità limitata*) are preferred to other legal forms. Thanks to limited liability and the fragmentation of share capital, they obstruct financial investigations and seizure; but, at the same time, they are easy to incorporate (€10,000 minimum share capital) and to manage, also from an accounting point of view (Sarno, 2015; Transcrime, 2013). Srl represent about 50 per cent of confiscated companies, and their weight in the mafia economy is two times higher than among legally registered businesses (see Figure 8.4).

Management strategies

Companies infiltrated by mafias have certain competitive advantages: they resort to criminal methods to increase profits, reduce costs, and limit competition. These methods include, among others, salary compression (which usually takes the form of black labour, tax and social security fraud), use of low-quality raw

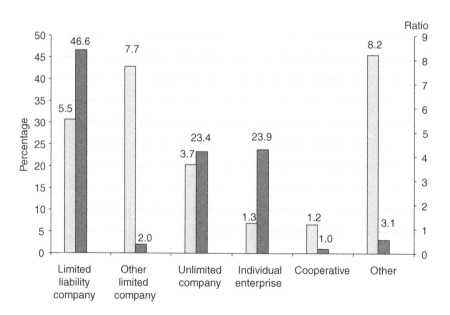

■% of total confiscated companies ▫Ratio on 10,000 registered companies

Figure 8.4 Business legal forms of confiscated companies in Italy (1983–2012) (source: authors' elaboration on Riccardi et al. (2015b)).

materials, corruption of public officials, accounting manipulations, market abuse crimes and discouragement of competition through intimidation and violence (Arlacchi, 1983; Lo Bello, 2011; Riccardi, 2014b; Transcrime, 2013). Moreover, they can rely on the high availability of financial resources originating from criminal activities (Di Bono et al., 2015; Transcrime, 2013).

Thanks to these advantages, there is no need for mafia companies to increase their productivity and competitiveness. Not surprisingly, these businesses are often not well managed (Sciarrone, 1998; Transcrime, 2013), are overstaffed, and incur extra costs which reduce their profits (Becchi & Rey, 1994). But their intent is not productive: they are primarily used as empty boxes to launder money, conceal criminal activities, destroy and occupy the market, or as treasury boxes from which to withdraw liquidity in case of need (Santino & La Fiura, 1990; Savona & Riccardi, 2015; Transcrime, 2013).

The unproductive nature of mafia companies is reflected in accounting terms: on average they have low assets, most of them kept in the form of cash or current assets, low financial debt (as there is no need for bank loans), high trade payables and receivables, which often hide illicit inflows or outflows (Di Bono et al., 2015; Transcrime, 2013). However, these patterns may change depending on the exact purpose for which the company is infiltrated (e.g. money laundering, VAT fraud, manipulating public procurements).

From infiltrated, to confiscated, to liquidated

The uncompetitive nature of these companies further complicates their management once seized. Judicial administration must abandon any mafia method and bear the costs of the 'return to legality': hiring irregular workers, paying trade debtors, cleaning up accounting manipulations, competing fairly in public bidding procedures (Riccardi, 2014a). As a result, most of the companies seized from organised crime lose their competitive advantages and are unable to survive in the legal market: out of the approximately 2,000 companies definitively confiscated from mafias in Italy since 1983, only 15 per cent are still active, while 85 per cent have been liquidated or gone bankrupt (Riccardi, 2014a).

The infiltration of legitimate businesses by foreign organised crime groups

The infiltration of foreign criminal groups in Italian businesses has often been neglected by research. In general, the study of organised crime in Italy has mainly focused on Italian mafias, with some exceptions related to Chinese (CNEL, 2011; Becucci, 2013) and Russian-speaking criminal groups (Varese, 2001).

Foreign organised crime in Italy: the missing link between illicit markets and the legitimate economy

Despite the key role played by 'Ndrangheta, Cosa Nostra and Camorra organisations, a significant number of foreign criminal groups operate in Italy, often in interaction with Italian mafias. A primary role is covered by foreign organised crime in illicit drug markets (e.g. by Albanian-speaking, North African and South American OCGs), in labour and sexual exploitation (Chinese, Eastern European and Nigerian criminal groups), counterfeiting (Chinese OCGs, often in joint ventures with Camorra clans), trafficking in firearms (Balkan and Eastern European OCGs), fraud and organised property crime (in particular Russian-speaking and Eastern European OCGs) (DIA, 2014a; Ministero dell'Interno, 2013).

All these actors exhibit different degrees of settlement and penetration in Italian society. According to police reports, some groups, in particular Chinese and Albanian-speaking, have increasingly acquired typical mafia features, including high levels of internal cohesion, a well-defined structure, capacity to intimidate victims and competitors, and ability to set up ad hoc alliances also at international level (DIA, 2014a, p. 166).

However, the large amount of evidence of activity in illicit markets by foreign OCGs seems not to be reflected in terms of infiltration in the legal economy, nor even of money laundering. In the first half of 2014, none of the €1.9 billion of assets seized or confiscated from OC by the Italian DIA were seized or confiscated from foreign groups (DIA, 2014a). In recent years, three large-scale operations have targeted the financial interests of foreign OCGs, but they have only focused on Chinese organisations (operations 'Qian Liu', 'Qian Ba' and 'Qian Ba II'). No patterns concerning Albanian-speaking or North African OCGs have emerged. Also the statistics on money laundering show that the weight of foreign criminals is still rather low (DIA, 2014a, p. 217).

The gap between activity by foreign OCGs in illicit and legitimate markets in Italy is even more surprising considering the key role that foreign nationalities have assumed in recent years in certain economic sectors. According to Italian business registry data, in the last five years Chinese nationals have increased their presence in wholesale and retail trade businesses, accommodation, bars, restaurants, real estate and personal services (e.g. beauty salons, massage parlours), accounting for almost half of foreign entrepreneurs in these sectors (CGIA, 2015). On the other hand Albanian and Romanian nationals are increasingly involved in construction companies in Italy, while Eastern European entrepreneurs play an important role in transportation companies. Overall the weight of foreign entrepreneurs is increasing especially in certain regions, such as Tuscany, Lombardy, Lazio and Emilia Romagna. Obviously this trend does not necessarily prove the infiltration of foreign OCGs in legal businesses, but it may suggest vulnerabilities which could be exploited by criminal infiltration, just as Italian communities abroad have likewise unwittingly facilitated infiltration by Italian mafias (Savona & Riccardi, 2015; Transcrime, 2013).

Geography of foreign organised crime infiltration

The first attempt to map the infiltration of foreign OC in Italy has been conducted within the EU co-funded project OCP (Savona & Riccardi, 2015) and
uses evidence taken from police investigations, institutional reports (e.g. annual
reports from DIA and DNA) and judicial files. It is reported in Figure 8.5.

According to the (limited) amount of cases collected, the regions with the
highest level of foreign OC infiltration are Tuscany and Lazio, followed by
Lombardy and Abruzzo. The concentration of foreign OC infiltration in 'non-
traditional mafia areas' may be due to various factors (Soriani & Riccardi,
2015, p. 186).

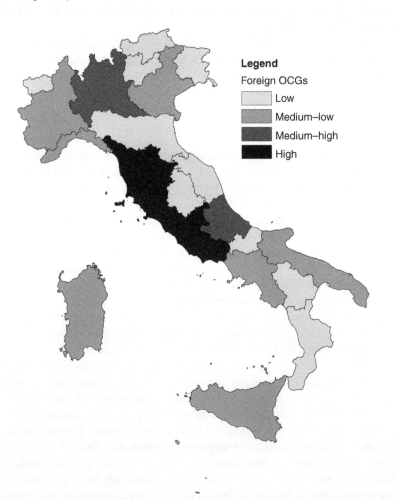

Figure 8.5 Geographical distribution of evidence of foreign organised crime groups'
investments in Italy (source: authors' elaboration on Soriani & Riccardi
(2015)).

First, foreign OCGs may avoid those territories that appear to be under monopolistic control by Italian mafias, and prefer to invest where business opportunities have not yet been fully absorbed by incumbent criminal organisations. Furthermore, the areas with higher levels of infiltration are also those characterised by a larger presence of communities of foreign origin which may, unwittingly or not, facilitate criminal investments, provide contacts and furnish a customer base or illegal manpower. Tuscany (and in particular the provinces of Prato and Florence) is an example with respect to Chinese OCG investments (CNEL, 2011; Becucci, 2013).

Finally, these are also the areas where, according to police evidence, foreign groups are most involved in illicit activities: for example Chinese OCGs producing counterfeit clothes in the Prato cluster may also launder money in the same area, not necessarily in the clothing sector (DIA, 2014a; Soriani & Riccardi, 2015).

Actors, business sectors and modus operandi

Chinese organised crime infiltration

Chinese are recognised in Italy as the foreign immigrants with the strongest entrepreneurial initiative, especially those originating from the southern Chinese regions of Zhejiang and Fujian, who are very numerous in the areas of Prato in Tuscany, and Naples. Similarly, Chinese OCGs are the foreign criminal groups which, according to available evidence, seem most active in terms of infiltrating the legal economy (CNEL, 2011; Becucci, 2013; DIA, 2014a).

The business sectors for which there is most evidence are those related to the illicit activities in which Chinese OCGs are involved. Infiltration in the manufacturing, wholesale and retail trade of clothing and apparel also serves to produce and sell counterfeits, often in connection with Camorra groups (CNEL, 2011, p. 123; DIA, 2014a, p. 178). The same mechanism applies, to a lesser extent, to the manufacturing and trade of counterfeit electronic equipment (DIA, 2014a). Sexual exploitation is often concealed behind legitimate massage parlours located in large urban areas of Northern and Central Italy and usually managed by Chinese women acting as figureheads of criminal groups (Da Rold & Rinaldi, 2014; DIA, 2014a). Evidence of infiltration can also be found in bars, restaurants and hotels (Tribunale di Firenze, 2010).

Businesses infiltrated by Chinese OC are often related to further illicit activities, including the exploitation of irregular workers, usually Chinese co-nationals, tax and VAT fraud, and illicit waste disposal (CNEL, 2011; DIA, 2014a). More recently, cases of corruption involving Chinese entrepreneurs and Italian public officials have emerged (La Repubblica, 2015).

Illegal proceeds are either laundered locally, for example in real estate and in legitimate businesses, or transferred abroad through cash-couriers and money transfer agencies controlled by the same Chinese criminal groups. Attention to this phenomenon is paid by Italian investigative agencies (UIF, 2014). The large-scale operations 'Qian Liu', 'Qian Ba' and 'Qian Ba II', conducted by the Italian

Guardia di Finanza (GDF) between 2010 and 2012, revealed that about €4.5 billion of illicit proceeds (from counterfeiting, sexual and labour exploitation, and tax fraud) had been transferred to China through money transfer businesses controlled by the same Chinese criminal groups. As a result of the investigation, about 200 companies were seized in the money transfer business but also in the clothing, import-export and restaurant industry in Tuscany, Lazio, Lombardy and Campania (Tribunale di Firenze, 2010).

Russian-speaking and Eastern European organised crime infiltration

According to the available evidence, two levels of infiltration by Russian-speaking and Eastern European OCGs can be identified. The first, which is common to other EU countries, is related to larger-scale and high-level money laundering by Russian citizens connected with criminal groups and investing in the real estate and hotel sector, often in tourist areas like Sardinia, Lake Garda or the Adriatic coast (DIA, 2014a; Toresini, 2014).

The second is of smaller scale and often functional to the illegal activity in which these OCGs are involved, primarily organised property crime. *Vor-Y-Zakone* criminal groups have set up import-export companies in several Italian regions in order to conceal the transfer of stolen goods to Eastern Europe and other destination countries (Bianconi & Santucci, 2012). Evidence of infiltration can also be found in the transportation sector, for example in North-Eastern Italy (DIA, 2014a, p. 187). An interesting case involved Russian citizens cooperating with Italian Camorra groups for the theft of anti-cancer pharmaceuticals from Italian hospitals, which were then 'laundered' through fictitious pharmaceutical wholesalers registered in Italy and in various Eastern European countries (Faucon, Plumridge & Falconi, 2014; Riccardi et al., 2015c).

Conclusions

Research implications

Despite the large amount of literature on organised crime infiltration in Italian legitimate businesses, there is still a need for further research in this field. The financial behaviour of different criminal groups within the same organisation (e.g. Camorra or 'Ndrangheta) should be studied more closely, for example by exploring how and by whom investment decisions (e.g. the selection of business sectors to infiltrate and the territories of action) are taken. For this purpose, it is necessary to expand the range of data beyond confiscated assets, for example by looking at the personal holdings of OC members and interviewing convicted entrepreneurs, accountants and professionals. In parallel, research on foreign OCGs' infiltration and money laundering behaviour should be improved.

The focus should pass from the analysis to the *assessment* of the risk of OC infiltration. This would yield better understanding of the related threats, vulnerabilities (i.e. the contextual factors facilitating penetration, such as cash-intensiveness or loopholes in the regulation) and consequences. Measuring the impact of OC infiltration will also require assessing the costs, for society, the economy and the environment, of the management of companies once they have been confiscated.

Policy implications

The Italian asset tracking and recovery system is widely recognised as a model for combating OC infiltration in the legal economy (European Commission, 2012; Forsaith et al., 2012). However, there is room for further intervention. Suggested measures should address four levels: prevention, investigation, confiscation, and management of confiscated businesses.

The prevention of criminal infiltration could be improved by developing risk assessment models and indicators to be adopted by both public bodies (e.g. in the screening of public procurements) and private entities (e.g. in AML KYC activities and in due diligence of suppliers and vendors). This would make it possible to identify and monitor businesses with greater vulnerability.

The investigation should be improved, especially at cross-border level, through stricter cooperation with foreign LEAs and increasing the use of software and tools able to search across different registers and databases.

In order better to adapt to the new forms of criminal infiltration, the regulation should allow greater use of asset recovery measures against new actors (e.g. foreign OCGs but also those entrepreneurs and public officials of the so-called 'grey area' facilitating OC infiltration) and for a wider range of offences often related to infiltration (e.g. public corruption or embezzlement of public funds). The modifications to the Italian Antimafia code (d.lgs 159/2011), which are under parliamentary debate, seem to go in this direction. Similarly, the introduction of a self-laundering offence (Art. 648-ter Italian criminal code) should help to target the financial aspects of criminal association more effectively.

Finally, the management of confiscated businesses should be improved: confiscation is not effective if not accompanied by good management. Problems of deterioration, depreciation and job-loss suffered by the companies under judicial administration, risk transforming a successful instrument like asset recovery into a public defeat, at least from a symbolic perspective (Fraschini & Putaturo, 2014; Riccardi, 2014a). In this sense, instruments alternative to confiscation could be used more extensively (Visconti, 2014). This is the case of the temporary suspension of the infiltrated companies' business administration (art. 34 of the Antimafia code, now under modification) or the administrative bans and disqualifications (e.g. *interdittive*), which would allow freezing of the infiltration process without resorting to radical measures (and dramatic for workers, suppliers and the local economy) such as seizure of the company.

Notes

1 The term *mafias* here encompasses all the main Italian mafia-type organisations, namely Cosa Nostra groups, Camorra groups, 'Ndrangheta groups and other less-known criminal organisations such as the Sacra Corona Unita and mafia-type groups active in the area of Rome. See Transcrime (2013), Savona and Riccardi (2015), Savona and Berlusconi (2015) for details.

2 The *Infinito* investigation, started in 2010, identified an 'Ndrangheta organisation operating in Northern Italy, in particular Lombardy, and was able to involve a wide network of professionals, public officials and local politicians used to obtain public procurements and favours in exchange for votes and bribes (Tribunale di Milano, 2010). The *Mondo di Mezzo* investigation, started in 2014, revealed a wide criminal organisation active in the Rome area both in illegal markets and infiltrating public procurements and legitimate businesses. It grouped representatives of the local municipal government, public officials, former political extremists and mafia members (Tribunale di Roma, 2014).

References

Anselmo, M., & Braucci, M. (2008). *Questa corte condanna. Spartacus, il processo al clan dei casalesi*. Napoli: L'Ancora del Mediterraneo.

Arlacchi, P. (1983). *La mafia imprenditrice. L'etica mafiosa e lo spirito del capitalismo*. Bologna: Il Mulino.

Becchi, A., & Rey, G. M. (1994). *L'economia criminale*. Roma: Laterza.

Becucci, S. (2013). La criminalità organizzata cinese in Italia. *Sicurezza E Scienze Sociali*, (3), 94–116.

Bianconi, G., & Santucci, G. (2012, 1 July). Il pugno della mafia russa nelle case degli italiani. *Corriere Della Sera*. Retrieved from http://lettura.corriere.it/il-pugno-della-mafia-russa-nelle-case-degli-italiani/.

Brunello, G. (2011). *Cittadino agricoltore in sicurezza 2011*. Roma: Confederazione Italiana Agricoltori.

Calderoni, F. (2014a). Measuring the presence of the mafias in Italy. In S. Caneppele & F. Calderoni (Eds.), *Organized crime, corruption and crime prevention* (pp. 239–249). New York, NY: Springer.

Calderoni, F. (2014b). Mythical numbers and the proceeds of organised crime: Estimating mafia proceeds in Italy. *Global Crime*, *15*(1–2), 138–163.

Campana, P. (2011). Eavesdropping on the mob: The functional diversification of mafia activities across territories. *European Journal of Criminology*, *8*(3), 213–228.

Caneppele, S. (2014). *Le mafie dentro gli appalti. Casi studio e modelli preventivi*. Milano: Franco Angeli.

Caneppele, S., Riccardi, M., & Standridge, P. (2013). Green energy and black economy: Mafia investments in the wind power sector in Italy. *Crime Law and Social Change*, *59*(3), 319–339.

Cantone, R., & Di Feo, G. (2010). *I gattopardi. Uomini d'onore e colletti bianchi: La metamorfosi delle mafie nell'Italia di oggi*. Milano: Arnoldo Mondadori Editore.

Catanzaro, R. (1988). *Il delitto come impresa. Storia sociale della mafia*. Padova: Liviana.

CENSIS. (2009). *Il condizionamento delle mafie sull'economia, sulla società e sulle istituzioni del mezzogiorno*. Roma: Centro Studi Investimenti Sociali.

CGIA. (2015, 14 August). Aumentano le imprese straniere: Boom di cinesi. Retrieved from www.cgiamestre.com/2015/08/aumentano-le-imprese-straniere-boom-di-cinesi/.

CNEL. (2011). *La criminalità cinese in Italia. Caratteristiche e linee evolutive*. Roma: Consiglio Nazionale dell'Economia e del Lavoro.

Commissione parlamentare d'inchiesta. (2000). *Relazione sulla Campania*. Roma: Commissione parlamentare d'inchiesta sul ciclo dei rifiuti e sulle attività illecite ad esso connesse.

CROSS. (2014). *Primo rapporto trimestrale sulle aree settentrionali, per la presidenza della commissione parlamentare di inchiesta sul fenomeno mafioso*. Milano: Osservatorio sulla criminalità organizzata, Università degli Studi di Milano.

Da Rold, A., & Rinaldi, L. (2014, September 29). Gli artigli della mafia cinese sull'Italia. *Linkiesta.it*. Retrieved from www.linkiesta.it/mafia-cinese-italia.

Daniele, V., & Marani, U. (2011). Organized crime, the quality of local institutions and FDI in Italy: A panel data analysis. *Journal of Political Economy, 27*(1), 132–142.

DIA. (2013). *Relazione del Ministero dell'Interno sull'attività svolta e sui risultati conseguiti dalla Direzione Investigativa Antimafia. Secondo semestre 2013*. Roma: Ministero dell'Interno.

DIA. (2014a). *Relazione del Ministero dell'Interno sull'attività svolta e sui risultati conseguiti dalla Direzione Investigativa Antimafia. Primo semestre 2014*. Roma: Ministero dell'Interno.

DIA. (2014b). *Relazione del Ministero dell'Interno sull'attività svolta e sui risultati conseguiti dalla Direzione Investigativa Antimafia. Secondo semestre 2014*. Roma: Ministero dell'Interno.

Di Bono, L., Cincimino, S., Riccardi, M., & Berlusconi, G. (2015). Management strategies of infiltrated businesses. In E. U. Savona & G. Berlusconi (Eds.), *Organized crime infiltration of legitimate businesses in Europe: A pilot project in five European countries* (pp. 102–112). Trento: Transcrime – Università degli Studi di Trento.

Di Vico, D. (2014, 6 April). La logistica hi-tech accanto al lavoro illegale. *Corriere Della Sera*. Retrieved from www.dirittiglobali.it/2014/04/logistica-hi-tech-accanto-illegale/.

Donato, L., Saporito, A., & Scognamiglio, A. (2013). *Aziende sequestrate alla criminalità organizzata: Le relazioni con il sistema bancario* (Occasional Papers No. 202). Roma: Banca d'Italia.

Dugato, M., Giommoni, L., & Favarin, S. (2015). The risks and rewards of organized crime investments in real estate. *British Journal of Criminology, 55*(5), 944–965.

EURISPES. (2015). *Agromafie. 3° Rapporto sui crimini agroalimentari in Italia 2015*. Roma: Istituto di Studi Politici, Economici e Sociali.

European Commission. (2012). *Confiscation and asset recovery: Better tools to fight crime*. Brussels: European Commission.

Europol. (2015). *Why is cash still king? A strategic report on the use of cash by criminal groups as a facilitator for money laundering*. The Hague: Europol.

Fantò, E. (1999). *L'impresa a partecipazione mafiosa. Economia legale ed economia criminale*. Bari: Edizioni Dedalo.

Faucon, B., Plumridge, H., & Falconi, M. (2014, 5 January). Italian officials probe criminal ties to cancer drug theft. *Wall Street Journal*. Retrieved from http://online.wsj.com/news/articles/SB10001424052702303678404579535143080068568.

Fijnaut, C., & Paoli, L. (Eds.). (2004). *Organised crime in Europe: Concepts, patterns and control policies in the European Union and beyond* (Vol. 4). Dordrecht: Springer.

Florio, P., Bosco, G., & D'amore, L. (2014). *Amministratore giudiziario: Sequestro, confisca, gestione dei beni, coadiutore dell'ANBSC*. Milano: IPSOA.

Forsaith, J., Irving, B., Nanopoulos, E., & Fazekas, M. (2012). *Study for an impact assessment on a proposal for a new legal framework on the confiscation and recovery of criminal assets*. Santa Monica, CA: RAND Corporation.

Fraschini, G., & Putaturo, C. (2014). *La confisca dei beni illeciti in Italia* (Enhancing integrity and effectiveness of illegal asset confiscation – European approaches). Transparency International Italia.

Giampietri, V., & Sarno, F. (2015). Italy. In E. U. Savona & G. Berlusconi (Eds.), *Organised crime infiltration of legitimate businesses in Europe: A pilot project in five European countries* (pp. 37–44). Trento: Transcrime – Università degli Studi di Trento.

Graebner Anderson, A. (1979). *The business of organized crime: A Cosa Nostra family*. Standford: Hoover Institution Publication.

Gurciullo, S. (2014). Organised crime infiltration in the legitimate private economy: An empirical network analysis approach. Retrieved from http://arxiv.org/abs/1403.5071.

La Repubblica. (2015, 28 November). Prato, il controllore chiede i soldi sottobanco all'imprenditore cinese. *La Repubblica*. Retrieved from http://firenze.repubblica.it/cronaca/2015/11/28/news/prato_il_controllore_chiede_i_soldi_sottobanco_all_imprenditore_cinese-128347013/.

Lisciandra, M. (2014). Proceeds from extortions: The case of Italian organised crime groups. *Global Crime*, *15*(1–2), 93–107.

Lo Bello, I. (2011). Mafia e mercato. In S. Danna (Ed.), *Prodotto interno mafia. Così la criminalità organizzata è diventata il sistema Italia*. Torino: Einaudi.

Marangon, M. (2015, 28 September). 'Ndrangheta a Latina: Coca, fiori e cioccolata per i traffici dei clan. *Corriere Della Sera*. Retrieved from http://roma.corriere.it/notizie/cronaca/15_settembre_28/ndrangheta-latina-coca-fiori-cioccolata-traffici-clan-185278fe-65fe-11e5-aa41-8b5c2a9868c3.shtml.

Ministero dell'Interno. (2013). *Relazione al Parlamento sull'attività delle Forze di Polizia, sullo stato dell'ordine e della sicurezza pubblica sulla criminalità organizzata*. Roma: Ministero dell'Interno.

Mugellini, G., & Caneppele, S. (2012). *Le imprese vittime di criminalità in Italia* (No. 16). Trento: Transcrime – Università degli Studi di Trento.

Pinotti, P. (2015). The causes and consequences of organised crime: Preliminary evidence across countries. *The Economic Journal*, *125*(586), 158–174.

Polo, M. (2011). L'espansione delle organizzazioni criminali: Quali effetti economici sui mercati legali. Presented at the Il sommerso e l'economia da svelare. Gli effetti dell'economia informale e illegale sullo sviluppo, Napoli.

Presidenza del Consiglio dei Ministri. (2014). *Per una moderna politica antimafia. Analisi del fenomeno e proposte di intervento e riforme*. Roma: Commissione per l'elaborazione di proposte per la lotta, anche patrimoniale, alla criminalità.

Riccardi, M. (2014a). The management of seized companies: Learning from the Italian experience. Presented at the 2nd Meeting of the European Commission Asset Recovery Office (ARO) Platform subgroup on Asset Management, Brussels.

Riccardi, M. (2014b). When criminals invest in businesses: Are we looking in the right direction? An exploratory analysis of companies controlled by mafias. In S. Caneppele & F. Calderoni (Eds.), *Organized crime, corruption and crime prevention* (pp. 197–206). New York, NY: Springer.

Riccardi, M., Dugato, M., Polizzotti, M., & Pecile, V. (2015c). *The theft of medicines from Italian hospitals, Transcrime Research in Brief – N.2/2015*. Trento: Transcrime – Joint Research Centre on Transnational Crime.

Riccardi, M., & Savona, E. U. (2011). Come proteggere l'economia legale dall'infiltrazione della criminalità organizzata: Il caso della Lombardia. Presented at the Legalità e cultura d'impresa: Risorse per il territorio, Milano.

Riccardi, M., Soriani, C., & Standridge, P. (2015a). Organised crime investments in Europe. In E. U. Savona & M. Riccardi (Eds.), *From illegal markets to legitimate businesses: The portfolio of organised crime in Europe* (pp. 150–165). Trento: Transcrime – Università degli Studi di Trento.

Riccardi, M., Soriani, C., & Standridge, P. (2015b). When the mafia is beneficial owner: Control strategies of mafia-owned companies. Presented at the European Society of Criminology meeting, Porto.

Sacco, S. (2010). *La mafia in cantiere. L'incidenza della criminalità organizzata nell'economia: Una verifica empirica nel settore delle costruzioni.* Palermo: Centro di studi ed iniziative culturali Pio La Torre.

Santino, U., & La Fiura, G. (1990). *L'impresa mafiosa. Dall'Italia agli Stati Uniti.* Milano: Franco Angeli.

Sarno, F. (2015). Control strategies of infiltrated businesses. In E. U. Savona & G. Berlusconi (Eds.), *Organised crime infiltration of legitimate businesses in Europe: A pilot project in five European countries* (pp. 90–101). Trento: Transcrime – Università degli Studi di Trento.

Savona, E. U. (2010). Infiltration of the public construction industry by Italian organised crime. In K. Bullock, R. V. Clarke, & N. Tilley (Eds.), *Situational prevention of organized crimes* (pp. 130–150). Cullompton: Willan Publishing.

Savona, E. U., & Berlusconi, G. (Eds.). (2015). *Organised crime infiltration of legitimate businesses in Europe: A pilot project in five European countries.* Trento: Transcrime – Università degli Studi di Trento.

Savona, E. U., & Riccardi, M. (Eds.). (2015). *From illegal markets to legitimate businesses: The portfolio of organised crime in Europe.* Trento: Transcrime – Università degli Studi di Trento.

Scaglione, A. (2014). Estimating the size of the loan sharking market in Italy. *Global Crime, 15*(1–2), 77–92.

Sciarrone, R. (1998). *Mafie vecchie, mafie nuove: Radicamento ed espansione.* Roma: Donzelli.

Sciarrone, R. (Ed.). (2011). *Alleanze nell'ombra. Mafie ed economie locali in Sicilia e nel Mezzogiorno.* Roma: Donzelli.

Sciarrone, R., & Storti, L. (2014). The territorial expansion of mafia-type organized crime. The case of the Italian mafia in Germany. *Crime, Law and Social Change, 61*(1), 37–60.

Soriani, C., & Riccardi, M. (2015). Organised crime investments in Italy. In E. U. Savona & M. Riccardi (Eds.), *From illegal markets to legitimate businesses: The portfolio of organised crime in Europe* (pp. 183–195). Trento: Transcrime – Università degli Studi di Trento.

Steinko, A. F. (2012). Financial channels of money laundering in Spain. *British Journal of Criminology, 52*(5), 908–931.

Toresini, M. (2014, 3 April). Così i russi operano sul Garda comprando immobili di pregio. *Corriere Della Sera.* Retrieved from http://brescia.corriere.it/notizie/cronaca/14_marzo_04/cosi-russi-operano-garda-comprando-immobili-pregio-c8f19f14-a39a-11e3-85bd-aff5c7c5e706.shtml.

Transcrime. (2013). *Progetto PON Sicurezza 2007–2013. Gli investimenti delle mafie.* Milano: Transcrime – Joint Research Centre on Transnational Crime.

Tribunale di Firenze. (2010). Ordinanza applicativa di misure cautelari personali e reali (Tribunale di Firenze 7 June).

Tribunale di Milano. (2010). Ordinanza di applicazione di misura coercitiva, No. 43733/06 DDA (Tribunale ordinario di Milano).

Tribunale di Roma. (2014). Ordinanza di applicazione di misure cautelari, No. 30546/10 R.G. Mod. 21 (Tribunale di Roma).

UIF. (2014). *Rapporto Annuale 2013*. Roma: Banca d'Italia.

Varese, F. (2001). *The Russian mafia: Private protection in a new market economy*. Oxford: Oxford University Press.

Varese, F. (2011). *Mafias on the move: How organized crime conquers new territories*. Princenton, NJ: Princeton University Press.

Visconti, C. (2014). Strategie di contrasto dell'inquinamento criminale dell'economia: Il nodo dei rapporti tra mafie ed imprese – Estratto. *Rivista Italiana Di Diritto E Procedura Penale, Anno LVII*(2).

9 *Grand banditisme traditionnel* and foreign groups

Organised crime infiltration in France

Michele Riccardi and Diana Camerini

Introduction

In the past decade, regulatory changes have been introduced in France to tackle more effectively money laundering and the financial interests of organised crime (FATF, 2011; TRACFIN, 2015b). A variety of agencies – at investigative, judicial and administrative level – have been created for improving the tracing, confiscation and management of criminal assets (AGRASC, 2012; Standridge, 2015).

However, despite the attention at political level, organised crime (OC hereafter) and OC infiltration have generally been neglected in terms of research (Gendarmerie Nationale-STRJD, 2013; Riccardi & Salha, 2015a). The reason for the gap may be attributed on the one hand to the lack of a notion of OC in French law (Calderoni, 2010; SIRASCO, 2013) which has inevitably resulted in a lack of statistics and data, despite the recent developments;[1] on the other, to a certain lack of interest by public opinion, with weak media coverage (with the exception of some investigative journalism) and lack of publicity of police and judiciary reports (Rizzoli & Colombié, 2015).

This chapter – largely based on the findings of the EU co-funded project OCP – Organised Crime Portfolio (Savona & Riccardi, 2015)[2] – provides a first insight into the study of OC infiltration in the French legitimate economy. It is structured in the following way: first it provides a review of the main OC actors and activities in France; then it analyses the patterns of OC infiltration in legitimate businesses, focusing on the *modus operandi*, the geographical distribution and the most targeted business sectors. Finally it discusses how OC infiltration is tackled in terms of criminal asset recovery, discussing future challenges at research and policy level.

Organised crime in France: an overview

The nature of criminal infiltration in the French legitimate economy strictly reflects the nature of organised crime active in the country and of the illicit activities therein carried out.

A transit and destination country

France is an important *transit* country for a range of illegal trafficking activities in Europe. It is located midway along the illicit drug route connecting North Africa and Spain to Northern Europe (in particular for cannabis and cocaine) and on the route from the Netherlands to Southern Europe – cocaine, heroin and synthetic drugs (Gendarmerie Nationale-STRJD, 2013; EMCDDA & Europol, 2013; Riccardi & Salha, 2015a; UNODC, 2014). French itineraries are involved in the trade of other illicit goods: firearms, illicit tobacco products, counterfeits (Calderoni, Favarin, Garofalo & Sarno, 2014; SIRASCO, 2013; Transcrime, 2015), stolen goods obtained from organised property crimes (Gendarmerie Nationale-STRJD, 2013), human trafficking and migrant smuggling (INHESJ-ONDRP, 2012; SIRASCO, 2013).

But France is also an important *destination* country: it is the third cannabis market in Europe in terms of revenues (€1.3 billion per year, according to Caulkins, Kilmer & Graf, 2013). Heroin, cocaine, cannabis, amphetamines and ecstasy as a whole are estimated to produce annual revenues of €3.2 billion (Giommoni, 2015), representing the main source of criminal proceeds in the country (SIRASCO, 2013). The consumption of illicit tobacco products is also high, with a market estimated at €2 billion in revenues per year, the biggest in the EU (Angelini & Calderoni, 2015; Transcrime, 2015).

A plurality of organised crime actors

A wide plurality of OC actors is active in all these illicit markets, with various roles, functions and different degrees of infiltration in society and the economy. Two broad categories can be identified (Gendarmerie Nationale-STRJD, 2013; SIRASCO, 2013; Riccardi & Salha, 2015a): indigenous and foreign organised crime.

Indigenous organised crime

According to police statistics, about 80 per cent of all serious and organised crime (SOC hereafter) offences committed in the country can be attributed to French indigenous (*autochtone*) groups (SIRASCO, 2013, p. 6). Two main subtypes can be identified, with very different structures, histories and drivers.

French grand banditry (*grand banditisme traditionnel*) originates in particular from Corsica and Provence–Alpes–Côte d'Azur (PACA hereafter), especially Marseille and Toulon, and is often referred to as *corso-marseillais* OC. It is historically active in the trafficking of illicit drugs (from the 1930s' heroin connection to cocaine and cannabis nowadays) but also in extortion racketeering (against bars, restaurants, nightclubs), usury, corruption, illegal gambling and organised fraud.

Gangs from difficult suburbs (*quartiers* or *cités sensibles*) have mostly a North African origin and are mainly involved in the trafficking of resin cannabis on the Morocco-Spain-France route, although the scope of their activity is expanding. If *grande banditisme* has often been attributed by scholars and practitioners the characteristics of a mafia-type OC, there are signs that also gangs from *quartier sensibles* are increasingly adopting mafia methods, including a stricter control of territory and a wider use of corruption of public officials (SIRASCO, 2013).

Foreign organised crime

According to police and judiciary evidence, a variety of foreign groups are also active in France. Their role often depends on the origin/destination country of the illicit goods trafficked and is influenced by migration flows and cultural links with neighbouring countries (Riccardi & Salha, 2015a). They include (Gendarmerie Nationale-STRJD, 2013; INHESJ-ONDRP, 2012; Riccardi & Salha, 2015a; SIRASCO, 2013): Moroccan and North African OC groups, connected with gangs from *quartiers sensibles* and playing a key role in the trafficking of resin cannabis from North Africa; Western Balkan groups, especially Albanian-speaking groups, involved in the trafficking of cocaine, heroin, firearms, cigarettes and, more recently, in the smuggling of migrants; Turkish-speaking criminals, involved in heroin trafficking but also in extortion, counterfeiting and money laundering activities, especially on the French north-eastern border with Germany and Belgium. Romanian and Bulgarian-speaking groups are active in the trafficking of human beings, especially for sexual exploitation purposes, and fraud (credit cards, *skimming*); other Eastern European groups (e.g. Lithuanian, Latvian, Georgian), structured in extremely mobile cells on French territory, are mainly involved in organised theft crimes (of metals, boats, cars, tractors); Chinese organised crime groups are active in labour and sexual exploitation (often concealed behind legitimate *salons de massage*), counterfeiting, drug trafficking and tax fraud. Other criminal groups include African and south-east Asian gangs.

An important (and perhaps less visible) role among foreign organised crime is played by Russian-speaking organised crime groups (OCGs hereafter) and Italian mafias. The first range from *Vor-y-zakone* cells to more structured organisations with links to Russian oligarchs and economic and political institutions in the homeland (SIRASCO, 2013). They are active in various criminal activities (using violence when necessary, including killings and attempted homicides) and also in terms of investments in the legal economy.

The presence of Italian mafias in France is often referred to as limited to the presence of *latitanti* (fugitives), especially from the 'Ndrangheta and Camorra OCGs, linked to the territories of origin or to neighbouring areas (such as the provinces of Imperia and Turin) (SIRASCO, 2013; Transcrime, 2013). However, their involvement in wider scale criminal activities is proven: illicit drug trafficking, often in connection with local *corso-marseillaise* and North African OCGs (such as in the 2015 'Trait d'Union' police operation – Polizia di Stato, 2015; Tribunale di Genova, 2015), counterfeiting of currencies, and fraud. And evidence of money laundering and infiltration into legitimate businesses can also be found.

Organised crime infiltration in French legal businesses

Such a diversity of actors, characterised by different structures, objectives and foreign connections, inevitably leads to different money laundering and investment strategies. As it is not possible to identify a dominant type of OC in the country, similarly it is not possible to identify a unique infiltration scope. The degree of infiltration not only changes according to the OC actor considered but also to the French region or the business sector where it takes place.

Infiltration occurs when an OCG or a natural person acting on behalf of an OCG invests financial and/or human resources to participate in the decision-making process of a legitimate business (Savona & Berlusconi, 2015, p. 19). It is often confused with the concept of 'money laundering' although it does not overlap as it does not necessarily entail the conversion of illicit monetary proceeds or financial resources (see Chapter 2 for details).

A classification of organised crime infiltration into French legitimate businesses

In an attempt to classify the evidence collected from judiciary cases, police investigations and institutional reports, and building on Riccardi and Salha (2015b), three main categories of OC infiltration in the French economy can be identified: occasional laundering, fraud-driven infiltration and mafia-type infiltration.

Occasional laundering

This refers to a rather unsophisticated type of infiltration, carried out by small and isolated OCGs who occasionally launder the proceeds of criminal activities (drug trafficking in particular) into legal businesses in France when illicit money is not entirely spent on consumable goods or transferred abroad. Indeed, there is wide evidence that foreign groups active in France may move criminal proceeds back to their home countries or into those where they have strong ties, using a variety of techniques such as cash mules, wire transfers, *hawala* systems and money transfer agencies (Europol, 2015; Gendarmerie Nationale-STRJD, 2013; INHESJ-ONDRP, 2008; SIRASCO, 2013).

This applies in particular to North African OCGs involved in the drug market: in 2012 a police operation revealed that a criminal organisation of Moroccan origin, located in Mayenne and trafficking cannabis, invested the proceeds of crime into flats, villas and other properties in Morocco, including a residence valued at €380,000 (Gendarmerie Nationale, 2012; Gendarmerie Nationale-STRJD, 2013). But these groups do not disdain investments in businesses in France, as proven by a 2012 investigation targeting a North African criminal organisation which laundered the proceeds of cannabis trade into restaurants (kebabs and fast food) in the area of Besançon and abroad (Gendarmerie Nationale-STRJD, 2013). The same strategy characterises Turkish OCGs involved in the trafficking of heroin: illicit funds are sent back to Turkey or laundered through bars and restaurants, in particular in those areas where their presence is stronger, such as across the French–German border (SIRASCO, 2013).

Evidence of Eastern European groups infiltrating businesses in France is weak, while it has been proven that they have invested criminal proceeds in their home country: in 2012, an international police operation dismantled a *Vor-y-zakone* organisation committing serial thefts in France and transferring funds to Georgia and Russia, where they were collected by the vertex of the OC and invested in the real estate sector (Gendarmerie Nationale-STRJD, 2013).

Fraud-driven infiltration

As in the rest of Europe, in France fraud is also emerging as a key SOC threat (Gendarmerie Nationale-STRJD, 2013; INHESJ-ONDRP, 2012), attracting both local OCGs and foreign ones. Fraudulent activities range from card skimming, cash-trapping or transaction reversal fraud to more sophisticated schemes of tax and VAT fraud or of social security fraud. Often the latter is enabled by infiltration into legitimate businesses, incorporated ad hoc or taken over in due course (especially those in financial difficulties), in order to commit the fraud. In all these cases companies are not only the recipient of illicit funds but rather themselves a further source of illicit financing (TRACFIN, 2015a, p. 20).

Tax fraud through legitimate businesses is largely committed by Chinese-speaking OCGs (SIRASCO, 2013): through complex systems of cross-shareholdings and credits between associate companies, facilitated by the use of strawmen, corruption and bankruptcy fraud, business incomes are not declared to the tax authority and are then illegally reinvested in the same company or transferred to China.

A good example of social security fraud is the one discovered by the French Gendarmerie in 2012: a construction entrepreneur connected to a Turkish-speaking OCG and located in the area of Forbach (on the French-German border) worked with a number of inactive companies on about 40 building sites from 2009 to 2011, employing irregular workers. The undeclared income, estimated at €1 million, was invested in the real estate sector through a *société civile immobilière* (Gendarmerie Nationale-STRJD, 2013).

Another case of fraud-driven infiltration is the one involving a local family clan which for years controlled the ferry service in the *vieux-port* of Marseille to the Frioul archipelago. The organisation set up a double-ticketing system which allowed it to conceal from the tax authority about €16 million from 1996 to 2006 (*Le Parisien*, 2009; Tribunal de Marseille, 2009). To facilitate the fraud scheme, a number of shell companies were established, even in tax havens. Besides tax fraud, members of the organisation were accused also of money laundering, embezzlement, bankruptcy fraud and asset misappropriation (Tribunal de Marseille, 2009).

Mafia-type infiltration

The third category of infiltration can be defined as mafia-type: it is a higher level penetration in the legitimate economy, and aims at controlling a business and managing it by making use of traditional mafia methods, such as intimidation of competitors, corruption of public officials, manipulation of public bids and other criminal behaviours. In the previous case of the *vieux-port* of Marseille, the fraudsters were also prosecuted because of intimidation and threat of violence, being accused of making use of 'terrorist practices against competitors' (Tribunal de Marseille, 2009) in order to keep the monopoly on the local ferry transports. Their long-term control of the sector was legitimised through public procurements granted by the municipal government and they apparently benefited from the support of the local community and of friendly public officials (*La Marseillaise*, 2010).

Mafia-type infiltration has historically characterised the French *grand banditisme*, in particular in Corsica and in the PACA in the urban areas of Nice, Toulon and Marseille (Riccardi & Salha, 2015a, 2015b). It is based on the one hand by the underground links with illicit markets (drugs, extortion, illegal gambling); on the other by high-level connections with local politicians, public officials and businessmen.

Not surprisingly, the business sectors most affected by this type of criminal infiltration are those characterised by high levels of public resources and public procurements, such as construction (BTP – *bâtiments et travaux publics*), waste management, public transport, or those passing through authorisation processes such as hotels, clubs and casinos. In all these economic activities OCGs can best use their arsenal made of violence, intimidation and corruption in order to infiltrate the legal markets with the aim of obtaining a semi-monopolistic regime. Large-scale investigations have been carried out in recent years (e.g. in Marseille and Aix-en-Provence) and revealed sophisticated schemes of corruption, money laundering and manipulation of public tenders involving local politicians and members of historical *corso-marsellaise* OCGs (Verne, 2014).

The question is whether this *modus operandi* is limited to indigenous French grand banditry groups or does it also characterise other OCGs active in the country. As mentioned, according to some police evidence, even gangs from *quartiers sensibles* are strengthening their mafia features (SIRASCO, 2013). This may also lead to changes in their money laundering strategy, with more pervasive infiltration plans. What about foreign organisations?

The infiltration into French legitimate businesses of Italian mafias is proven. Evidence of Cosa Nostra, Camorra and 'Ndrangheta investments in France can be found, in Côte d'Azur in particular but also in Rhône-Alpes and Île-de-France (Forgione, 2009; Transcrime, 2013, pp. 236–237). But its magnitude is still questionable: some refer to it as *colonisation* (Grasso, 2015), others depict it as 'occasional' and limited to the presence of some *latitanti* (fugitives); others stress the risk of an integration of mafia representatives into the French economic texture, also as a result of 'Ndrangheta activity in the neighbouring Italian province of Imperia (Grasso, 2015; Riccardi & Salha, 2015b; SIRASCO, 2013; Zancan, 2014).[3]

Indeed it would be mistaken to think that mafia businessmen would change their modus operandi once they have crossed the Ventimiglia border, as confirmed by the case of the Pellegrino brothers: the two entrepreneurs, sentenced in 2011 in Italy because of mafia association, corruption, intimidation and attempted extortion (Tribunale di Genova, 2015) and linked to an 'Ndrangheta clan, established a flourishing construction business in France. With their company registered in Menton they were able to obtain several contracts and subcontracts for building flats, apartments, hotels and public properties in Côte d'Azur. One of these buildings has become the main office of a local municipalities association; another, a police station (FLARE Network France, 2011; France 2, 2013).

Geography of organised crime infiltration

The infiltration patterns described above are reflected also in terms of geography. According to the collected literature and police evidence, the areas of France with the highest evidence of OC infiltration are Provence–Alpes–Côte d'Azur (PACA), Corsica, Rhône-Alpes, Île-de-France, the north-eastern border and in particular the regions of Nord-Pas-de-Calais, Lorraine, Alsace and France-Comté. In these areas the asset recovery activity of French judicial authorities has also been stronger, measured in terms of seizures of cash and of real estate properties, although there is little data as regards companies seized, see below (see Figure 9.1).

Côte d'Azur and south-eastern France

South-eastern France, and in particular Côte d'Azur and the area of Marseille, may be considered the most vulnerable area to OC infiltration in businesses for

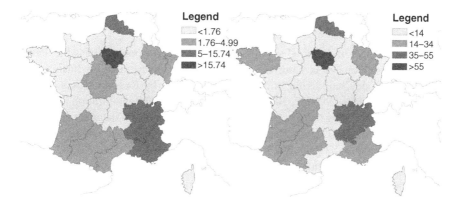

Figure 9.1 Value (million euro) of seized cash (left) and number of real estate seizures (right) in France (NUTS2, 2011–2012) (source: authors' elaboration on Camerini & Riccardi (2015)).

various reasons. First, it is a strategic area for illicit trafficking. It is a border area (France, Switzerland, Monaco, Italy); it comprises important commercial harbours such as Marseille and Toulon and a galaxy of touristic ports, increasingly used for the trafficking of cocaine and cannabis through small boats (as confirmed by the latest 'Trait d'Union' investigation – Grasso, 2015; Tribunale di Genova, 2015). Second, together with Corsica, it is the historical area of influence of the French *grand banditisme* and the one where its 'underworld' (*milieux*) of connections within the social, political and business fabric, as discussed above, is stronger. Third, Côte d'Azur is an attractive market for investors, in particular in the real estate and hotel sectors. Properties in this area record a surge in sales, unlike the rest of France and of Europe, accounting for 25 per cent of all the international sales in the country (Sullivan, 2014). The booming real estate market, the strong tourist appeal, the proximity to centres of financial excellence like Monaco may expose this area to both legal and illicit investments, also from foreign OCGs, in particular Russian-speaking OCGs who see Côte d'Azur, together with Savoie and Paris, as the preferred location for money laundering in luxury real estate (Riccardi & Salha, 2015b).

Another vulnerability of south-eastern France is the geographical proximity to Italy and in particular, as mentioned, the province of Imperia. There is the risk that the strong business activity of 'Ndrangheta in that area may extend across the border, thus creating a sort of *continuum* open to criminal investments (Zancan, 2014; Riccardi & Salha, 2015b; Grasso, 2015). In this sense, the *latitanti* resident on the French Riviera may not only act as logistic bases for illicit trafficking, but also as facilitators for criminal investments in the region.

Similarly to southern France, Corsica is also characterised by the strong activity of local grand banditry OCGs (e.g. the *Brise de Mer* or the Colonna clan). The control of local businesses may take the form of extortion racketeering, intimidation and usury but also of investment, especially in restaurants, hotels, beach properties and housing complexes (Pelletier, 2012).

Paris and north-eastern France

Given the range of criminal groups and of business opportunities, the Paris region (Île-de-France) is naturally exposed to OC investments in businesses. Signals of money laundering in the real estate sector by Russian OCGs can be identified (INHESJ-ONDRP, 2008; SIRASCO, 2013), while infiltration by North African OCGs, gangs from *quartiers sensibles*, Turkish-speaking criminal groups, Chinese OCGs and Italian organised crime has also been recorded (Gendarmerie Nationale-STRJD, 2013; Transcrime, 2013).

In north-eastern regions of France (Nord-Pas-de-Calais, Lorraine, Alsace, France-Comté and, to a similar extent, Rhône-Alpes) OC infiltration in the legal economy depends on the strategic position played by these areas on cross-border illicit routes, especially of drugs. The OCGs involved in these markets (in particular gangs from *quartiers sensibles*, North African and Turkish OCGs) set up businesses in these regions as deposits, logistic bases, but also to occasionally launder illicit proceeds, as highlighted by the case studies discussed above. According to the collected evidence, particularly involved may be the cities on the French–German and French–Belgian border, such as Lille, Metz, Strasbourg or Besançon (SIRASCO, 2013).[4]

Business sectors of organised crime infiltration

A variety of business sectors attract the interests of organised crime. The most frequent ones are discussed below.

Real estate sector

The real estate sector represents a preferred area of investment and money laundering of both indigenous and foreign OCGs active in France, in particular Russian-speaking OCGs (Gendarmerie Nationale-STRJD, 2013; Riccardi & Salha, 2015b; TRACFIN, 2011). Properties also represent, in monetary value, the most important asset confiscated in relation to SOC crimes, according to AGRASC data (AGRASC, 2013, 2014; Camerini & Riccardi, 2015).

Investments may be made in personal names or, increasingly, through holding companies. In particular there is evidence of a growing use of *société civile immobilière* (SCI) or *société de gestion immobilière* (SGI) (Gendarmerie Nationale-STRJD, 2013; INHESJ-ONDRP, 2012): they offer tax and management advantages, a wider range of trading possibilities, and they make it more difficult to trace and seize properties.

For example, in Aix-en-Provence, a number of affiliates to the Corsican *Brise de Mer* OCG had invested in the real estate sector through *société civile immobilière* – SCI. Among them was an important representative of the local hotel sector, using holding companies to launder money and purchasing properties in Corsica and in the PACA region (*L'Alsace*, 2011).

Bars, restaurants, clubs

Wide evidence of infiltration in this sector by both local and foreign criminal groups can be found. Almost all the main OCGs active in the country (*grand banditisme*, North African groups, Turkish groups, Chinese, Italian and Russian organised crime) have at least one case related to the HoReCa industry. Evidence of laundering usually relates to pizzerias, fast food restaurants, street food stalls (e.g. kebabs) and bars across the whole of France, and in particular in those areas where the OC activity is stronger (Gendarmerie Nationale-STRJD, 2013; SIRASCO, 2013).

As in many other countries, also in France bars and restaurants are attractive to OC because of their *multi-purpose* nature: they are labour intensive (useful for exploiting or concealing irregular workers), do not require high-level management skills, can facilitate laundering due to their cash-intensive nature (TRACFIN, 2015b) and are also crucial for public relations purposes (Riccardi

& Salha, 2015b). Moreover, bars may also serve as logistic bases and cover illegal activities such as drug retail trade.

Nightclubs and casinos

Evidence of laundering through discos and nightclubs can also be found, in particular in relation to *corso-marseillaise* grand banditry, Corsican OC, Italian mafias, Eastern European and Russian OC (Riccardi & Salha, 2015b). The management of nightclubs also creates the opportunity for related illicit and legitimate business activities, such as private security and guarding services ('bouncers'), which themselves have attracted the interest of Russian and Chechnya clans on the French Riviera (SIRASCO, 2013).

Legal gambling activities represent well-known money laundering opportunities (FATF, 2009). Judicial evidence shows that French OCGs, Corsican groups and Italian mafias have invested in casinos in the PACA region and Paris (Rizzoli & Colombié, 2015; Transcrime, 2013). Both casinos and nightclubs are also common targets of extortion racketeering, in particular related to the imposition of slot-machines, video-lottery (VLT) and other gambling machines.

Public procurements: construction, public transportation, waste management

As mentioned, infiltration in the public procurements sector represents a higher level penetration in legitimate businesses, as it may imply the use of traditional mafia methods such as the corruption of public officials, the intimidation of competitors and other market abuse offences (Calderoni, 2014; Caneppele, 2014). According to the evidence discussed above, the public construction industry, public transport (e.g. see the case in the *vieux-port* of Marseille) and waste management (Verne, 2014) have been particularly targeted.

Infiltration in the construction sector is most common in the PACA region and Corsica, where the underground connections between *grand banditisme*, entrepreneurs and the public administration are stronger (*Le Mentonnais*, 2012; Pelletier, 2012) and where the buoyant real estate market (see above) offers numerous opportunities for investment. Besides French OCGs, the interest of 'Ndrangheta in the construction market in Côte d'Azur is emerging (see above). Cases could be found also with Turkish OCGs (Gendarmerie Nationale-STRJD, 2013).

Other business sectors

Massage parlours (*salons de massage*) are a frequent target of Chinese OC infiltration and often used, as in many other European countries, to cover prostitution rings (Savona & Riccardi, 2015). Chinese-speaking OCGs also invest in wholesale and retail trade businesses, in particular clothing, food, electronic appliances (SIRASCO, 2013) and are often related to tax fraud offences (see above). In this sector evidence of infiltration by Italian mafias (Camorra in particular) and

Turkish OCGs can also be found (Forgione, 2009; Transcrime, 2013): wholesale and import–export companies are often used as fronts for illicit trafficking, e.g. drugs or stolen goods.

Contrasting organised crime infiltration through asset recovery: state of the art and future challenges

The confiscation of organised crime assets in France

How is the infiltration of organised crime in French businesses contrasted in terms of asset recovery? In the past decade, there have been major changes in the French criminal justice system regarding the seizure and confiscation of criminal assets (see Standridge, 2015 for a review). These include the introduction of a form of *extended confiscation*, the establishment of the national agency for the management of seized and confiscated assets (the AGRASC)[5] and the adoption of measures to improve international cooperation in asset recovery, including the mutual recognition of confiscation orders in accordance with the EU Framework Decision 2006/783/JHA.

All these developments have brought a steady increase in the number and value of seized and confiscated assets in the country (Camerini & Riccardi, 2015). Although AGRASC data represent only a partial picture of the situation, Figure 9.2 reveals that the number of confiscated assets managed by the agency

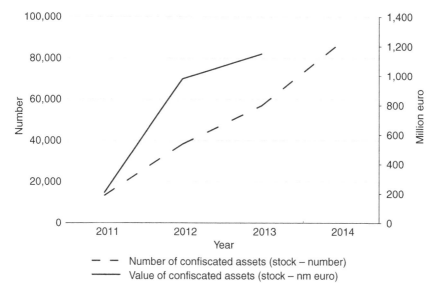

Figure 9.2 Number and value of seized and confiscated assets between 2011 and 2014 (stock) (source: authors' elaboration on AGRASC (2014) and AGRASC (2015) data).

Note
No data are available for the value of confiscated and seized assets at the end of the year 2014.

went from 13,354 in the first year of operation (2011) to 87,278 in 2014, with an increase of 550 per cent (53 per cent only in the last year). Similarly, the value also increased by over 450 per cent reaching €1,148.5 million at the end of 2013.

In terms of predicate offences, the highest share is represented by assets confiscated in drug-trafficking cases (54.5 per cent of the total number of assets between 2011 and 2014), which confirms its role as the primary source of OC proceeds in France. Theft (13.4 per cent) and fraud (6.0 per cent) follow. In contrast, the weight of other important SOC offences, such as illegal immigration, tax evasion, corruption or misappropriation of public funds, is still very low (Figure 9.3).

Inspection of the breakdown by type of assets (AGRASC, 2012, 2013, 2014) reveals that the vast majority of seized and confiscated assets in France consist of cash and bank accounts (87 per cent of total stock in 2013). Real estate constitutes a minor share in terms of number of assets (1.6 per cent) but the highest in terms of value (approximately €587 million, 51 per cent of the total value – see Figure 9.4). It must be noted that the number of confiscated companies is very low (only two between 2011 and 2013).[6]

The evidence of OC infiltration into French legal businesses, described in previous paragraphs, is not fully reflected in terms of *confiscation* of businesses. A gap exists between where OC invests and what is seized. Why does this happen?

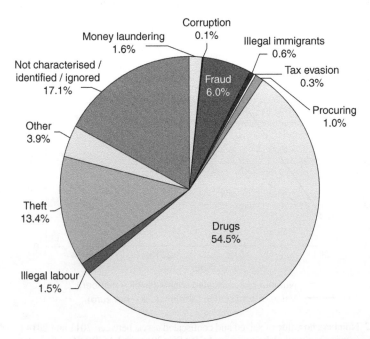

Figure 9.3 Breakdown of seized and confiscated assets by type of offence (per cent on total number of assets 2011–2014) (source: authors' elaboration on AGRASC (2015) data).

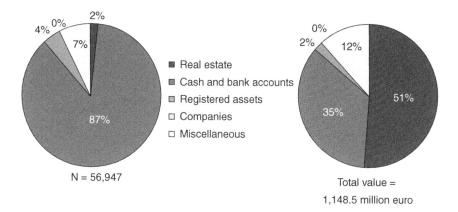

Figure 9.4 Breakdown by type of confiscated and seized assets in number (left) and value (right) (2011–2013) (source: authors' elaboration on AGRASC (2014) data).

The problems in tracing and confiscating infiltrated businesses

The reasons are various. First, especially in cases of fraud-driven infiltration, OC-controlled businesses often have a very ephemeral nature (TRACFIN, 2015a) as they are used as shell companies or only for money laundering purposes: they have low assets, mostly cash and liquidity, few or no employees and have no actual productive nature (Di Bono, Cincimino, Riccardi & Berlusconi, 2015; Transcrime, 2013). They are not seized or they are quickly liquidated before confiscation, as there is no reason to keep them alive (Riccardi, 2014b).

Second, there may be problems of asset tracing. Financial investigations on companies require accessing a wide range of information (e.g. financial accounts, ownership data, tax records) from a wide range of sources (e.g. business registers, land registries, bank records, income and tax authorities) in France and abroad. The difficulties for law enforcement agencies in accessing – and analysing – these sources is well known (Riccardi & Savona, 2013; Unger & van der Linde, 2013).

Third, businesses are often not seized because, once seized, they are difficult to manage (European Commission, 2015; Riccardi, 2014b). They cannot be disposed of like cash or parked like station-wagon cars. Especially in the case of companies, a good management system is a precondition for an effective confiscation. Despite the developments introduced with the establishment of AGRASC, management problems can still dampen the seizure of infiltrated businesses.

Conclusions

This chapter has represented one of the first attempts to analyse organised crime infiltration in French legitimate businesses on the basis of police reports, investigative evidence, judicial files and previous research.

The analysis reveals a variety of OC infiltration strategies, which reflect the plurality of OC groups active in France. Three main types of infiltration can be identified: occasional money laundering, fraud-driven infiltration, mafia-type infiltration, mostly targeting, for different reasons and to a different extent, the PACA area, Île-de-France and the regions on the north-eastern border. The evidence of OC infiltration is not fully reflected in terms of asset recovery, as only a few businesses have been confiscated by French authorities in relation to SOC offences.

Research challenges

What are the future challenges to be faced in this field? From a research perspective there is the need to improve the study of the involvement of organised crime in the French economy, to gain a better understanding the OC infiltration strategy in terms of types of assets, business sectors, *modus operandi* and of the interactions (joint-ventures) between different OCGs. To do so, more and better data should be collected and made available by the French authorities, first of all data on seized and confiscated assets, now limited to the public statistics provided by AGRASC. A higher publicity of police reports (e.g. SIRASCO reports) would also help to strengthen academic research and public awareness around this issue.

The analysis of the collected information, together with other social, economic and accounting data, would help to identify the *macro* and *micro* factors that increase the risk of OC infiltration in France. This would also help to respond to the money laundering *risk assessment* obligations foreseen by the latest EU Anti-Money Laundering Directive (2015/849) and Financial Action Task Force (FATF/GAFI) recommendations (FATF, 2012).

Policy and regulatory implications

Improvements could also be considered at policy and regulatory level: the financial investigation capacity of French law enforcement agencies and prosecutors could be strengthened, by increasing the number of available instruments and datasets, increasing cooperation with financial investigation authorities in other countries[7] and eventually with tools able to search across different registers and jurisdictions.[8]

From a regulatory perspective, despite the introduction of a form of *extended confiscation* by Law no. 2010–768, further powers in terms of third-party confiscation and non-conviction-based measures could be envisaged (Standridge, 2015). Moreover, alternative measures to confiscation could be explored, such as the introduction of temporary suspension of business administration, as successfully implemented in Italy – Art. 34 of the Italian Antimafia code, now under modification (Riccardi, 2014a).

Finally, and most importantly, in order to support AGRASC in the management of confiscated businesses, the networking among notaries, judicial administrators, managers and business schools should be strengthened. More concrete options for the social re-use of seized assets could also be explored (Rizzoli & Colombié, 2015).

Notes

1 From April 2013 French crime statistics allow the distinguishing of offences related to a new category of high-level crime (*grande criminalité*) (SIRASCO, 2013, p. 3).
2 The reader is addressed to the final report of the project in order to collect more details about methodology, definitions, data and sources mentioned in this chapter.
3 Two local councils in the Imperia province (Bordighera and Ventimiglia) have been dissolved in recent years because of mafia infiltration. A high number of investigations by Italian police has proven the involvement of 'Ndrangheta-controlled companies in the area. Imperia ranks as the 17th province in Italy according to the MPI – the Mafia Presence Index developed by Transcrime (Transcrime, 2013) – and the first among northern provinces.
4 For example, investigative evidence suggests that bars and restaurants in the neighbouring areas of Strasbourg (France) and Kehl (Germany) have served as logistic bases for Turkish OCGs active in the trafficking of heroin on the North-west–South-east route (SIRASCO, 2013).
5 AGRASC – Agence de gestion et de recouvrement des avoirs saisis et confisqués (Agency for the Recovery and Management of Seized and Confiscated Assets) – is a public administrative institution under the joint supervision of the Ministries of Justice and Finance. It was created by Law no. 2010–768, 9 July 2010, with the purpose of managing seized and confiscated assets (www.justice.gouv.fr/justice-criminal-11330/agrasc-12207/).
6 It has to be remarked that this number cannot be fully representative for two reasons: first, because some of the other confiscated goods (e.g. real estate, equipment, bank accounts) may be held by legal persons – in these cases it is possible that only companies' assets are seized without seizing the company share capital; second, because AGRASC statistics are only a partial picture of the assets recovered in France. It would be interesting to see if in previous stages of the asset recovery process the weight of companies is higher. This could be examined, for example, through statistics of the police and in particular of the PIAC – Plateforme d'identification des avoirs criminels.
7 In this sense, the signature, in September 2015, of a protocol to foster the exchange of judicial information in the field of organised crime and OC asset recovery between the French JIRS (Juridiction inter-régionale spécialisée) and the Italian DNA (Direzione Nazionale Antimafia) is to be welcomed.
8 Such as the IT system developed by the EU co-funded project EBOCS (www.ebocs.eu).

References

AGRASC. (2012). *Annual report for 2011*. Paris: Agency for the Recovery and Management of Seized and Confiscated Assets. Retrieved from www.justice.gouv.fr/art_pix/rapport_ARMSCA_anglais_2011.pdf.

AGRASC. (2013). *Annual report for 2012*. Paris: Agency for the Recovery and Management of Seized and Confiscated Assets. Retrieved from www.justice.gouv.fr/art_pix/agrasc_rapport_activite_2012_english_.pdf.

AGRASC. (2014). *Annual report for 2013*. Paris: Agency for the Recovery and Management of Seized and Confiscated Assets. Retrieved from www.justice.gouv.fr/publication/rap_agrasc_2013_en.pdf.

Angelini, M., & Calderoni, F. (2015). Illicit trade in tobacco products. In E. U. Savona &

M. Riccardi (Eds.), *From illegal markets to legitimate businesses: The portfolio of organised crime in Europe* (pp. 64–68). Trento: Transcrime – Università degli Studi di Trento.

Calderoni, F. (2010). *Organized crime legislation in the European Union. Harmonization and approximation of criminal law, national legislations and the EU framework decision on the fight against organized crime.* Berlin-Heidelberg: Springer.

Calderoni, F. (2014). Measuring the presence of the mafias in Italy. In S. Caneppele & F. Calderoni (Eds.), *Organized crime, corruption and crime prevention* (pp. 239–249). New York, NY: Springer.

Calderoni, F., Favarin, S., Garofalo, L., & Sarno, F. (2014). Counterfeiting, illegal firearms, gambling and waste management: An exploratory estimation of four criminal markets. *Global Crime, 15*(1–2), 108–137.

Camerini, D., & Riccardi, M. (2015). Confiscated assets in France. In E. U. Savona & M. Riccardi (Eds.), *From illegal markets to legitimate businesses: The portfolio of organised crime in Europe* (pp. 257–263). Trento: Transcrime – Università degli Studi di Trento.

Caneppele, S. (2014). *Le mafie dentro gli appalti. Casi studio e modelli preventivi.* Milano: Franco Angeli.

Caulkins, J. P., Kilmer, B., & Graf, M. (2013). Estimating the size of the EU cannabis market. In F. Trautmann, B. Kilmer, & P. Turnbull (Eds.), *Further insights into aspects of the EU illicit drugs market* (pp. 289–323). Luxembourg: Publications Office of the European Union.

Di Bono, L., Cincimino, S., Riccardi, M., & Berlusconi, G. (2015). Management strategies of infiltrated businesses. In E. U. Savona & G. Berlusconi (Eds.), *Organized crime infiltration of legitimate businesses in Europe: A pilot project in five European countries* (pp. 102–112). Trento: Transcrime – Università degli Studi di Trento.

EMCDDA, & Europol. (2013). *EU drug markets report: A strategic analysis.* Luxembourg: European Monitoring Centre for Drugs and Drug Addiction – Europol.

European Commission. (2015). *Report of the ARO platform sub-group on asset management.* Brussels: European Commission, DG Home Affairs.

Europol. (2015). *Why is cash still king? A strategic report on the use of cash by criminal groups as a facilitator for money laundering.* The Hague: Europol.

FATF. (2009). *Vulnerabilities of casinos and gaming sector.* Paris: The Financial Action Task Force.

FATF. (2011). *Lutte contre le blanchiment de capitaux et le financement du terrorisme. Rapport d'evaluation mutuelle. France.* Paris: The Financial Action Task Force – Organization for Economic Cooperation and Development.

FATF. (2012). *International standards on combating money laundering and the financing of terrorism & proliferation. The FATF Recommendations.* Paris: The Financial Action Task Force.

FLARE Network France. (2011, 20 April). La Riviera 'infiltrée' par la mafia calabraise. Retrieved from http://flarenetworkfrance.blogspot.it/2011/04/la-riviera-infiltree-par-la-mafia.html.

Forgione, F. (2009). *Mafia export: Come 'Ndrangheta, Cosa Nostra e Camorra hanno colonizzato il mondo.* Milano: Baldini Castoldi Dalai.

France 2. (2013). *13h15 mafia calabraise.* France 2. Retrieved from www.youtube.com/watch?time_continue=3&v=IBsb-0qxLKQ.

Gendarmerie Nationale. (2012). Pays-de-la-Loire, fin d'un réseau de stupéfiants. Retrieved from www.gendarmerie.interieur.gouv.fr/fre/Sites/Gendarmerie/Actualites/2012/Juillet/Pays-de-la-Loire-fin-d-un-reseau-de-stupefiants.

Gendarmerie Nationale-STRJD. (2013). Contribution for the Project OCP.

Giommoni, L. (2015). Illicit drugs market. In E. U. Savona & M. Riccardi (Eds.), *From illegal markets to legitimate businesses: The portfolio of organised crime in Europe* (pp. 43–56). Trento: Transcrime – Università degli Studi di Trento.

Grasso, M. (2015, 16 June). La colonizzazione: Costa Azzurra in mano alle cosche calabresi. *Il Secolo XIX*. Retrieved from http://mafieinliguria.it/wp-content/uploads/2015/06/16-Giugno-2015-Il-Secolo-XIX.pdf.

INHESJ-ONDRP. (2008). *La criminalité en France. Rapport de l'Observatoire national de la delinquance 2008*. Paris: Institut National des Hautes études de Sécurité et de la Justice – Observatoire National de la Délinquance et des Réponses Pènales.

INHESJ-ONDRP. (2012). *La criminalité en France. Rapport de l'Observatoire national de la délinquance et des réponses pénales 2012*. Paris: Institut National des Hautes Études de Sécurité et de la Justice – Observatoire National de la Délinquance et des Réponses Pènales.

L'Alsace. (2011, 24 March). Affaire Barresi: La piste du blanchiment relie Mulhouse à Aix-en-Provence. *L'Alsace*. Retrieved from www.lalsace.fr/actualite/2011/03/24/affaire-barresi-la-piste-du-blanchiment-mene-a-aix-en-provence.

La Marseillaise. (2010, 31 December). Les faits marquants de l'année. Le commissaire plonge avec les navettes du Frioul. *La Marseillaise*. Retrieved from www.lamarseillaise.fr/les-archives/12526-les-faits-marquants-de-lannee.

Le Mentonnais. (2012). La mafia à Menton. Retrieved from www.mentonnais.org/html/extranet/presse_citron_00.html.

Le Parisien. (2009, 5 October). Les parrains du Vieux-Port avaient bâti un empire mafieux. *Le Parisien*. Retrieved from www.leparisien.fr/faits-divers/les-parrains-du-vieux-port-avaient-bati-un-empire-mafieux-05-10-2009-662406.php#xtref=https%3A%2F%2Fwww.google.it%2F.

Pelletier, E. (2012, 3 November). L'emprise du Milieu en Corse. *L'Express*. Retrieved from www.lexpress.fr/actualite/societe/l-emprise-du-milieu-en-corse_1182351.html.

Polizia di Stato. (2015, 15 June). Operazione Trait D'Union. Retrieved from http://questure.poliziadistato.it/Genova/articolo-6-198-82776-1.htm.

Riccardi, M. (2014a). The management and the disposal of confiscated companies: From Italy to France. Presented at the Gestion optimale des biens saisis et confisqués, quelle implication des partenaires institutionnels de l'AGRASC, Paris.

Riccardi, M. (2014b). The management of seized companies: Learning from the Italian experience. Presented at the 2nd Meeting of the European Commission Asset Recovery Office (ARO) Platform subgroup on Asset Management, Brussels.

Riccardi, M., & Salha, A. (2015a). Organised crime groups in France. In E. U. Savona & M. Riccardi (Eds.), *From illegal markets to legitimate businesses: The portfolio of organised crime in Europe* (pp. 101–106). Trento: Transcrime – Università degli Studi di Trento.

Riccardi, M., & Salha, A. (2015b). Organised crime investments in France. In E. U. Savona & M. Riccardi (Eds.), *From illegal markets to legitimate businesses: The portfolio of organised crime in Europe* (pp. 172–177). Trento: Transcrime – Università degli Studi di Trento.

Riccardi, M., & Savona, E. U. (Eds.). (2013). *Identifying the beneficial owner of legal entities in the fight against money laundering networks. Final report of project BOWNET*. Trento: Transcrime – Università degli Studi di Trento.

Rizzoli, F., & Colombié, T. (2015). France: un crime organisé entre puissance et impunité. *Revue Diplomatie, 26*.

Savona, E. U., & Berlusconi, G. (Eds.). (2015). *Organised crime infiltration of legitimate businesses in Europe: A pilot project in five European countries*. Trento: Transcrime – Università degli Studi di Trento.

Savona, E. U., & Riccardi, M. (Eds.). (2015). *From illegal markets to legitimate businesses: The portfolio of organised crime in Europe*. Trento: Transcrime – Università degli Studi di Trento.

SIRASCO. (2013). *Rapport sur la criminalité organisée en France 2012–2013*. Paris: Ministère de l'Intérieur – Direction Générale de la Police Nationale – Direction Générale de la Gendarmerie Nationale.

Standridge, P. (2015). The regulatory framework: Confiscation in France. In E. U. Savona & M. Riccardi (Eds.), *From illegal markets to legitimate businesses: The portfolio of organised crime in Europe*. Trento: Transcrime – Università degli Studi di Trento.

Sullivan, R. (2014, 8 August). Why Menton on the Cote d'Azur stands apart from the rest of France. *Financial Times*. Retrieved from www.ft.com/intl/cms/s/2/a7682e4e-1807-11e4-a82d-00144feabdc0.html#axzz3E21gs300.

TRACFIN. (2011). *Rapport d'Activité 2010: Traitement du renseignement et action contre les circuits financiers clanderstins*. Paris: Ministère de l'Economie et des Finances.

TRACFIN. (2015a). *Rapport Annuel d'Activité 2014*. Paris: Traitement du Renseignement et Action contre les Circuits Financiers Clandestins.

TRACFIN. (2015b). *Tendances et analyse des risques de blanchiment de capitaux et de financement du terrorisme en 2014*. Paris: Traitement du Renseignement et Action contre les Circuits Financiers Clandestins.

Transcrime. (2013). *Progetto PON Sicurezza 2007–2013. Gli investimenti delle mafie*. Milano: Transcrime – Joint Research Centre on Transnational Crime.

Transcrime. (2015). *European outlook on the illicit trade in tobacco products*. Trento: Transcrime – Università degli Studi di Trento.

Tribunal de Marseille. (2009, 25 March). Ordonnance de non-lieu partiel et de renvoi devant le Tribunal Correctionnel. Tribunal de Grande Instance de Marseille.

Tribunale di Genova. (2015, 6 December). Fermo di indiziato di delitto. Tribunale di Genova.

Unger, B., & van der Linde, D. (2013). *Research handbook on money laundering*. Cheltenham: Edward Elgar Publishing.

UNODC. (2014). *The illicit drug trade through South-Eastern Europe*. Vienna: United Nations Office on Drugs and Crime.

Verne, J.-M. (2014). *Main basse sur Marseille et la Corse*. Paris: Nouveau Monde Éditions.

Zancan, N. (2014, 19 August). Dai furti ai reati tributari. Imperia 'capitale' del crimine. *La Stampa*. Retrieved from www.lastampa.it/2014/08/19/italia/cronache/dai-furti-ai-reati-tributari-imperia-capitale-del-crimine-ojlX7FWmgvyOrBp20yGUpO/pagina.html.

10 From bikers to entrepreneurs

The infiltration of motorcycle gangs into legitimate business in Finland

Sarianna Petrell and Jarmo Houtsonen

Organised crime and its infiltration in Finland

Introduction: an overview of organised crime in Finland

Organised crime, as understood nowadays in the form of organised crime groups (hereafter OCGs) and other criminal alliances cooperating with extensive partner networks is a relatively new phenomenon in Finland (NBI, 2012). The first international outlaw motorcycle gangs, Hells Angels and Bandidos, entered the country in the 1990s. Since then, organised crime has become more serious and professional operating both in illegal markets and the legal economy. Although organised crime groups, and particularly motorcycle gangs, are hierarchically structured and governed by formal rules (Mölsä, 2008), their criminal activities are exercised through flexible networks and skilled criminal alliances with varying actors and compositions (Junninen, 2006).

The number of criminal groups in Finland has increased steadily over the past 10 years or so. According to police estimates, criminal underground groups in 2000 consisted of eight outlaw gang chapters, increasing to more than 60 groups in the autumn of 2013. The National Bureau of Investigation (hereafter NBI) estimates that these groups currently have approximately 1,000 members (NBI, 2013).

Members of OCGs commit around 2,500 crimes annually, most of which are rather mundane or commonplace crimes and violations such as driving under the influence of alcohol, public disorder offences or traffic offences. Twenty per cent of these crimes are more violent or typical of OCGs, including aggravated narcotics and violent crimes, and various kinds of financial crime ranging from fraud to tax evasion and black labour. Members of OCGs have recently been convicted of money laundering, firearms offences, extortion, property crime and illegal serving of alcohol (Huhtanen, 2010; Kerkelä, 2006, 2011, 2013; Nevala & Ranta, 2006; Salovaara, 2013a, 2013b).

The most striking feature of the Finnish organised crime scene is various outlaw motorcycle gangs (hereafter OMCGs) with their vests, badges and tattoos. The largest, most active and most notorious motorcycle gangs in Finland are Hells Angels Motorcycle Club (hereafter HAMC), Bandidos MC (hereafter BMC) and Cannonball MC (hereafter CMC). The Finnish HAMC and BMC belong to the international organisations of Hells Angels and Bandidos, whereas Cannonball is a domestic group. In addition to these three OMCGs, United Brotherhood (hereafter UB) is one of four major organised crime groups in Finland (Petrell & Houtsonen, 2015).

According to Mölsä (2008), the structures of the Finnish motorcycle gangs are hierarchical consisting of various positions such as president, vice-president, treasurer, arms sergeant, members, prospective members and hang arounds. Formal rules defining authority, tasks and duties together with official symbols are important features of OMCGs. The executive level makes decisions and plans activities. The middle level has a certain degree of autonomy, takes part in decision making and distributes tasks to the rank and file members and street gangs. Some members or cooperating gangs are also specialised in carrying out certain criminal activities, such as contract violence, extortion, violent debt collections, economic crime and money laundering. Often 'prospective members', 'hang arounds', or even 'wannabes' carry out dirty tasks or take responsibility for criminal actions (Petrell & Houtsonen, 2015).

Underworld financiers, who have made their wealth both in legal and illegal business, operate close to top criminal authorities. Other specialists also play a significant role, mainly lawyers, accountants and business professionals. The lowest stratum of the criminal community consists of habitual criminals who commit crimes in order to satisfy their daily needs, which often relate to addictions (NBI, 2013; Perälä, 2011).

Although the Finnish HAMC and BMC are part of an international organisation, their members, and the members of other organised crime groups, are largely Finnish citizens. There are only a few OCGs comprising only non-Finnish members. Finnish OCGs have some foreign members, who mainly come from neighbouring countries. Nevertheless, organised crime operations of non-Finnish origin still extend to Finland, because non-Finnish crime groups supply illicit goods and services to Finnish groups, commit crimes in Finland, and route their activities through Finland. The Finnish citizens engaged in drug crime have good contacts and cooperation partners abroad, especially in Estonia, Russia, Lithuania and Sweden (NBI, 2013).

Methodological challenges to studying organised crime in Finland

There are few studies of organised crime in Finland, and particularly of organised crime involvement in illegal markets and the legitimate economy. Research into organised crime infiltration in the legal economy in Finland is hard, because especially the upper levels of OCG members tend to control their properties using legitimate fronts or façades (Junninen, 2006, 2009).[1] The use of frontmen – a representative of an organisation utilised to hide the people in real power – and shell companies – a legal entity existing mainly on paper and utilised for fraudulent activities – not only hinders police investigations, but also make it difficult to obtain a complete, up-to-date picture of the situation on OCGs' infiltration of the legal economy in Finland.

Although it is known (mainly) through police intelligence and media reports that OCGs in Finland invest illicit proceeds in various sectors of the legitimate economy, including companies, it is hard to estimate systematically how illicit proceeds are divided according to different needs, goals, markets, offences and actors. Furthermore, it is difficult to identify any patterns of investment by different OCGs and to estimate what proportion of criminal assets is actually recovered by the Finnish authorities (Petrell & Houtsonen, 2015).

The first systematic academic effort to produce comprehensive information about OCGs' involvement in illegal markets and the legitimate economy in Finland was offered by Savona and Riccardi (2015) and Petrell and Houtsonen (2015). Important sources were crime situation reports, threat assessments and the annual reports of the NBI.[2] In addition to media reports, in particular from main newspapers and TV channels, data was obtained and analysed from the Police Information System (hereafter PATJA) on assets confiscated from organised crime by police (Petrell & Houtsonen, 2015; Savona & Riccardi, 2015).

In Finland, criminal investigations are carried out and led by the police, the customs and the border guard. They can use seizure for security to ensure forfeiture and the enforcement of compensation to the injured party. The Finnish Coercive Measures Act (806/2011) regulates seizure, that is, freezing the asset in the custody of the law: in this case it is not in the full control and availability of the suspect or accused person, but is administrated by the pre-trial authorities or the Executive Office (Korkiatupa, 2015). The primary legislative provisions on forfeiture are contained in the Criminal Code of Finland (875/2001). Forfeiture means that the natural or juridical person subjected to the measure loses all rights to the confiscated asset, and the asset belongs to the Finnish State. The asset can be used as a compensation or restitution for the victim or injured party. The court, at the request of the prosecutor, decides on forfeiture based on the criminal offence (Korkiatupa, 2015).

PATJA – maintained by the National Police Board (under the Ministry of the Interior) – contains crime reports and measures of executive assistance by the police. Information is available on crimes, suspects' personal details, locations, addresses, crime-related assets, and coercive measures such as prohibition of transfer and confiscation for security. The added value of PATJA is that it includes a classification and definition of organised crime.[3] None of the other databases, including those of the Finnish Asset Recovery Office, Financial Intelligence Unit, National Administrative Office for Enforcement, National Board of Patents and Registration of Finland, and Legal Register Centre, do this. For this reason, it is very difficult to identify cases or to collect statistics on confiscated assets in relation to serious and organised crime using these databases.

However, there are some weaknesses in the quality of the data obtained from PATJA:

- OC classification is not used systematically, e.g. if the connection to organised crime is found later during the pre-trial investigations, it is not always marked retrospectively.

- The changes in the state of seizure are not recorded in PATJA retrospectively after the trial, so that the final outcome of seizure or the type of confiscation, e.g. if it is a forfeiture based on a criminal offence decided by the court, is unknown.
- It is impossible to say in which phase of the confiscation process the data are collected.
- The search results are not comprehensive, because access is forbidden to those sections and cases in PATJA that contain confidential and restricted information. It is also practically impossible to assess the proportion of lost information.
- The number of cases is not shown in the database, so that it is impossible to say whether the confiscation pertains to one or more cases.

The information collected from these various sources yields a limited set of references on criminal investments and infiltration into the legal economy. Where available, for each case, Petrell and Houtsonen (2015) gathered information about geographical region, type of asset or business sector and type of criminal actor involved. Given the limited amount of cases, the information collected hardly constitutes a representative sample. Yet, this is the most comprehensive and systematic information on organised crime activities and confiscations, and it also offers the best evidence of criminal infiltration and investments into the legal economy.

The portfolio of organised crime in Finland

Assets confiscated from organised crime by the police

Confiscations recorded in the PATJA information system cannot be regarded as a totally valid picture of the situation of organised crime assets portfolio in Finland. However, they can be seen as a proxy for assets of criminal groups in Finland. Between 1 January 2005 and 30 June 2013, altogether 302 assets were confiscated for serious and organised crimes (see Figure 10.1).

Movable assets represent about 63 per cent of the total and mainly consist of cash (about 86 per cent of the confiscated movables). Their economic value varies from a few euro to hundreds of thousands of euro. Also, some bank accounts, jewellery, and stock certificates of e.g. apartments (with values up to €800,000) have been confiscated (see Figure 10.2) (Petrell & Houtsonen, 2015).

Registered assets represent the other notable macro-type of assets confiscated from OCGs in Finland (103 items, or about 34 per cent of the total). The majority of them consist of motor vehicles,[4] mainly cars and motorcycles. It should be noted that, as regards motorcycles, the most common brand is Harley-Davidson. Motorbikes are an integral part of the OMCG culture: they can serve both as 'investments' and as instruments to exercise power and to commit crimes. The values of motor vehicles were usually not available, but, when available, they varied from a few thousand to €50,000. The motor vehicles were

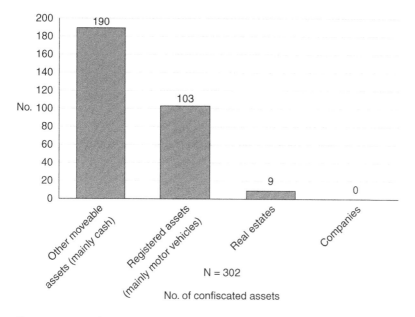

Figure 10.1 Confiscated assets (2005–2013) per macro-type (source: authors' elaboration on Petrell & Houtsonen (2015) and PATJA data).

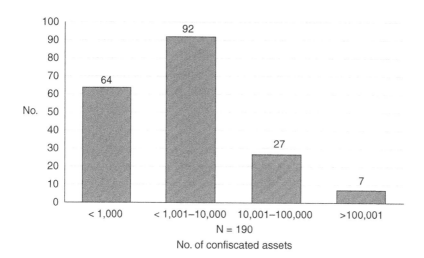

Figure 10.2 Confiscated movable assets (2005–2013) per number and value (source: authors' elaboration on Petrell & Houtsonen (2015) and PATJA data).

confiscated especially in cases of aggravated narcotics offences and tax fraud. Car dealers specialising in serving criminal customers often own the cars used by criminals, which makes confiscation more difficult (Junninen, 2006; Petrell & Houtsonen, 2015).

For example, an expensive Ferrari Testarossa was confiscated in a case of aggravated money laundering, in which an attempt was made to conceal the origin of the proceeds of crime and loan arrangements by bringing the valuable car from Spain to Helsinki. In another case of aggravated money laundering, which also included aggravated narcotics offences, the suspect tried to transfer his possessions, for example a valuable BMW, into the name of his girlfriend in order to avoid confiscation measures. Also, several stock certificates, with values up to €800,000, were confiscated because they had been used to cover illegal profits and change them into cash (PATJA) (Petrell & Houtsonen, 2015).

A search of the Police Information System revealed the confiscation of only nine real estate properties, and not a single company. Real estate properties represented roughly 3 per cent of all confiscated items. However, it should be borne in mind that real estate properties are usually owned by legal fronts and reported under their name, which makes it difficult to determine whether they are a preferred form of investment by criminal groups. The values of the properties varied from €15,000 to €200,000, while in three cases the value was unknown. The offences related to confiscated real estate were two frauds and one case of drug trafficking, tax fraud, money laundering, extortion, a doping offence and alcohol offences (Petrell & Houtsonen, 2015).

Even though no companies were found in the database regarding confiscated assets, according to media reports the police believe that hundreds of Finnish companies are in the grip of organised crime (Passi, 2011a, 2011b). The police estimate that more than half of the members of the most significant OCGs have companies of their own or occupy responsible positions in other companies. Infiltration of business activities is an important means to gain influence, obtain crucial information, earn and launder illegal money, and carry out other criminal activities. Yet, infiltration by organised crime of companies is difficult to trace because relatives, façades, or other legal fronts usually own the latter (Petrell & Houtsonen, 2015). Companies and business sectors will be discussed later in the section 'Business sectors: construction, renovation and private security industry'.

Differences across geographical regions and organised crime groups

Given the limited amount of evidence, it is challenging to determine which geographical areas of Finland are most exposed to criminal infiltration. Some information can be derived from an analysis of confiscated assets. The analysis of the confiscation locations offers a similar picture to the one that is obtained from police intelligence reports and media sources. Confiscations vary from southern to northern Finland, concentrating in the richest areas with large populations and

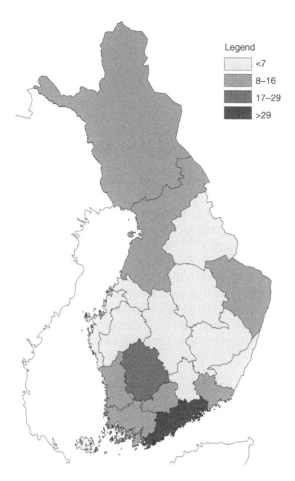

Legend

- <7
- 8–16
- 17–29
- >29

Figure 10.3 Confiscated assets per Finnish region (NUTS3) (source: authors' elaboration on Petrell & Houtsonen (2015) and PATJA data).

criminal opportunities (see Figure 10.3). Most of the confiscations were recorded in the province of Uusimaa (147 items), which includes the three biggest cities in the Helsinki metropolitan area, namely Helsinki (56), Vantaa (44), and Espoo (20) (Petrell & Houtsonen, 2015).

The four most significant organised crime groups are active throughout the country and are expanding their operations in new areas that are logistically significant from the point of view of being illegal. Confiscated assets cluster in the areas which have strong OCG presence, such as the Helsinki metropolitan area, the City of Tampere, south-eastern Finland close to the routes leading to Russia and to the sea, northern Finland close to the land border between Finland and Sweden, and south-western Finland close to the sea routes to Sweden and the Baltic states (NBI, 2013; Petrell & Houtsonen, 2015).

The confiscation database shows that the Finnish organised crime scene is heavily in the hands of Finns. In almost all cases the nationality of the owner of the confiscated assets was Finnish (280 items, or about 93 per cent). Other nationalities that appear more than once in the PATJA database were Russian (12), Estonian (4) and Swedish (2). This can be seen as a consequence of the fact that the cooperation partners of the Finnish OCGs mainly come from the neighbouring countries of Russia, Estonia and Sweden (Petrell & Houtsonen, 2015).

The activity of four major gangs was reflected in the data on confiscations, since almost 57 per cent of confiscated assets (171 out of 302 items) were obtained from the three major outlaw motorcycle gangs, Bandidos MC (75 or 44 per cent), Cannonball MC (65 or 38 per cent), and Hells Angels (11 or 6 per cent) and the one criminal alliance, namely United Brotherhood (20 or 12 per cent) (Petrell & Houtsonen, 2015).

When the type of offence is related to confiscation, we get a picture of the main criminal activities these organisations are involved in. Confiscations are most often related to drug trafficking (120 items), tax fraud (40), fraud (23), money laundering (21), alcohol offences (18), receiving offences (15), and extortion (13). There were also cases of arms trafficking, robbery, human trafficking, accounting offences and manslaughter (Petrell & Houtsonen, 2015).

Motorcycle gangs and other Finnish OCGs are the criminal groups most active in terms of investments in the country's legitimate economy. There is scanty information about the differences between groups in terms of investment

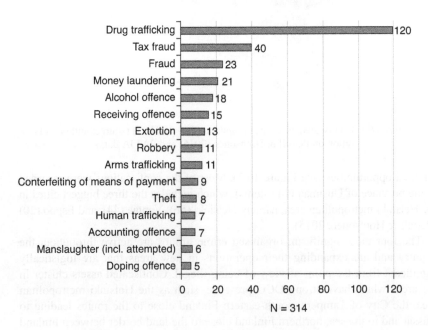

Figure 10.4 Confiscated assets per type of offence (source: authors' elaboration on Petrell & Houtsonen (2015) and PATJA data).

strategy. However, there is some evidence of foreign financial interests, especially in the 'grey area' between legitimate companies and illegal markets (NBI, 2013, 2014; Petrell & Houtsonen, 2015).

In addition to cooperation between Finnish OCGs, there is also cooperation between Finnish and Estonian OCGs in the field of financial crime. Estonian partners are able to provide low-wage labour for the purpose of OCG-related grey economy enterprises in construction and renovations, which try to avoid various statutory payments, e.g. taxes and social security contributions. In the case of joint criminal projects with Estonian criminals, especially in the construction sector, money is transferred to Estonia, for example using companies registered in that country (NBI, 2012). According to Rajamäki (2006), the use of cheap black market labour from Estonia and the other Baltic states occurs particularly in the metropolitan area, in the construction, catering and accommodation sectors.

Money laundering by Russian OCGs is also a threat, especially in the construction sector. Financing from Russia may involve illegally obtained money, and therefore strengthen the strategies of action typical of Russian organised crime in the construction sector to launder money (NBI, 2012). In addition, financial crime related to foreign trade and transportation via freight forwarders is conducted by Russian perpetrators with links to Russian criminal groups. Small logistics and forwarding agencies have been set up by Russian OCGs in southern Finland in order to commit fraud and financial crime in connection with foreign trade and commercial transit transport to the Russian market (Saarinen, 2007).

However, it is necessary to be cautious in drawing conclusions. With this data, it is not possible to differentiate criminal groups in terms of their asset portfolios or investment strategies on the basis of an analysis of confiscated assets.

Business sectors: construction, renovation and private security industry

Based on academic research (Petrell & Houtsonen, 2015; Savona & Riccardi, 2015), police intelligence reports (NBI, 2013) and various media sources, it can be conjectured that the business sectors most typically infiltrated by OCGs in Finland are construction and renovation, maintenance and cleaning, bars and restaurants, machine repair, second-hand machine and car retailing, tattoo and sex shops, and private security (including 'bouncers' in popular nightclubs). Business networks in the above-mentioned sectors provide opportunities to seek new crime opportunities, conceal criminal earnings and launder money. For these purposes, OCGs use legitimate business structures and companies, as well as professional business and law specialists. However, typically Finnish organised crime uses fronts or façades to hide the real ownership and control of properties and business firms (NBI, 2013; Petrell & Houtsonen, 2015; Savona & Riccardi, 2015).

It can be suggested that organised crime is interested in companies in these particular business sectors for several reasons. First, OCGs prefer concentrating on labour intensive (e.g. construction and renovation) and low tech (e.g. bars and restaurants) sectors. Second, some sectors are close to OCG cultures and life-styles, such as sex shops and tattoo parlours, machine repair and car retailing, and private security. These are also branches in which OCG members can utilise the knowledge, skills and contacts that they typically possess. Finally, the lack of supervision, e.g. in the construction industry and the restaurant business, makes them vulnerable to exploitation by the OCGs. The resources to monitor these labour-intensive sectors are inadequate, and as a consequence the risk of being caught is rather low (NBI, 2013, 2014; Petrell & Houtsonen, 2015; Savona & Riccardi, 2015).

For example, police suspected that a criminal organisation linked to Bandidos MC (BMC) lay behind a very large series of economic crimes in the construction sector. Altogether, 100 people were suspected of committing crimes in 200 different companies. Twenty million euro of suspicious money was transferred through these companies. At least €1 million was confiscated. The types of crimes ranged from aggravated tax frauds to accounting offences. Most of the companies acted on the border between the legal and illegal sectors, and they used black labour and bogus receipts. The targets of the construction projects included a prison, a garrison, and a ministry building (Kerkelä, 2006).

To take another example, it was discovered that the heating, piping, and air conditioning (HPAC) company that was hired to renovate the mansion of a Finnish minister in 2010 was owned by Hells Angels (Salovaara, 2013a). The same company had also been hired by a police station in south-eastern Finland (Nieminen, 2013). Another example of organised crime activity in the construction business is provided by a staffing company owned by a Romanian man who was also in charge of an OCG that brought 21 Romanians into Finland to work on construction sites for very low wages. The man was convicted of human trafficking in Romania (Passi, 2011a).

A significant phenomenon emerged in the early 2000s in the security sector services related to bars and restaurants when OCGs started to use their members as bouncers on the doors of nightclubs or to establish their own companies in the door supervision sector. The 'bouncer business' is used by OCGs to gain influence and control over a territory and to acquire a legal façade for criminal actions, since the same companies are also active in money laundering and the drug and doping business. Cannonball MC in particular has gained control of the doors to the big nightclubs in Helsinki (Palovaara & Passi, 2011).

A notable case arose in the security service sector at the end of 2013. The police authorities, the Finnish Customs, and the Ministry of Foreign Affairs had purchased security devices, mainly electronic tags, from a company partly owned by an investment company founded and headed by the sister of the leader of the United Brotherhood (UB). Economic crimes, aggravated frauds, bribery and abuse of public office were also connected to the case. UB is a new underworld alliance that was established by members of certain significant gangs in 2010. The gang is notorious for narcotics offences and its use of violence, for example, in debt collection. Half of its approximately 90 members are currently in prison (Passi & Reinboth, 2013).

Ownership and management strategies and infiltration drivers

The most typical method used to launder illegal proceeds in Finland is still to report them as the property of close intimates or other frontmen (Junninen, 2006; NBI, 2013): wives, cohabitants, lawyers, children, friends, or any reliable person who may legally own and run a business. The front is used as a façade so that the authorities find it difficult to confiscate assets. The reliable front is formally responsible for ownership and management of the business in return for a small compensation amount.

Fronts seeking easy money are not difficult to find in Finland (Junninen, 2006). Needy or credulous people are willing to serve the purpose of money launderers.[5] False identities are rather easily available in public data sources too (NBI, 2012). It is also possible to use ghost companies as fronts, or individuals who themselves are not even aware of the fact that there are companies registered in their name. Both companies registered in Finland and abroad are involved in money laundering by organised crime members. One method of hiding and re-investing the proceeds of crime is to deposit the money abroad in different currencies, e.g. in Russia or in tax haven countries (Junninen, 2006).

Today, however, money laundering is increasingly carried out with systematic and professional methods, e.g. by making use of business structures and companies both at home and abroad, as well as by using the expertise of professional business and law professionals. Financiers of criminal projects operate in close cooperation with the organised crime figures because they know how to carry out both legal and illegal business operations. There are also a number of underworld bankers who finance criminal projects in Finland. Professionals and company service providers are exploited in all phases of the criminal project, from preparation and commission to the laundering of the proceeds. The infiltration of business by organised crime figures has brought violence and extortion connected to financial crime into companies (NBI, 2012, 2013).[6]

Even more sophisticated money laundering schemes are used. Illegal money obtained, for example in narcotics crime, is laundered by using business companies to pay unreported wages and make investments. The beneficiaries of criminal projects get their share (also laundered) as well as other benefits such as cars. Vehicles are obtained by entering into agreements with car dealers cooperating with the OCGs (Junninen, 2006).[7]

The reports by the National Bureau of Investigation (NBI 2012, 2013) indicate that OCGs use illicit proceeds to cover the operating costs of illegal activities, to buy property, and to invest in the illegal and legal economy. Money laundering and profits, together with the facilitation of future crime, seem to be important drivers behind investments. However, it is difficult to estimate with currently available data and research how illicit proceeds are divided according to different needs, goals, markets, offences and organised crime actors. It is also hard to identify any patterns of investments by different OCGs. The companies related to OCGs are often fairly small, but OCGs also control some multi-business firms which often provide a variety of services, such as security combined with various other services, such as maintenance, cleaning and recruitment. Companies in these sectors can be used to acquire information and gain entry into places and buildings that later become targets of criminal activity (NBI, 2013).

One method commonly used to invest criminal money is to purchase a restaurant. Organised crime members engaged in smuggling are often also involved in the restaurant business. Restaurants are constructed and renovated and illegal workers using stolen equipment and materials make refurbishments. Alcohol and tobacco sold in these restaurants may often be smuggled or stolen (Junninen, 2006). Many OCGs, such as Hells Angels, have been accused of illegal sales of alcohol and tobacco for profit (Salovaara, 2013a). For instance, police suspected that a chapter of Bandidos MC earned tens of thousands of euro by running an illegal drinking place in their clubhouse in southern Finland. The activity lasted for at least a year, and the customers were both members and non-members of Bandidos. The alcohol was apparently bought in Estonia where alcohol is much cheaper than in Finland (Vähäsarja, 2011).

The most significant outlaw motorcycle gangs have established tattoo parlours in the biggest cities of Finland. Setting up a tattoo business serves to mark the gang's foothold in the area and to support marketing and recruiting. These premises attract local young people interested in the biker lifestyle and perhaps wishing to become familiar with criminal subculture. The premises introduce them to the ideology and activities of the gang (NBI, 2013). Hells Angels MC, Bandidos MC and Cannonball MC have their own tattoo parlours around Finland. Hells Angels and Bandidos have stores where they sell their support products (Mölsä, 2008).

The infiltrated companies seek to avoid restrictions by legislation and public regulation so that they can react more rapidly to changes in the economy and consumer demand than legal companies. By using black market labour and avoiding taxes, infiltrated companies can save money, offer cheap services, and win competitive biddings. As with all business, organised crime is also increasingly shifting its activities to the internet, where anonymity, topicality and a lack of borders are substantial advantages. Finland is among the top countries in combating corruption. Nevertheless, companies run by OCGs try to affect competition, for example in the construction business, by means of corruption and bribery (NBI, 2013).

One example of how OCGs can rapidly adjust to changes in different sectors and extend their actions into new branches was apparent a few years ago during an exceptionally snowy winter. OCGs set up 'snow business' companies and offered to plough roads and clear roofs. The work was done by cheap black labour hired from abroad (Palovaara & Passi, 2011). When spring came, the house owners noticed that the workers had damaged their roofs, but the companies responsible for the snow clearance were no longer to be found. Instead, cheap repair work was soon on offer (NBI, 2013).

Conclusions

The lack of research into organised crime in general and infiltration in legitimate business in particular makes it difficult to estimate the economic activities of the Finnish OCGs, and to identify their investment patterns and business strategies. Consequently, research has necessarily relied on media reports, estimates made by the National Bureau of Investigation and data on confiscations obtained from the Police Information System, PATJA. However, these data have their limitations (Petrell & Houtsonen, 2015; Savona & Riccardi, 2015).

As described in the introduction, an organised motorcycle gang is a hierarchical organisation with different roles for the *brains* and *hands* in criminal activity. Indeed, the structure of organised crime groups in Finland is usually composed of two main layers, which offer specific roles and powers to individual organised crime members, something that conditions their possibilities to invest and infiltrate into legitimate business.

The lowest level of criminal community carries out the dirtiest tasks such as contract violence, extortion and violent debt collection. Consequently, these OCG members are pushed to live hand-to-mouth and commit crimes in order to satisfy their daily needs. The small sums of money that these OCG members can earn from criminal activities are used for everyday expenditure. There is not much left to buy expensive property or to invest in business (Mölsä, 2008; NBI, 2013).

The executive level of organised crime in Finland consists of the more powerful and experienced OCG members, who are in a position to plan and commit well-organised and more lucrative crimes in cooperation with other top criminals, financiers and specialists. This upper level of organised crime is connected through flexible networks to various actors in both the criminal spheres and legitimate business (NBI, 2013).

Typical criminal activities of organised crime in Finland are illicit drug trafficking and various economic crime offences, such as tax fraud, fraud and money laundering. Economic crime can be greatly facilitated by using various business structures and companies as was described in sections on business sectors and ownership and management strategies.

The business branches most typically with OCG involvement in Finland are construction and renovation, maintenance and cleaning, bars and restaurants, machine repair, second-hand machine and care retailing, tattoo and sex shops, and private security services. These sectors are labour intensive, low tech and relatively loosely supervised by authorities. Business networks in these sectors provide a number of opportunities to obtain information, gain influence, launder money and commit further crime.

The concealment of criminal earnings is an integral part of organised crime. Criminal proceeds must be laundered in order to become part of the legal economy. In Finland, relying on frontmen, often chosen among close intimates, usually does this. Today, however, money laundering is increasingly carried out in a systematic and professional manner, e.g. by making use of business structures and companies both at home and abroad, as well as by using the expertise of professional business and legal specialists. The use of fronts and façades to hide the real ownership of organised crime properties complicates not only police investigations but also the production of analyses and situational awareness.

OCGs use illicit proceeds to cover the operating costs of illegal activities, to buy property, and to invest in the illegal and legal economy. Even so, it is difficult to reach reliable estimates of how illicit proceeds are divided according to different needs, goals, offences, and organised crime actors. Similarly, the patterns of investments by different OCGs are impossible to identify.

In terms of types of assets, movable and registered assets comprise the majority of assets confiscated from organised crime. There are only a few confiscated pieces of real estate and no companies at all. Confiscations give a picture of organised crime assets made up mostly of cash and motor vehicles, but the police intelligence and media reports give more diverse information: there is evidence that criminal groups do invest in real estate and can exploit company structures.

Infiltration into business activities is an important means not only for establishing relations with the licit sphere, gaining influence, and obtaining critical information, but also making and laundering illegal money and carrying out other criminal activities.

Therefore, it is quite plausible to conclude that companies cannot be found in the Police Information System because the holdings of the upper-level OCG members, who would probably invest in companies and immovable properties, are often reported under legal fronts and reliable façades which could make it harder for the police to trace and confiscate their assets.

New data and a new research strategy will be needed in the future. One option would be to use the personal details of notorious organised crime members in the analysis of company information available from the Finnish business register. Combining personal details of upper-level organised crime members with the registered information about the ownership and control of companies and real estate would give us a much better picture of organised crime infiltration in legitimate business.

Notes

1 Unlike in some other countries, members of Finnish organised crime are not listed openly as owners, managers or employers, and it is highly unusual if the names of the criminals appear e.g. in company documents.

2 The NBI's main task is to combat serious, international and organised crime and to produce up-to-date and reliable situational awareness on these crime areas. The NBI has the most extensive information on organised crime in Finland. Its surveys are based on criminal intelligence gathered in cooperation between the police authorities, Finnish Customs and Finnish Border Guard Services. The reports also include police and other agencies' reports, judicial evidence, crime and administrative statistics and open sources. Most of the NBI reports are not publicly available because they contain confidential information.

3 The classification of organised crime in the PATJA includes four criteria, which differ

slightly from the EU criteria for organised crime. A case can be classified as pertaining to organised crime if the actions meet the following minimum criteria: (i) there is cooperation between more than two persons; (ii) there is a suspicion of the commission of serious offences; (iii) it has been going on for a long time; (iv) it is motivated by substantial profit or power.

4 The values of motor vehicles were usually not available.

5 Gullible persons interested in extra money and ready to lend their bank accounts are easily found on the internet, and they are exploited by OCGs from abroad. Individuals in difficult economic circumstances are also easily available in the criminal environment, and they are used as money mules to conceal the origin of proceeds.

6 For example, certain car dealers specialise in serving criminal customers and providing them with underworld banking services. Holding companies are used to channel illegal proceeds into, for example, vehicles to be used by the perpetrators and organisers (NBI, 2012).

7 Car dealers specialising in serving criminal customers often own the cars used by criminals. The dealers know that the criminals work in illegal businesses and accept payments in cash. In return, they register the cars in the names of their companies.

References

Huhtanen, J. (2010, 3 February). Rikollisjengit yhä useammin mukana talousrikoksissa. *Helsingin Sanomat*. Retrieved from www.hs.fi/paivanlehti/#arkisto/.

Junninen, M. (2006). *Adventures and risk-takers: Finnish professional criminals and their organisations in the 1990s cross-border criminality*. Helsinki: European Institute for Crime Prevention and Control, affiliated with the United Nations (HEUNI).

Junninen, M. (2009). Finnish professional criminals and their organisations in the 1990s. *Crime, Law and Social Change, 51*(5), 487–509.

Kerkelä, L. (2006, 4 August). Keskusrikospoliisi tutkii jättimäistä rakennusalan kuittitehtailua. *Helsingin Sanomat*. Retrieved from www.hs.fi/paivanlehti/#arkisto/.

Kerkelä, L. (2011, 9 September). Helvetin enkeleitä epäillään valtavasta huumebisneksestä. *Helsingin Sanomat*. Retrieved from www.hs.fi/paivanlehti/#arkisto/.

Kerkelä, L. (2013, 10 August). Aseita ja huumeita kätkenyt mies sai 11 vuotta vankeutta. *Helsingin Sanomat*. Retrieved from www.hs.fi/paivanlehti/#arkisto/.

Korkiatupa, J. (2015). Finland. In E. U. Savona & M. Riccardi (Eds.), *From illegal markets to legitimate business: The portfolio of organised crime in Europe* (pp. 227–229). Trento: Transcrime – Università degli Studi di Trento.

Mölsä, M. (2008). *Prosenttijengit. Moottoripyöräkerhot ja järjestäytynyt rikollisuus Suomessa*. Helsinki: Johnny Kniga Kustannus.

NBI. (2012). *Threat assessments, crime situation reports, and annual reports*. Helsinki: National Bureau of Investigation.

NBI. (2013). *Threat assessments, crime situation reports, and annual reports*. Helsinki: National Bureau of Investigation.

NBI. (2014). *Threat assessments, crime situation reports, and annual reports*. Helsinki: National Bureau of Investigation.

Nevala, S., & Ranta, R. (2006, 1 September). Kansainvälinen terrorismi on järjestäytynyttä rikollisuutta. *Helsingin Sanomat*. Retrieved from www.hs.fi/paivanlehti/#arkisto/.

Nieminen, T. (2013, 14 April). Tarvittaessa poistakaa myös heidät krp:n rekisteristä. *Helsingin Sanomat*. Retrieved from www.hs.fi/paivanlehti/#arkisto/.

Palovaara, J., & Passi, M. (2011, 5 October). Portsariyritysten valvontaa kiristetään. *Helsingin Sanomat*. Retrieved from www.hs.fi/paivanlehti/#arkisto/.

Passi, M. (2011a, 1 June). Krp: Kerjäläisilmiöön liittyy Suomessakin ihmiskauppaa. *Helsingin Sanomat*. Retrieved from www.hs.fi/paivanlehti/#arkisto/.

Passi, M. (2011b, 5 October). Paritusta Helsingin keskustassa. *Helsingin Sanomat*. Retrieved from www.hs.fi/paivanlehti/#arkisto/.

Passi, M., & Reinboth, S. (2013, 12 September). Poliisin laitehankinnat kytkeytyvät rikollisryhmään. *Helsingin Sanomat*. Retrieved from www.hs.fi/paivanlehti/#arkisto/.

Perälä, J. (2011). *'Miksi lehmät pitää tappaa?' Etnografinen tutkimus 2000-luvun alun huumemarkkinoista Helsingissä*. Helsinki: National Institute of Health and Welfare (THL).

Petrell, S., & Houtsonen, J. (2015). Finland. In E. U. Savona & M. Riccardi (Eds.), *From illegal markets to legitimate businesses: The portfolio of organised crime in Europe* (pp. 166–171). Trento: Transcrime – Università degli Studi di Trento.

Rajamäki, K. (2006, 27 February). Talousrikostorjunta edellyttää jatkuvia tehokkaita toimia. *Helsingin Sanomat*. Retrieved from www.hs.fi/paivanlehti/#arkisto/.

Saarinen, J. (2007, 11 January). Venäjän järjestäytynyt rikollisuus juurtunut idän tavaralikenteeseen. *Helsingin Sanomat*. Retrieved from www.hs.fi/paivanlehti/#arkisto/.

Salovaara, O. (2013a, 27 March). Hautala ei osannut epäillä remonttifirmaa. *Helsingin Sanomat*. Retrieved from www.hs.fi/paivanlehti/#arkisto/.

Salovaara, O. (2013b, 7 December). Helvetin enkeleille tuomioita. *Helsingin Sanomat*. Retrieved from www.hs.fi/paivanlehti/#arkisto/.

Savona, E. U., & Riccardi, M. (Eds.). (2015). *From illegal markets to legitimate businesses: The portfolio of organised crime in Europe*. Trento: Transcrime – Università degli Studi di Trento.

Vähäsarja, I. (2011, 13 February). Poliisi: Bandidos tienasi Hangossa salakapakalla. *Helsingin Sanomat*. Retrieved from www.hs.fi/paivanlehti/#arkisto/.

Part IV

Research and policy implications

11 The impact of organised crime infiltration on the European legitimate economy

John Walker

Introduction

In the history of criminology, it is not too many years since the first studies of the costs of crime emerged (Walker, 1992). Early research into the costs of crime typically focused on the direct costs of the crimes themselves, in terms of impacts on victims, and the costs of crime prevention, law enforcement and justice, with indirect costs being relegated to a secondary role, in part because of the inherent difficulties of measurement. However, researchers such as Mayhew (2003) and Brand and Price (2000) established that these indirect costs were indeed measurable (although with difficulty) and significant. More recently, the European Commission has issued a formalised approach entitled 'Mainstreaming Methodology for Estimating the Costs of Crime' (University of York, 2009), which aims to encourage a standard 'costs of crime' approach across European Union countries. Building on this history of research, the European Commission's approach includes, in its 'Costs as a consequence of crime' section, some elements that would have been considered rather 'third-order' impacts in early attempts to measure the costs of crime. Together with 'traditional' elements such as property losses and medical and mental health care costs, they include productivity losses (e.g. the time lost from work by victims of crime), household services (additional costs imposed as a result of crime), lost school days, pain, suffering and lost quality of life, victim support services, tort claim expenses and 'long-term consequences'.

While these same categories of costs can be taken as a starting point for an analysis of the costs imposed by the criminal groups' patterns of investment, organised crime investments are not necessarily criminal in themselves. They may have an even wider range of impacts on the community – and particularly on the economies in which they operate – including, for example, their impacts on business management, labour markets, real estate values, and the corrosive impacts of corruption on public and private life. Actual measurement of costs of investment are difficult to obtain because of the extreme scarcity of hard data on the magnitude of the problem. However, several significant threads emerged from previous research on the topic. They can be classified as: sub-optimal investments, market distortion, and interference in government and judicial decision making.

Sub-optimal investments

According to Italian studies (Arlacchi, 1983; Calderoni, 2014; Riccardi, 2014; Transcrime, 2013) most of the companies controlled by organised crime groups are poorly managed by operators not necessarily familiar with the business. Furthermore, these companies are not necessarily profitable, have more employees than necessary, and only survive in the market because they use corruption, accounting manipulations and other criminal means. In this sense the business activities managed by criminal groups may be somehow 'sub-efficient' or 'sub-optimal' thus implying loss of productivity and profitability.

Impacts of sub-optimal investments include irregular work, consequences of confiscation, and environmental and health implications.

Irregular work

According to the cases analysed in this book, most of the companies controlled by organised crime groups use more employees than necessary and often hire irregular workers (or even exploit the labour of trafficked persons), making them dependent on welfare or petty crime to generate income. Australian studies (e.g. Australian Crime Commission, 2015; Australian Taxation Office, 2014) show that criminal groups, particularly those operating in the building and construction industries, may illegally employ and underpay migrant workers, and may systematically run a company into debt, and transfer the assets into a new company to avoid paying creditors, tax or employee entitlements (this is known as 'phoenix activity' after the mythical bird that is continually reborn from its own ashes). The new company, usually operated by the same director, continues the business under a new structure to avoid responsibilities to creditors, but the employees are abandoned without hope of receiving their entitlements. Australian Taxation Office studies are underway to estimate the costs and impacts of the use of such schemes by criminal groups in Australia. The Australian Crime Commission's report states that

> visa and migration fraud is being used by organised crime as a means of obtaining cheap labour and potentially expanding their criminal networks; this is done by facilitating unlawful entry, visa extensions and employment for individuals, while extorting, underpaying and exploiting employees.
>
> (Australian Crime Commission, 2015, p. 75)

To the extent that this is true, then:

- Productivity losses occur across the part of the workforce that is employed by organised crime-controlled businesses.
- Tax losses occur as a result of tax-evasive business practices by organised crime-controlled businesses and as a result of the lower incomes paid to employees.

- Dependency on welfare may become an issue for income support for poorly paid and laid-off workers, and for their dependents.
- Stress related to working conditions may lead to long-term physical and mental health problems for employees of organised crime-controlled businesses, and for their dependents.
- Children of poorly paid and laid-off workers may miss out on educational opportunities, with the consequence of long-term disadvantage.

Consequences of confiscation

Once confiscated, criminal assets are often not efficiently managed and hence soon lose productivity or fail. For example, most confiscated companies in Italy go bankrupt or are liquidated. Transcrime (2013) found that 65–70 per cent of the businesses confiscated from organised crime groups in Italy ended in liquidation, 15–20 per cent went bankrupt, while only 15–20 per cent remained active. This will result in further loss of jobs, of productivity and of wealth. The reasons for this may include (Flare Network, 2014, pp. 1–4):

- '[E]xcessive length of the court proceedings […] which often leads to depreciation or deterioration of the assets.'
- Poor 'coordination between stakeholders and factors hampering timely and effective sale or transfer of property (e.g. mortgage liens, legal disputes over the assets, unfavourable market conditions)'.
- Excessive costs of administration 'so that often the costs of management receivers outweigh what is recovered'.
- '[T]he bad conditions of seized assets: for example, […] seized assets are frequently unusable or soiled'.
- '[A] scant sensitivity toward the importance of the management of seized assets among prosecutors and judges.'

Environmental and health implications

Most companies controlled by criminal organisations use criminal means to survive in the market. For example, in order to reduce operating costs they avoid any kind of rule regarding waste disposal (including toxic waste) or use lower-quality products (e.g. cement with high percentages of sand, chemical additives in food products) which represent risks from the environmental and public health points of view. This will result in sickness, miscarriage and birth defects from tainted food (CSPI, 2000). Some forms of illegal dumping such as chemicals or asbestos can lead to pollution of the environment, and directly cause harm or injury to humans and wildlife.

A clear example of this is the contamination of the Caserta plain (near Naples) due to environmental damage caused by Camorra companies. It is often referred to as the 'triangle of death' (Senior & Massa, 2004), and, for example, the annual death rate per 100,000 inhabitants from liver cancer is close to 34.5 for men and 20.8 for women, as compared to the national average of 14.

A report for the European Commission (Fröhlich, 2003) identified 122 cases of environmental crime in EU member states between 1994 and 2003, thought to be the responsibility of organised crime groups, although for some cases the available data could not definitively prove organised crime involvement. Twenty of these offences involved illegal waste dumping, 27 involved the emission of ozone depleting substances and 32 involved the mishandling of radioactive waste. The total estimated profits, from those cases where data were available, amounted to almost €100 million from illegal waste dumping alone, over €60 million for the emission of ozone depleting substance and €200,000 from radioactive substances, indicating a significant level of activity in this sector.

Market distortion

The ability of organised crime groups to pay 'over-the-top' prices for the purchase of registered assets (e.g. cars, boats, motorcycles), moveable assets (e.g. fine arts, jewels or fur coats), real estate properties and companies (including hotels, bars and restaurants, construction, wholesale and retail trade), as part of their money laundering activities, can drive out legitimate investors from these markets. The use of corruption, intimidation and impositions (e.g. on suppliers' materials) by the companies controlled by criminal groups, reducing their operating costs relative to legitimate forms of business, produces further distortions for legal competitors in the market, again leading to sub-optimal economic equilibrium. Of particular concern is the ability of organised crime-controlled businesses to corrupt and co-opt professionals, including accountants and lawyers, distorting the markets for professional services. Impacts of market distortion may include capital loss and capital flight amongst competitor businesses, price bubbles for registered assets, moveable assets, real estate properties and companies, loss of confidence in the professions, loss of neighbourhood prestige/ reputation, reduced municipal services, and increased fear of crime.

Capital loss and capital flight amongst competitor businesses

Legitimate businesses may lose revenues, or leave an industry or an area in extreme circumstances if they have incurred significant or sustained loss from the unfair competition of organised crime-controlled companies, or have been threatened by standover men. Or businesses that would otherwise have invested in the region prefer to invest in less organised crime-controlled regions.

On the basis of a statistical analysis of international data, Pinotti (2015, p. 169) finds that 'organised crime is associated with significantly lower levels of economic output per capita – of the order of 35 percent for a 1 standard deviation increase in the [World Economic Forum's] organised crime index'. As an extreme example, the American University's 'InSightCrime' research group estimated that extortion and threats by criminal groups led to the shutdown of 17,500 small businesses in Honduras during 2012 (Cawley, 2013). Citing La Prensa, they estimated that 'some 25,000 Hondurans are affected either directly or indirectly by the closure of these businesses, which include stores, restaurants, transportation companies, and street vendors'. To the extent that this is typical of regions with high organised crime investment levels, it will result in loss of services and amenities to the community, including retail outlets, cafes and restaurants, loss of jobs in the region and consequent emigration to more prosperous regions, reductions in productivity, as better qualified staff leave the businesses, and a spiral of economic decline.

Daniele and Marani (2008, p. 3) have shown that in Italy 'the correlation between organized crime and FDI (foreign direct investment) inflow is both negative and significant', indicating that businesses are deterred from investing in the areas most affected by organised crime. What is needed, they say, is 'the improvement of security conditions (and, possibly, of the quality of the local socio-economic context)' as 'a fundamental prerequisite for increasing the regional level of attractiveness and, presumably, to increase the effectiveness of direct policy interventions to attract foreign investment in the less developed areas of the country' (Daniele & Marani, 2008, p. 3).

Price bubbles for registered assets, moveable assets, real estate properties and companies

The Global Agenda on Organized Crime of the World Economic Forum (WEF, 2011) stated that the

> [p]urchase of expensive homes by crime figures and corrupt officials shows that crime really does pay. Economic bubbles can be exacerbated by money laundering into real estate and ordinary citizens can be priced out of markets distorted by money launderers.

There is consequently the risk that these markets will collapse when the organised crime groups' investment strategies change, because the cheap money entering the markets from criminal sources will have the same overpricing effects as cheap money from mortgage providers. An analysis of house prices in the US through the 1980s and 1990s found negative correlations ranging from 0.65 to 0.83 between overvaluation and subsequent prices (Chen, Carbacho-Burgos, Mehra & Zoller, 2013, p. 5). Legitimate investors in these markets therefore risk losing much of their investment, mirroring the impacts of the residential housing 'bubbles' experienced in many EU countries during the global financial crisis (Zemcik & Zabrodska, 2012, p. 3).[1]

Loss of confidence in the professions

Although it is difficult to find research to demonstrate the point, the employment of professionals, including corrupted accountants, police officers and lawyers, to facilitate the operations of businesses infiltrated by organised crime groups, may drive out legitimate operators from these professions. 'Corruption can take many forms that can include graft, bribery, embezzlement and extortion. Its existence reduces business credibility and profits when professionals misuse their positions for personal gain' (Ray, 2015). This may result in a significant loss of confidence by the community in the integrity of these professions, and a reluctance, by legitimate businesses, to engage the services of these professionals, due to fears that they may infiltrate their business. 'When the news about corrupt business professionals breaks, customers lose respect and trust, requiring company officials to spend valuable time and resources to monitor the fallout and reassure clients the company is still viable' (Ray, 2015). Failure to employ legitimate professionals may lead to reduced efficiencies and/or productivity.

Corruption in the legal profession may be particularly problematic. A global survey of legal professionals in 2010, conducted by the International Bar Association, the OECD and the UNODC (International Bar Association, 2010, p. 6) found that '[n]early half of all respondents stated corruption was an issue in the legal profession in their own jurisdiction. The proportion was even higher – over 70 per cent – in the following regions: CIS, Africa, Latin America, Baltic States and Eastern Europe.' 'Nearly a third of respondents said a legal professional they know has been involved in international corruption offences' and '[n]early 30 per cent of respondents said they had lost business to corrupt law firms or individuals who have engaged in international bribery and corruption' (International Bar Association, 2010, p. 6). Corruption on this scale may result in a reluctance, by legitimate businesses, to use the courts to resolve business disputes (for example, customers who fail to pay for goods and services provided), due to fears that they may have been corrupted by organised crime groups. Failure to pursue such civil cases may reduce profitability. Corruption may also result in the loss of professionals who may leave the profession or the area as a result of intimidation or in search of more legitimate careers, reducing the attractiveness of the region for investment and employment opportunities.

Loss of neighbourhood prestige/reputation

Although studies on the impact of criminal investments on neighbourhoods are lacking, there is considerable evidence that the levels of crime may affect property prices and the reputation of neighbourhoods. Linden and Rockoff (2006) combined data from the housing market with data from the North Carolina Sex Offender Registry to estimate how individuals value living in close proximity to a convicted criminal. House prices within a one-tenth of a mile area around the home of a sex offender fall by four per cent on average (about 5,500 US dollars) while those further away show no decline. Linden and Rockoff (2006) estimated victimisation costs of over US$1 million – far in excess of estimates taken from the criminal justice literature. In a study of several US cities, Shapiro and Hassett (2012, p. 4) found that '[t]he largest economic benefits, however, arise from the impact of lower rates of violent crime on the housing values in the cities sampled here.' On average, a reduction in a given year of one homicide in a zip code causes a 1.5 per cent increase in housing values in that same zip code the following year. At least one study has found that crime impacts the real estate market differently in poor, middle class and rich neighbourhoods, and that violent crime has the most significant impact (Tita, Petras & Greenbaum, 2006). To the extent that organised crime-controlled businesses use violence, or are even reputed to use illegal business practices, this may impair the reputation of the neighbourhood, reducing property values to legitimate property owners.

Reduced municipal services

When organised crime fails to pay its taxes or intimidates businesses and residents to leave the area, local governments inevitably lose revenue and are less able to provide the public services, such as urban planning, public transport, water supply or waste removal, that support local businesses and residents, thereby creating something of a downward spiral in public amenity. Shapiro and Hassett (2012) estimated savings for municipal budgets from a 25 per cent reduction in violent crime ranging from US$6 million per year in Seattle to US$12 million per year in Boston and Milwaukee, to US$42 million per year in Philadelphia and US$59 million for Chicago. Lower out-of-pocket medical costs were also identified for those who would otherwise have been victims, as well as their averted pain and suffering. Again, to the extent that organised crime-controlled businesses use violence, or are even reputed to use illegal business practices, this may impact on municipal budgets and hence on services.

Increased fear of crime

As discussed above, there is copious evidence to show that fear of crime itself, and the knowledge of criminal activity in the neighbourhood, impacts on real estate prices. Fear of crime can also have a range of other negative impacts on a community. Poor health caused by fears of intimidation in organised crime-controlled businesses may impact on workers' performance, and therefore on company profits. World Bank findings suggest that fear of crime 'leads to loss of output because of reduced hours of operation (including avoiding night shifts) or loss of workdays arising from outbreaks of violence, and avoidance of some types of economic activity' (World Bank, 2003).

Interference in government and judicial decision making

The costs of justice in the civil and criminal courts have increased, along with costs caused by delays in proceedings, due to the ability of organised crime groups to pay high fees to lawyers and accountants to protect their investments. The cost of tax scrutiny is increased, and the heightened need for vigilance by tax authorities imposes delays and costs on honest tax payers. Corrupt payments to politicians, public servants, police, court and customs officials result in loss of public confidence in government and state officials.

Caneppele, Calderoni and Martocchia find that

> the evolution of organised crime infiltration in public procurement has most recently shifted towards more subtle and sophisticated forms of infiltration, which now require complex knowledge on how to participate in public procurement, how to submit a bid, and how to run a company. This entails direct control over one or more companies, which in return provide powerful means to launder dirty money and exert social control over the local economic system.
>
> (Caneppele et al., 2009, p. 154)

Comparing international data, Pinotti (2015, p. 159) finds that 'politicians are on average more corrupt and, also, more exposed to the risk of violence in countries with a greater presence of criminal organisations'.

In an interview with L'Espresso in 2008 (Di Feo & Fittipaldi, 2008), the boss of the Casalesi clan, G.V., admitted to systematically working for 20 years to bribe local police, politicians and officials to facilitate dumping toxic waste in the Caserta plain. A submission to the Parliamentary Joint Committee on the Australian Crime Commission (2009, p. 25) said that 'organised criminal activity in South Australia involves [...] a reliance [...] on professionals, such as lawyers and accountants, to create complicated structures to hide the proceeds of their crimes'.

Impacts of interference in government and judicial decision making include higher costs to all legitimate users of the courts: while hard evidence is impossible to find, it is inevitable that law enforcement and civil litigants face higher costs in courts as a result of organised crime groups' ability to pay high fees for lawyers. It is perhaps significant that website searches find many law firms – particularly in the US – stressing their competence in fighting charges relating to organised crime. New Jersey lawyer Seymour Wishman notes that

> [s]ince most white-collar defendants had stolen large sums of money, their lawyers were usually well paid. A small percentage of lawyers represented Mafia figures, or large, established, drug rings. These lawyers were highly competent, more so than most, and they earned a great deal of money.
>
> (Wishman, 2013, p. 53)

Impacts of interference in government and judicial decision making also include corruption of public officials. This section has already identified instances in which organised crime have employed or bribed corrupt public officials in order to protect their investments. World Bank and IMF studies (Kaufmann, 2004) find that

> corruption and bribery is a regressive tax. Not only smaller enterprises pay a higher share of their revenue in bribes than their larger counterparts, but also poorer households bear a disproportionate share of the bribery burden,

paying a much higher share of their incomes than higher income households – often for public services that were expected to be provided for free.

Researchers at the International Monetary Fund, utilising worldwide data on income distribution, also find that corruption is associated with increased income inequality. Gupta, Davoodi and Alonso-Terme (2002) provide evidence of significant adverse distributional effects of corruption. They find that high and rising corruption is associated with higher income inequality and poverty. A worsening of the corruption index of a country by one standard deviation increases the Gini coefficient by 11 points, and one standard deviation increase in the growth of corruption reduces income growth of the poor by 4.7 percentage points a year. Lanza (2004) finds that institutionalised bribery also introduces a new set of transaction costs – the costs of negotiating, monitoring and enforcing illicit agreements and avoiding detection by those not a party to the agreement. And since corruption involves the arbitrary use of discretionary power, uncertainty – the 'great bogeyman' of business confidence – grows, and the business environment becomes less secure. Furthermore, political corruption undercuts free markets and hampers efficiency, and firms with political connections can be less cost conscious since they are shielded from competition. Corruption also distorts the allocation of resources toward projects that can generate (illicit) payoffs. Besides the undesirable efficiency consequences arising from this distortion, the effect is likely to aggravate social inequalities, because the poor and powerless suffer, by definition, a comparative disadvantage in securing special favours (Lanza, 2004).

UNAFEI (2008) finds that

> [e]ven minor acts of corruption are damaging, breeding feelings of distrust and unfairness toward the government among ordinary citizen. As a consequence, it may ultimately weaken or collapse the national or local ruling government and economic structure of a country.

The above suggests that the costs to the community of organised crime groups' investing in legal, administrative and political resources are measured in terms of corruption – of the economy, of the processes of government and of the courts – the three lynchpins of democracy. The fact that hard data are at present so difficult to find should prompt the development of new systems of monitoring corruption and related activities, with a focus on professional occupations that are currently self-regulated.

Conclusions

This chapter has provided some suggestions to measure – or, in the absence of hard data, to describe – the impacts of organised crime infiltration on the European legal economy. Impacts are widespread and impose very significant costs on society and the legitimate economy. Moreover most – if not all – of these impacts *could* be measured. Indeed, most of the impacts described here have been measured, at least in some context and at some point in time.

In the same way that the development of population surveys of crime victimisation, during the 1980s and later, provided much-needed data on the costs of crime in general, it may be possible to develop appropriately targeted data-gathering techniques to address the impacts of organised crime groups and their investment strategies. Owing to the transnational nature of the problem, such techniques themselves would inevitably have to involve international collaboration. A good starting point may be the UNODC International Classification of Crime for Statistical Purposes (UNODC, 2015) which recommends the use of 'situational context' flags in crime incidence data. It is suggested that these might indicate, for example, where participation in 'an organized criminal group'[2] or 'a gang'[3] was an integral part of the *modus operandi* of the crime. This is already the case in, for example, Italy, where homicides, mass murders and some types of assault are distinguished between mafia and non-mafia related (Ministero dell'Interno, 2008), and in Mexico, where crime statistics indicating the extent of organised crime involvement are produced (Centro Nacional de Informacion, 2015). Another useful data development is the assessment of the wealth of an organised crime group, which is the subject of a special investigation by the Australian Crime Commission (2015) designed to disrupt and deter criminal groups by collecting evidence and intelligence about financially motivated crime. This type of evidence not only provides an indication of the resources that organised crime groups have at their disposal, and that could be invested, but also has the potential to identify where and how it is invested. It is important that new data sources such as these are developed and implemented internationally, before the impacts of organised crime investments can genuinely be measured.

Notes

1 Prices fell by an average of 13.9 per cent per annum in Ireland between the third quarter of 2008 and the third quarter of 2011; by 5.1 per cent per annum in Spain, by 4.9 per cent per annum in the UK and to lesser extents in Hungary, Greece, Denmark, the Netherlands, Portugal, Poland and France during the same period (Zemcik and Zabrodska, 2012, p. 3).

2 Where 'organised criminal group' is defined as 'a structured group of three or more persons, existing for a period of time and acting in concert with the aim of committing one or more serious crimes or offences in order to obtain, directly or indirectly, a financial or other material benefit', aligning with the United Nations Convention Against Transnational Organized Crime and the Protocols Thereto.

3 A gang is defined as 'a group of persons that is defined by a set of characteristics including durability over time, street-oriented lifestyle, youthfulness of members, involvement in illegal activities and group identity'.

References

Arlacchi, P. (1983). *La mafia imprenditrice. L'etica mafiosa e lo spirito del capitalismo.* Bologna: Il Mulino.

Australian Crime Commission. (2009). *Inquiry into the legislative arrangements to outlaw serious and organised crime groups*. Canberra: Parliamentary Joint Committee on the Australian Crime Commission.

Australian Crime Commission. (2015). *Organised crime in Australia 2015*. Canberra: Australian Crime Commission.

Australian Taxation Office. (2014). *The fight against tax crime*. Canberra: Australian Taxation Office.

Brand, S., & Price, R. (2000). *The economic and social costs of crime*. London: Home Office, Economics and Resource Analysis Research, Development and Statistics Directorate.

Calderoni, F. (2014). Measuring the presence of the mafias in Italy. In S. Caneppele & F. Calderoni (Eds.), *Organized crime, corruption and crime prevention* (pp. 239–249). New York, NY: Springer.

Caneppele, S., Calderoni, F., & Martocchia, S. (2009). Not only banks: Criminological models on the infiltration of public contracts by Italian organized crime. *Journal of Money Laundering Control, 12*(2), 151–172.

Cawley, M. (2013). Extortion shuts down over 17,000 Honduras businesses. *InSight Crime*. Retrieved from www.insightcrime.org/news-briefs/economic-impact-honduras-extortion.

Centro Nacional de Informacion. (2015). *Reporte de incidencia delictiva del fuero federal por entidad federativa 2012–2015*. Mexico City: Centro Nacional de Informacion. Retrieved from http://secretariadoejecutivo.gob.mx/docs/pdfs/fuero_federal/estadisticas%20fuero%20federal/Fuerofederal012015.pdf.

Chen, C., Carbacho-Burgos, A., Mehra, S., & Zoller, M. (2013). The Moody's Analytics case-shiller home price index forecast methodology. *Moody's Analytics*. Retrieved from www.moodysanalytics.com/~/media/Brochures/Economic-Consumer-Credit-Analytics/Examples/case-shiller-methodology.pdf.

CSPI. (2000). *Miscarriage, birth defects 'too high a price to pay' for tainted food charge victims and health group*. Washington, DC: Center for Science in the Public Interest.

Daniele, V., & Marani, U. (2008). Organized crime and foreign direct investment: The Italian case. *Trends in Organized Crime, 11*(3), 296–300.

Di Feo, G., & Fittipaldi, E. (2008, 9 November). Così ho avvelenato Napoli. *L'Espresso*. Retrieved from http://espresso.repubblica.it/palazzo/2008/09/11/news/cosi-ho-avvelenato-napoli-1.9911.

Flare Network. (2014). The management and disposal of confiscated assets in the EU member states: Laws and practices. Flare Network. Retrieved from http://flarenetwork.org/media/files/recast/recast_summary_report_1_eng.pdf.

Fröhlich, T. (2003). *Organised environmental crime in the EU Member States*. Kassel: Betreuungsgesellschaft für Umweltfragen.

Gupta, S., Davoodi, H. R., & Alonso-Terme, R. (2002). Does corruption affect income inequality and poverty? In G. T. Abed & S. Gupta (Eds.), *Governance, corruption, & economic performance*. Washington, DC: International Monetary Fund.

International Bar Association. (2010). Risks and threats of corruption and the legal profession. *Anti-Corruption Strategy for the Legal Profession*. Retrieved from www.oecd.org/corruption/anti-bribery/46137847.pdf.

Kaufmann, D. (2004, 29 September). World Bank finds corruption is costing billions in lost development power. *Probe International*. Retrieved from http://journal.probeinternational.org/2004/09/29/world-bank-finds-corruption-is-costing-billions-in-lost-development-power/.

Lanza, S. (2004). The economics of ethics: The cost of political corruption. *The Connecticut Economy Quarterly*, winter issue.

Linden, L. L., & Rockoff, J. E. (2006). *There goes the neighborhood? Estimates of the impact of crime risk on property values from Megan's Laws* (NBER Working Paper No. 12253). Cambridge, MA: National Bureau of Economic Research.

Mayhew, P. (2003). *Counting the costs of crime in Australia: Technical report* (Technical and Background Paper Series No. 4). Canberra: Australian Institute of Criminology.

Ministero dell'Interno. (2008). *Rapporto sulla criminalità in Italia. Analisi, prevenzione, contrasto*. Roma: Ministero dell'Interno.

Pinotti, P. (2015). The causes and consequences of organised crime: Preliminary evidence across countries. *The Economic Journal*, *125*(586), 158–174.

Ray, L. (2015). The effects of corruption on business. *Huston Chronicle*. Retrieved from http://smallbusiness.chron.com/effects-corruption-business-52808.html.

Riccardi, M. (2014). When criminals invest in businesses: Are we looking in the right direction? An exploratory analysis of companies controlled by mafias. In S. Caneppele & F. Calderoni (Eds.), *Organized crime, corruption and crime prevention* (pp. 197–206). New York, NY: Springer.

Senior, K., & Massa, A. (2004). Italian 'triangle of death' linked to waste crisis. *The Lancet Oncology*, *5*(9), 525–527.

Shapiro, R. J., & Hassett, K. A. (2012). *The economic benefits of reducing violent crime. A case study of 8 American cities*. Washington, DC: Center for American Progress.

Tita, G., Petras, T., & Greenbaum, R. (2006). Crime and residential choice: A neighborhood level analysis of the impact of crime on housing prices. *Journal of Quantitative Criminology*, *22*(4), 299–317.

Transcrime. (2013). *Progetto PON Sicurezza 2007–2013. Gli investimenti delle mafie*. Milano: Transcrime – Joint Research Centre on Transnational Crime.

UNAFEI. (2008). *International training course on the criminal justice response to corruption*. Tokyo: United Nations Asia and Far East Institute for the Prevention of Crime and the Treatment of Offenders.

University of York. (2009). *Mainstreaming methodology for estimating the costs of crime*. York: Centre for Criminal Justice, Economics and Psychology, University of York.

UNODC. (2015). *International classification of crime for statistical purposes*. Vienna: UNODC. Retrieved from www.unodc.org/documents/data-and-analysis/statistics/crime/ICCS/ICCS_final-2015-March12_FINAL.pdf.

Walker, J. (1992). *Estimates of the cost of crime in Australia*. Canberra: Australian Institute of Criminology.

WEF. (2011). *Global Agenda Council on Organized Crime*. Cologne: World Economic Forum. Retrieved from www3.weforum.org/docs/WEF_GAC_OrganizedCrime_Report_2010-11.pdf.

Wishman, S. (2013). *Confessions of a criminal lawyer: A memoir*. New York: Open Road Media.

World Bank. (2003). *Jamaica: The road to sustained growth* (No. 26088-JM). Washington, DC: The World Bank.

Zemcik, P. & Zabrodska, A. (2012). The varied cycles of European housing markets. *Moody's Analytics*. Retrieved from www.moodysanalytics.com/~/media/Insight/Economic-Analysis/Housing/2012/2012-08-02-The-Varied-Cycles-of-European-Housing-Markets.pdf.

12 From the analysis of criminal infiltration to the assessment of its risk

Lorella Garofalo

Why assess the risk of infiltration

Risk assessment (hereafter RA) is the process of determining the likelihood that a specified event will occur and of preventing and/or reducing its negative consequences (Albanese, 2008; Albrecht & Kilchling, 2002; Covello & Merkhofer, 1993; Dawe, 2013; FATF, 2012). RA is an approach commonly used in both public and private sectors to support the decision-making process. It is applied in several fields pertaining to different industries, such as the environment, engineering, aerospace, military, medical products, social services and food. In the past decades RA has also been applied to crime issues, such as money laundering, terrorism and corruption, due to growing international pressure in combating these phenomena. Indeed, several international and European provisions have been issued to mandate countries to adopt legal, regulatory and operational measures for combating money laundering, terrorist financing and other related threats. Countries and businesses are obliged to implement these standards within their regulations.

The Financial Action Task Force (FATF) has developed a series of recommendations that are recognised as the international standards for combating money laundering, the financing of terrorism, and the proliferation of weapons of mass destruction. These recommendations form the basis for a coordinated response to these threats to the integrity of the financial system, and they help ensure a level playing field. They were first issued in 1990 and further revised in 1996, 2001, 2003, and most recently in 2012. Recommendation no. 1 states that:

> [c]ountries should identify, assess, and understand the money laundering and terrorist financing risks for the country, and should take action, including designating an authority or mechanism to coordinate actions to assess risks, and apply resources, aimed at ensuring the risks are mitigated effectively. Based on that assessment, countries should apply a risk-based approach (RBA) to ensure that measures to prevent or mitigate money laundering and terrorist financing are commensurate with the risks identified.
>
> (FATF, 2012, p. 11)

The EU Directive 2015/849 on prevention of the use of the financial system for the purposes of money laundering or terrorist financing (often known as the fourth 'anti-money laundering directive') came into force in June 2015.[1] It takes the latest recommendations of the FATF into account and obliges member states to evidence that they have taken appropriate steps to identify, assess, understand, and mitigate the risk of money laundering and terrorism. Moreover, it requires states to carry out national risk assessments. The United Nations convention against corruption (resolution no. 58/4 of 2003) declares that businesses have the responsibility to act as good corporate citizens; if not, they are held criminally, civilly and/or administratively liable (art. 26). All the international provisions have a feature in common: they stress the need to identify, assess and understand the risk deriving from money laundering or corruption by adopting specific risk-based approaches and complying with the international standards (FATF, 2013).

Criminal infiltration into the legitimate economy is undoubtedly linked to money laundering and corruption (Buscaglia & van Dijk, 2003; Europol, 2015; Savona & Riccardi, 2015; Transcrime, 2013a; UIF, 2015; van der Does de Willebois, Halter, Harrison, Park & Sharman, 2011; Vannucci, 1997). Indeed, criminal organisations infiltrate various sectors of the legal economy that allow them to invest in, and launder profits from, illegal activities, as well as providing additional opportunities for extra gain. RA may help the constant monitoring of changes in the legal economy and the vulnerabilities that may be exploited by criminal organisations; it could help to anticipate or mitigate the negative consequences and develop appropriate actions to recognise and prevent the criminal infiltration itself. Risk-based models for assessing criminal infiltration are also useful for evaluating the threats to which a certain economic sector/territory/business is exposed, its vulnerabilities, and the resulting consequences (i.e. the harm to the economic system, institutions, or society). Moving from mere analysis of the phenomenon to the assessment of risk could be useful for developing effective preventive strategies and complying with the international requirements and standards in the field. Moreover, the RA approach is useful for policymaking. Indeed, it may help to identify areas in which to concentrate counteractions and factors to be mitigated through the implementation of specific interventions. Finally, it assists governments in the prioritisation and efficient allocation of resources (FATF, 2013).

Risk assessment and criminal infiltration of the legitimate economy

RA as defined by the international standards has not yet been applied to criminal infiltration. The existing literature in the field comprises some qualitative and quantitative models which attempted to identify the risk factors of the economic sectors/activities/territories most vulnerable to criminal infiltration. The main existing models of criminal infiltration of the legitimate economy are presented below.

One of the first models was developed by Albanese (1987) in order to predict a company's risk of being infiltrated by organised crime. Albanese identified six predictors, which defined the company's vulnerabilities (Table 12.1). The author

Table 12.1 Preliminary predictive model on organised crime infiltration of legitimate businesses

Predictors	Low risk	High risk
Supply	Few available small, financially weak businesses	Readily available small, financially weak businesses
Customers	Elastic demand for product	Inelastic demand for product
Regulators	Difficult to enter the market	Easy to enter the market
Competitors	Monopoly/oligopoly controlled market	Open market with many small firms
Patronage	Entrepreneurs are professional managers	Entrepreneurs are non-professionals ill-equipped to deal with business problems
Prior record	No prior record of organised crime involvement in the market	Prior history of organised crime infiltration in the industry

Source: author's elaboration on Albanese (1987).

considered two different ways in which criminal infiltration of the legal economy can be assessed: the use of legal businesses as covers for illegal activities, and corruption.

Albanese then developed a second model which used illicit markets as the units of analysis (2008). Its purpose was to assess the presence of organised crime groups in 'areas that may or may not have a history of organised crime involvement' (Albanese, 2008, p. 263). Albanese sought to assess comparative risk levels of criminal activities and illicit markets. Indeed, he stated that if illegal activities are properly assessed and ranked, targeting these activities will make it possible to tackle the high-risk organised crime groups involved. He identified three main categories of organised crime activities: provision of illicit services; provision of illicit goods; and infiltration of legitimate businesses. Each of these activities was further divided into more specific offences. The provision of illicit services encompassed commercialised sex, illegal gambling, and human trafficking, subcontracting to others (provision of services such as illicit dumping of waste, trafficking in human organs or protected animal species). The provision of illicit goods involved drug trafficking, property theft, and counterfeiting. The infiltration of businesses included extortion of business owners, racketeering, money laundering and fraud. The following are the fundamental dimensions on which to assess which markets are at higher risk:

- Supply indicators: objective availability of the product or service; easily transported/sold;
- Regulation indicators: ease of entry into the market due to market regulations; skills needed; law enforcement capability and competence; level of local government corruption;

- Competition indicators: history of organised crime in the market; profitability; harm;
- Demand indicators: current customer demand for the product; nature of the demand.

Rozekrans and Emde (1996) developed a conceptual model based on the preventive screening of economic sectors. They stressed that business processes rather than industries are the level of analysis that should be considered by preventive screening for organised crime infiltration. Their research introduced a diagnostic review model named the PST (primary, secondary, tertiary) risk analysis model for analysing business processes. The PST risk analysis model distinguishes among primary (basic illegal criminal activities); secondary (activities to generate profits: money laundering); and tertiary (investments) types of criminal activities. These different forms of crime are linked to the specific characteristics and vulnerabilities of each business process. The use of indicators (which differ according to the diverse forms of crime that may affect the sector) helps measure these elements. They assess the vulnerabilities to crime of each phase in the process (PST risk profile). The model identifies indicators either facilitating or discouraging criminal activities, and it is built by first identifying the key phases of the business process.

The MAVUS model (Method for Assessment of the Vulnerability of Sectors), developed in 2005 by the Institute for International Research on Criminal Policy (IRCP) of the University of Ghent and Transcrime – Joint Research Centre on Transnational Crime, is a method of analysis, which aims at assessing the degree of vulnerability of the legitimate economic sectors to organised crime. It is based on a multidisciplinary approach comprising economic, sociological and criminological methodologies. In Europe, the model has been applied to several economic sectors, such as the diamond industry, transport, music, pharmaceuticals, fashion, and waste management (Vander Beken, 2005, 2007). The MAVUS model comprises three different levels of analysis: *macro, meso* and *micro*. At the *macro* level, it analyses the environment surrounding the economic sector; the *meso* level analyses the sector itself; while the *micro* level analyses the individual economic entity and its business processes. The application of MAVUS moves through two main phases, each of them divided into further steps:

- Descriptive phase: analysis of the sector (sector analysis); analysis of the environment and the cluster around the sector (environmental scan and cluster analysis); analysis of the economic entity and its business processes (reference model analysis);
- Analytical phase: width scan; depth scan.

In the descriptive phase, the first two steps involve the collection of information on the cluster around the sector (*macro* level), the sector itself (*meso* level), and the activities within the sector (*micro* level). The data collected lead to the development of indicators and the construction of a reference model for the economic sector under investigation that describes how the business is organised. The third step (reference model analysis) deals with definition of the business's structure: it analyses its business processes by collecting data on the operating rules that guide the choices and information derived directly from the sector. The information gathered in the descriptive phase is used in the analytical phase to develop the vulnerability profile of the sector. In particular, the indicators identified from the information gathered at the macro and meso level is analysed to define a width profile of vulnerability of the entire sector (width scan). Analysis of the indicators identified at the micro level leads to the creation of an in-depth vulnerability profile of the business (depth scan).

Between 2011 and 2013, Transcrime developed two risk models: Me.Tri.C. and Mo.Vu.S. The first had the purpose of analysing the vulnerabilities of the economic sector in the Italian province of Trento which might facilitate infiltration of the legal economy by criminal organisations (Transcrime, 2013a). Me. Tri.C. consisted of two different macro dimensions created from the identification of several risk factors: the first focused on the territory; whereas the second one focused on the economic sector. The risk factors were operationalised into indicators so that they could be directly measured. Table 12.2 summarises the indicators and variables included in each model.

The Mo.Vu.S. model was developed to assess the vulnerabilities of the legal economy to organised crime infiltration for all the Italian provinces (Transcrime, 2013b). Mo.Vu.S. identified the risk of infiltration by organised crime for 12 economic sectors at provincial level. The model consisted of the combination of two different macro dimensions: the territory (R_t), which is related to the characteristics of the territory that might facilitate infiltration by criminal organisations, and the economic sector (R_s), determined by the characteristics of each sector at provincial level. Each dimension was operationalised into different risk factors, indicators and variables (Table 12.3).

Table 12.2 Me.Tri.C. model. Indicators included in the territory and economic sector models

Risk factor	Indicator
Territory	Small business
	Bankruptcy
	Business turnover
	Economic crime index
	Organised crime index
	Wealth index
Economic sector	Business structure
	Business structure static index
	Business structure dynamic index
	Economic crime index of the sector

Source: author's elaboration on Transcrime (2013a).

Table 12.3 Mo.Vu.S. model, indicators included in the territory and economic sector risk dimensions

Risk factor	Indicator
Territory	Organised crime presence
	Wealth
	Shadow economy
	Market structure
Economic sector	Business size
	Business crisis
	Competitiveness
	Previous infiltration

Source: author's elaboration on Transcrime (2013b).

The risk factors facilitating infiltration

Several risk factors can be identified as facilitators of criminal infiltration into the legitimate economy, and they should be taken into account when developing an ad hoc RA model. They can be grouped into four main dimensions: those referring to the territory where infiltration takes place; those related to the economic sector; and risk factors linked to the business ownership structure and the economic and financial management.

Territory

Previous studies on organised crime investments in the legitimate economy have shown that businesses located in territories with specific characteristics present more evidence of criminal infiltration (Savona & Riccardi, 2015; Transcrime, 2013b). Table 12.4 summarises the main hypotheses on the characteristics of infiltrated territories, which can change depending on the country/region/city subject to analysis. For instance, what is tested as regards the criminal infiltration in one country may be different in other countries. Some hypotheses have already been statistically tested and proved, although not yet in a multivariate model (Transcrime, 2013b; Riccardi, 2014).

The literature suggests that areas with a historical, well-rooted presence of organised crime groups are likely to present evidence of the involvement of such groups in the legal economy (Caneppele, Riccardi & Standridge, 2013; Riccardi, 2014; The Dutch Parliament, 1996; Vander Beken, 2004; Varese, 2011). Territories with a stable presence of criminal groups are thus vulnerable to the criminal infiltration of legitimate businesses. Criminal groups may favour territories with which they are familiar because of past cases of criminal infiltration into legal businesses.

Organised crime groups may favour areas characterised by low competition – and thus low openness to international investments and high territorial specificity – in order to benefit from a monopolistic position (Daniele & Marani, 2008).

Table 12.4 Hypotheses on the characteristics of infiltrated territories

Assumption	Dimension
Organised crime groups invest in businesses operating in the same territory where they are present and active	Organised crime presence
Organised crime groups invest in areas with 'protected' economies characterised by low competition levels and low openness to foreign investments	Openness to foreign countries
Organised crime groups invest in areas characterised by traditional economic activities, low technological levels, and low R&D rates	Technology
Organised crime groups infiltrate businesses located in areas characterised by low levels of wealth and low levels of infrastructure development	Income and infrastructural equipment
Organised crime groups infiltrate businesses that operate in contexts characterised by high levels of tax evasion, black economy, and economic-financial crimes	Shadow economy, corruption, and money laundering

Source: author's elaboration on Transcrime (2013a, 2013b), Riccardi (2014) and Savona and Berlusconi (2015).

Other characteristics of territories that may favour criminal infiltration in legal businesses include: high incidence of traditional economic activities (e.g. construction and mining, retail, hotels and restaurants, transport and distribution), low technological levels and low rates of research and development (Transcrime, 2013b); high levels of tax evasion and shadow economy; widespread corruption and money laundering activities (Albanese, 2008; Caneppele et al., 2013; Marine, 2010; Riccardi, 2014; Transcrime, 2013).

Criminal groups may also exploit the fragility of the industrial, commercial, financial and banking systems, acting as last resort creditors to businesses with financial difficulties and eventually take them over (Bertoni & Rossi, 1997; Masciandro & Ruozi, 1999; Riccardi, 2014). Moreover, areas with low levels of regulation may facilitate infiltration by organised crime groups and the concealment of criminal activities (Albanese, 2008; Blum, Levi, Naylor & Williams, 1999; FATF, 2004; Savona & Riccardi, 2015; Suendorf, 2001; Vander Beken, 2005).

Criminal infiltration may be facilitated by high levels of shadow economy, money laundering and corruption. Indeed, the literature has confirmed that the unobserved economy and the use of cash are the most prevalent facilitators for laundering profits deriving from all different types of criminal activities (Ardizzi, Petraglia, Piacenza, Schneider & Turati, 2012; Ardizzi, Petraglia, Piacenza & Turati, 2014; Europol, 2015; Schneider, 2010; Schneider, Buehn & Montenegro, 2010; UIF, 2015). The presence of widespread corruption and market illegalities is exploited by criminal groups because it facilitates illicit activities and reduces the risks of being reported to law enforcement agencies (Buscaglia & van Dijk,

2003; FATF, 2010; Kelly, 2012; van der Does de Willebois et al., 2011; van Duyne, Jager, von Lampe & Newell, 2004).

Business sectors

Risk factors can be linked with the characteristics of the business sector. Indeed, sectors with past evidence of organised crime infiltration, or characterised by low levels of competition and openness to foreign investments and low levels of technology, may favour the criminal infiltration of legal businesses (Savona & Berlusconi, 2015). Other risk factors include a small average company size, low barriers to entry, and a weak or developing regulation. Table 12.5 summarises the main hypotheses on the characteristics of infiltrated sectors.

The literature suggests that organised crime groups invest in sectors with high profitability in order to maximise their profits (Albanese, 2008; Calderoni & Caneppele, 2009; Riccardi, 2014; Transcrime, 2013). However, available studies in which this hypothesis has been tested either show the opposite or do not confirm that profitability, at macro or micro level, is correlated with the prevalence of criminal infiltration (Donato, Saporito & Scognamiglio, 2013; Transcrime, 2013b; Riccardi, 2014; Savona & Berlusconi, 2015). Criminal groups may also favour sectors characterised by an inelasticity of demand and where the number of competitors is limited (i.e. sectors with low openness to international investments and low competition) (Berghuis & de Waard, 2011; Calderoni & Caneppele, 2009; Daniele & Marani, 2008; Fiorentini, 2000; Gambetta & Reuter, 2000; Vander Beken, 2005).

Organised criminals may favour economic sectors characterised by low labour productivity and high labour intensity, so as to create new jobs and

Table 12.5 Hypotheses on the characteristics of infiltrated business sectors

Assumption	Dimension
Organised crime groups invest in sectors with high profitability	Profitability
Organised crime groups invest in sectors with low competition	Competition
Organised crime groups invest in sectors characterised by a low level of foreign investments	Openness to foreign investments
Organised crime groups invest in sectors characterised by low technological levels and low R&D rates	Technology
Organised crime groups invest in sectors characterised by low capital intensity, high labour intensity, and low labour productivity	Labour intensity
Organised crime groups invest in sectors with small-medium (often unlisted) enterprises	Business entity size

Source: author's elaboration on Transcrime (2013a, 2013b), Riccardi (2014) and Savona and Berlusconi (2015).

increase their social consensus (Calderoni & Riccardi, 2011; Gambetta & Reuter, 2000; Transcrime, 2013b; Vander Beken, 2005). The consensus may also be increased by being active in sectors characterised by public utility, such as health care, thus ensuring high visibility, social prestige, and legitimation by the local population (Transcrime, 2013b; Savona & Riccardi, 2015; Savona & Berlusconi, 2015). Traditional activities, or activities with low technological levels, may also be vulnerable to infiltration by criminal groups because they ensure high profits without entailing high research and development costs (Becchi & Rey, 1994; Calderoni, Dugato & Riccardi, 2010; Lavezzi, 2008; Sciarrone, 2009).

Organised crime groups frequently infiltrate small–medium size and unlisted businesses in order to reduce their visibility and minimise the risk of controls (Becchi & Rey, 1994; Lavezzi, 2008; Riccardi, 2014; Transcrime, 2013b; Vander Beken, 2004). They may also exploit sectors with weak or changing regulations that make it possible to conceal criminal activities easily (Berghuis & de Waard, 2011; Calderoni & Caneppele, 2009; Transcrime, 2000; Vander Beken & van Daele, 2008).

Business sectors with low barriers to entry may also be favoured. These latter include few requirements to set up a company (e.g. registration with the national business registry and absence of disqualifications from being a company director); no need for a licence (e.g. in the wholesale and retail trade, there is no need for an import licence except for particular goods); low start-up costs – i.e. low capital-intensiveness (Brå, 2011, p. 7; Brå, 2014, p. 10). Generally, low capital-intensive sectors have lower barriers to entry and thus are easier to infiltrate. Finally, sectors with a high availability of public resources may be infiltrated by criminal groups, especially if there exist collusive relationships between criminals and public officials and politicians (Becchi & Rey, 1994; Centorrino & Signorino, 1997; Fantò, 1999; Sacco, 2010; Savona & Riccardi, 2015; Sciarrone, 2009; Transcrime, 2013b).

Ownership structure of legal business

A third category of risk factors includes characteristics of the business ownership structure, which comprise, among others, the legal form, i.e. the type of company (e.g. limited company, unlimited company, individual enterprise, cooperative);[2] the nature of shareholders[3] and directors;[4] and the use of other forms of control (e.g. cross shareholding, foreign registered seats).

Legal form

Depending on the specific goals that they intend to pursue, organised crime groups may prefer some legal forms rather than others. Table 12.6 summarises the hypotheses on the legal forms of infiltrated businesses.

Organised crime groups may need to conceal their criminal activities and identity. In these cases, they will prefer legal forms, such as private limited companies, which allow for greater fragmentation of the share capital, thus making it

Table 12.6 Hypotheses on the legal form of infiltrated businesses

Driver	Strategy	Proxy
Concealment of illicit activities and beneficial ownership	Fragmentation of company's issued share capital to conceal the beneficial owner and reduce the risk of seizure of the whole company	Limited companies
	Use of non-transparent legal entities	Use of individual companies as holding companies; use of trusts, fiduciary companies, associations, foundations; use of shell companies
Direct control and exposure	Direct control over the company without the need to involve professionals or external managers	Unlimited companies; individual companies
	Legal forms easy to establish and manage, and not requiring accounting of financial transactions	Individual companies; unlimited companies; limited companies

Source: author's elaboration on Transcrime (2013a, 2013b) and Savona and Berlusconi (2015).

more difficult for law enforcement agencies to identify the beneficial owners of the infiltrated businesses. Limited liability also reduces the potential impact of seizure and confiscation. Indeed, in case of seizure or confiscation, only the shares of the person indicted are usually restricted (FATF, 2006; Gup & Beekarry, 2009; Steinko, 2012; Transcrime, 2013b). For the same reasons, organised criminals may also choose legal forms with low transparency requirements, such as trusts or foundations, especially those registered in countries with low transparency regimes (FATF, 2006; Transcrime, 2013b; van der Does de Willebois et al., 2011). Individual companies (e.g. sole traders/proprietorships) or unlimited companies (e.g. partnerships) may be favoured by criminal groups, which want to exert direct control over their assets. The same consideration also applies to organised crime members who want to achieve visibility and social prestige by being publicly recognised as 'successful entrepreneurs' (Gup & Beekarry, 2009; Transcrime, 2013b).

Shareholders and directors

The need to conceal criminal activities and identity and to exert direct control over infiltrated businesses may also influence the control strategies adopted by organised crime groups in terms of shareholders and directors of infiltrated companies. Table 12.7 summarises the hypotheses drawn from the literature.

Table 12.7 Hypotheses on shareholders and directors of infiltrated businesses

Driver	Strategy	Proxy
Concealment of illicit activities and beneficial ownership	Legal persons as shareholders	Use of corporate shareholders
	Natural persons as figureheads	Relatives among the shareholders; professionals among the shareholders; legal entrepreneurs among the shareholders; young people, old/retired people or women among the shareholders/ directors; presence of people with low levels of education
Direct control and exposure	Direct control on mafia companies; use of 'family companies'	Organised crime affiliates included as shareholders; Organised crime affiliates included as employees; Family members among the shareholders and/or directors

Source: author's elaboration on Transcrime (2013a, 2013b) and Savona and Berlusconi (2015).

The use of figureheads as company shareholders is a strategy commonly used by organised crime groups to conceal their criminal activities and hide the identity of the ultimate beneficial owners (Brå, 2011; FATF, 2006; Schneider, 2004; Transcrime, 2008b, 2013b; van der Does de Willebois et al., 2011). Persons frequently used as figureheads include relatives of organised crime members, legal entrepreneurs and professionals. The use of figureheads is particularly frequent if the members of the criminal organisation have criminal records which prevent them from directly participating in the ownership and management structure of the infiltrated business (Sarno, 2015; Transcrime, 2013b). Legal companies as corporate shareholders may also be used to conceal the beneficial ownership of infiltrated businesses.

Nonetheless, the inclusion of relatives among the company shareholders can be used not only as a means to conceal the criminal activities and identity of organised crime members, but also as a strategy to maintain control that is as direct as possible on the infiltrated business when they cannot do this personally (Sarno, 2015; Transcrime, 2013b). Alternatively, organised crime groups will include some of their affiliates among the shareholders and the employees of the infiltrated businesses in order to exert direct control or to achieve visibility and social prestige (Calderoni & Caneppele, 2009; Transcrime, 2008b, 2013b).

Other forms of control

Organised crime groups may resort to other strategies of control over infiltrated businesses in order to make it more difficult for law enforcement agencies to identify their criminal identity and beneficial ownership. The main hypotheses drawn by the literature are summarised in Table 12.8.

Table 12.8 Hypotheses from the literature on other forms of control of infiltrated businesses

Driver	Strategy	Proxy
Concealment of illicit activities and beneficial ownership	Use of complex corporate ownership schemes	Pyramidal structures; frequent transformations (e.g. registered address, name, business sector), transfers of business lines or business branches, dissolution of a company and transfer of its business activities to a newly incorporated company
	Foreign countries with low transparency requirements	Tax havens; use of multi-jurisdictional structures
Direct control and exposure	Direct control on mafia companies	Small or medium-sized companies

Source: author's elaboration on Transcrime (2013a, 2013b) and Savona and Berlusconi (2015).

One strategy commonly used by criminal groups is the creation of complex corporate ownership schemes (FATF, 2006; Schneider, 2004; Suendorf, 2001; Transcrime, 2008a, 2008b, 2013b). In particular, the literature distinguishes between static and dynamic schemes. The former involve the creation of large networks of companies interconnected by cross-shareholdings (so-called 'Chinese boxes'). The latter are more dynamic strategies which include: frequent transformations of company details (e.g. registered address, name), transfers of business lines or business branches, dissolution of a company and transfer of its activities to a newly incorporated one (Transcrime, 2013b).

Financial management

'Management strategies' refer to the financial management of infiltrated businesses, i.e. how infiltrated businesses are financed and if they are able to produce profits. Analysing the management strategy of infiltrated businesses may mean looking at the financing sources, use of assets and profitability.

Financing sources

Among the drivers of organised crime infiltration of legal businesses, money laundering and the concealment of illegal activities may influence the financial statement items (i.e. equity and liabilities) of infiltrated businesses. Criminal groups may have a large amount of illicit proceeds to be invested and laundered through legal businesses. As a consequence, infiltrated businesses may not need to resort to bank credit, and they may have low levels of financial indebtedness (Di Bono, Cincimino, Riccardi & Berlusconi, 2015; Transcrime, 2013b).

At the same time, criminal groups need to conceal the origin of the money used to finance the infiltrated businesses. Possible options include the creation of complex corporate schemes to account loans as debts towards companies of the same group, or towards subsidiaries, shareholders and parent companies. Infiltrated businesses may also incorporate (fictitious) supplier companies and disguise the injection of money as debts to suppliers (i.e. trade payables) (Di Bono et al., 2015; Transcrime, 2013b). Finally, infiltrated companies may show levels of trade payables higher than the sector's average in the case of actual indebtedness to suppliers, especially if they are able to intimidate them and delay payments (Steinko, 2012; Transcrime, 2013b). Table 12.9 summarises the hypotheses on the financing sources of infiltrated businesses

Available empirical evidence seems to confirm these hypotheses, although in most cases it does so on the basis of case studies (Transcrime, 2013b). In one of the few large-scale empirical studies (Di Bono et al., 2015), only the level of financial net debt of infiltrated businesses is significantly lower than the average level of legal and non-infiltrated companies belonging to the peer group of the analysis.[5]

Use of assets

An infiltrated business's use of assets may be influenced by the type of company, i.e. whether the business is productive or a shell business entity. Productive businesses aim to produce revenues and maximise their profits through (formally) legal activities. Therefore, like any other legal business, they are likely to invest the capital in buildings, machinery and other means of production. By contrast, legal businesses infiltrated with the aim of laundering money or committing fraud are likely to keep their assets in liquidity (e.g. cash, bank deposits) or other current assets (Catanzaro, 1988; Di Bono et al., 2015; Transcrime, 2013b). Businesses infiltrated by criminal groups to conceal criminal activities may also show levels of receivables and a number of debtors higher than the sector's average if

Table 12.9 Financing sources of infiltrated businesses

Driver	Strategy	Proxy
Large availability of illicit resources for laundering and for financing the firm	Low levels of financial debt	Low level of financial debts on total assets
	Low levels of debts	Low level of debts
Need to conceal illicit resources	Little use of shareholders' funds	Low level of equity on total assets
	Use of covert forms of funding	High level of other debts; high level of trade payables
Intimidation of suppliers	High exposure to suppliers	High level of trade payables

Source: author's elaboration on Transcrime (2013a, 2013b), Di Bono et al. (2015) and Savona and Berlusconi (2015).

they use them to disguise outflows to organised crime members or other companies controlled by the criminal group (Schneider, 2004; Transcrime, 2013b). Table 12.10 summarises the hypotheses on the use of assets of infiltrated businesses.

These hypotheses have been tested and some of them have also been confirmed (Di Bono et al., 2015). For instance, businesses managed by organised crime groups show levels of non-financial current assets significantly higher than the peer group composed of legal and non-infiltrated businesses used for the analysis. Some financial ratios instead show a trend which is in contrast with the one expected from the review of the literature. This may be due to the nature of the company included in the analysis (shell and paper companies, companies with no production activities).

Profitability

Also the level of profitability may be influenced by the type of company, i.e. whether the business is productive or a shell company. Productive companies are likely to be similar to legal businesses in terms of revenues and costs. However,

Table 12.10 Use of assets of infiltrated businesses

Driver	Strategy	Proxy
Shell companies: no production and investments, use of the companies only for money laundering	Low levels of fixed assets	Low levels of fixed assets and non-current assets out of total assets
	High levels of current assets	High level of current assets out of total assets; high level of cash and cash equivalents out of total assets; high level of trade receivables out of total assets; High level of non-financial current credits out of total assets
Shell companies: need to conceal outflow to organised crime members and/or colluding companies	Use of receivables and debtors to screen outflows to members	High levels of trade receivables; high levels of other debtors; high levels of receivables and debtors
	False invoicing	Use of false invoices
	Structuring and smurfing	Large financial transaction parcelled into a series of smaller transactions
	Deposits to foreign countries with low transparency requirements	Deposits to foreign bank accounts

Source: author's elaboration on Transcrime (2013a, 2013b), Di Bono et al. (2015) and Savona and Berlusconi (2015).

businesses infiltrated by organised crime groups can exploit competitive advantages guaranteed by the coexistence of formally legal activities and criminal methods (e.g. threats, corruption). Therefore, infiltrated businesses may be able to minimise their labour and production costs (Arlacchi, 2007; Fantò, 1999; Transcrime, 2013b; see also Chapter 8 in this book). The former can be reduced by not paying social security contributions, insurance, and overtime work; the latter can be minimised by using poor-quality materials. Infiltrated companies may instead be used to conceal outgoing flows to the members of the criminal group who are hired as employees. In this case the salaries – and thus labour costs – are likely to be higher than the sector's average (Schneider, 2004; Steinko, 2012; Transcrime, 2013b). Finally, shell and paper companies are characterised by no or minimum productive activities (Catanzaro, 1988). At accounting level, this may result in low revenues or in revenues characterised by high variance across time (Transcrime, 2008c, 2013b). Table 12.11 summarises the hypotheses on the profitability of infiltrated businesses.

According to available empirical studies, only one financial ratio used to assess the profitability of infiltrated companies provides statistically significant results (Di Bono et al., 2015). In general, companies controlled and managed by criminal groups are characterised by profits lower than those of the peer group of non-infiltrated businesses, regardless of the driver of infiltration. This may be partly due to the fact that infiltrated businesses often face economic difficulties, either because of the management by the members of the criminal group or because organised criminals target businesses with financial difficulties. However, these results may be biased by the presence of accounting

Table 12.11 Profitability of infiltrated businesses

Driver	Strategy	Proxy
Productive companies: profit maximisation and costs minimisation through criminal methods	Costs minimisation in the purchase of raw materials and services	Use of poor-quality materials
	Minimisation of production costs	Low production costs
	Advantages from illegality and discouragement of competition	Profitability higher than the sector's average
Shell and paper companies: concealing and laundering of criminal resources	No productive activity	Low revenues and profitability
	Concealment of cash outflows to organised crime members in the form of wages or as purchases of services	High levels of services costs or ones above the sector's average

Source: author's elaboration on Transcrime (2013a, 2013b), Di Bono et al. (2015) and Savona and Berlusconi (2015).

manipulations which, in the case of income statements, are easier and more frequent than in balance sheets.

Assessing the risk of criminal infiltration: challenges and opportunities

Assessing the risk of criminal infiltration into the legitimate economy may encounter several challenges. One of the main difficulties arises from the lack of a shared definition and the related complexity of the issue (Savona & Berlusconi, 2015, pp. 18–19). The boundaries between legal and illegal economy are often fuzzy. Economic activities are distributed along a continuum with criminal activities at one extreme and completely legal ones at the other (Ruggiero, 2008; Smith, 1975, 1980). Between these two extremes lie several other possible ways in which criminal organisations engage in activities that are formally legal yet organised and managed illegally.

Moreover, criminal infiltration into the legal economy is not criminalised per se (see Chapter 2); rather, national and international criminal laws usually punish several types of crime carried out during the infiltration process (e.g. fraud, money laundering, accounting manipulation/falsification). However, legal definitions may differ from country to country, or a specific criminal conduct may not even be criminalised in certain countries. Moreover, there is also the problem of data availability (neither police nor judicial data are available at the European and country level) and comparability among different countries.

Determining the risk of organised crime infiltration into the legitimate economy requires specific local assessments rather than more general conclusions because the phenomenon may exhibit different characteristics depending on the country/region/city subject to analysis. For instance, what is tested as risky for criminal infiltration in one country may be different in other countries. Moreover, broad assessments are able to draw attention to the problem, but they are not useful in assessing the risk of a specific area, economic sector or entity, given the huge variation from one country to another and within the same country.

The concept of criminal infiltration cannot be directly assessed and measured. Rather, it should be deconstructed and operationalised into simpler elements which are directly measurable (i.e. risk factors and proxy variables). This process entails the choice among several dimensions and variables, which should be carefully selected keeping in mind the evidence of already-existing studies on the same issue and the final aim of the risk assessment process. Both qualitative and quantitative information is needed in order to develop a comprehensive framework. Quantitative data derived from official sources are suggested in order to standardise the base for comparative purposes among countries. In addition, qualitative information derived from multiple sources at country level should be collected in order to customise an interpretative framework aimed at better interpreting quantitative data understanding. Table 12.12 presents an example list of risk factors, which can be grouped into four categories: territory, business sector, ownership structure, financial management.

Table 12.12 Operationalisation of risk factors for organised crime infiltration of legal businesses

Dimension	Indicator
Territory	Past evidence of organised crime infiltration
	Presence of organised crime
	Large urban areas
	High level of infrastructural equipment
	High level of shadow economy
	High level of corruption
Business sector	Past evidence of organised crime infiltration
	Low level of competition
	Low level of openness to foreign investments
	Low level of technology
	Small average company size
	Low barriers to entry
	Weak or developing regulation
Ownership structure	Limited company
	Characteristics of shareholders (young/old, female shareholders)
	Corporate shareholders
	Complex corporate ownership schemes and cross-shareholding
	Frequent change of company details
	Small company size
Financial management	Lower level of financial debt than peer group
	Higher level of current assets than peer group
	Low revenues and profitability

Source: author's elaboration on Transcrime (2013a, 2013b); Riccardi (2014); Savona and Berlusconi (2015); Di Bono et al. (2015).

The risk of infiltration can be identified as a function of the features of the territory (R_{ter}), business sector (R_{sec}), the business's ownership structure (R_{own}), and financial management of legal businesses (R_{man}), as shown in Figure 12.1.

Other challenges for the assessment of criminal infiltration concern the methodology to be adopted, the selection and interpretation of the risk factors and their dimension, and the different scenarios in which the phenomenon is analysed. Moreover, there is a well-proved lack of quantitative data on this issue, which could affect the inclusion of certain indicators in the final risk-assessment model. The selection of tools and methodologies to be used for the assessment of criminal infiltration into the legitimate economy relates to the final aim pursued by the risk assessment exercise. The general purpose when assessing criminal infiltration is to protect legitimate economies from the misuse of legal businesses for illicit purposes, as well as to improve prevention and enforcement by identifying the factors facilitating and/or promoting the infiltration and to orient policy measures. The methodology and risk factors adopted should be suitable to the country specificities of the phenomenon, and they should be customised to highlight the peculiarities of the areas analysed or to enable comparison among different economic sectors and countries.

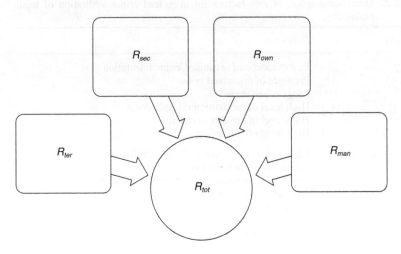

Figure 12.1 Risk model of organised crime infiltration of legitimate businesses (source: author's elaboration on Savona & Berlusconi (2015, p. 123)).

Conclusions

Risk assessment as defined by the international standards has not yet been fully applied to criminal infiltration. The existing literature in the field comprises both qualitative and quantitative approaches, which have attempted to identify the economic sectors/activities/territories most vulnerable to criminal infiltration according to several risk factors. These approaches cannot be helpful for developing effective prevention strategies as requested by the international standards (e.g. anti-money laundering and corruption assessment, public procurement screening). The infiltration process is often difficult to detect and assess, especially when there lacks a common definition and the boundaries between legal and illegal economy are often blurred.

There is a need for the systematic monitoring of changes and vulnerabilities of the legal economy that could be exploited by criminal organisations. Such monitoring could anticipate the negative consequences and assist development of the appropriate counter-actions. Risk assessment models can help law enforcement agencies and policymakers to evaluate the extent to which a certain economic sector, territory or business is exposed to criminal infiltration. These models should go beyond the mere description and analysis of the phenomenon by identifying the factors facilitating and/or promoting infiltration, and they are helpful for developing a more comprehensive knowledge. Indeed, the more that is known about the phenomenon, better and more reasonable decisions can be taken for prevention and for orienting policymakers.

Notes

1 Directive EU 2015/849 of the European Parliament and of the Council of 20 May 2015 on prevention of the use of the financial system for the purposes of money laundering or terrorist financing, amending Regulation EU 648/2012 of the European Parliament and of the Council, and repealing Directive 2005/60/EC of the European Parliament and of the Council and Commission Directive 2006/70/EC.

2 The legal form of a company is the general type that it may legally use to identify itself according to the local, regional, national or international law governing it. This is normally reflected in the abbreviation after the company's name (e.g. Inc., Corp., S.A.).

3 A shareholder is any person, company or other institution that owns at least one share of a company's stock. Shareholders are a company's owners. They have the potential to profit if the company does well, but they may also suffer losses if the company does poorly. Moreover, depending on the type of stock held, they may have the right to vote in the shareholders' meeting of the company. A shareholder may also be referred to as a 'stockholder'.

4 The director is an appointed or elected member of the board of directors of a company who, with other directors, is responsible for determining and implementing the company's policy. A company director does not necessarily have to be a stockholder (shareholder) or an employee of the firm, and may only hold the office of director. Directors act on the basis of resolutions made at directors' meetings, and derive their powers from the corporate legislation and from the company's articles of association.

5 The level of financial net debt was measured as the difference between current financial liabilities plus medium/long-term financial liabilities minus cash and cash equivalents on net equity. For further details on the methodology see Savona & Berlusconi (2015).

References

Albanese, J. S. (1987). Predicting the incidence of organized crime: A preliminary model. In T. S. Bynum (Ed.), *Organized crime in America: Concepts and controversies*. New York, NY: Criminal Justice Press.

Albanese, J. S. (2008). Risk assessment in organized crime: Developing a market and product-based model to determine threat levels. *Journal of Contemporary Criminal Justice, 24*(3), 263–273.

Albrecht, H.-J., & Kilchling, M. (2002). Crime risk assessment, legislation, and the prevention of serious crime: Comparative perspectives. *European Journal of Crime, Criminal Law and Criminal Justice, 10*(1), 23–38.

Ardizzi, G., Petraglia, C., Piacenza, M., Schneider, F., & Turati, G. (2012). *Estimating money laundering through a 'Cash Deposit Demand' approach*. Pavia: Università di Pavia.

Ardizzi, G., Petraglia, C., Piacenza, M., & Turati, G. (2014). Measuring the underground economy with the currency demand approach: A reinterpretation of the methodology, with an application to Italy. *Review of Income and Wealth, 60*(4), 747–772.

Arlacchi, P. (2007). *La mafia imprenditrice. Dalla Calabria al centro dell'inferno*. Milano: Il Saggiatore.

Becchi, A., & Rey, G. M. (1994). *L'economia criminale*. Roma: Laterza.

Berghuis, A. C., & de Waard, J. (2011). Geen kansen bieden aan de georganiseerde misdaad. *Justitiële Verkenningen, 2*.

Bertoni, A., & Rossi, E. (1997). I rapporti tra impresa criminale e l'economia legale di riferimento. La gestione del patrimonio cumulato con attività criminose. In A. Bertoni (Ed.), *La criminalità come impresa*. Milano: EGEA.

Blum, J. A., Levi, M., Naylor, T. R., & Williams, P. (1999). Financial havens, banking secrecy and money-laundering. *Criminal Justice Matters, 36*(1), 22–23.

Brå. (2011). *Storskaliga skattebrott. En kartläggning av skattebrottslingens kostnader* (No. 2011:7). Stockholm: Brottsförebyggande rådet.

Brå. (2014). *Gå På Pengarna! Antologi Om Tillgångsinriktad Brottsbekämpning.* (No. 2014:10). Stockholm: Brottsförebyggande rådet.

Buscaglia, E., & van Dijk, J. (2003). Controlling organized crime and corruption in the public sector. *Forum on Crime and Society, 3*(1–2), 3–34.

Calderoni, F., & Caneppele, S. (Eds.). (2009). *La geografia criminale degli appalti. Le infiltrazioni della criminalità organizzata negli appalti pubblici nel Sud Italia.* Milano: Franco Angeli.

Calderoni, F., Dugato, M., & Riccardi, M. (2010). *Mafia Inc.: Analysis of the investments of the Italian mafia.* Presented at the 10th European Society of Criminology meeting, Liege.

Calderoni, F., & Riccardi, M. (2011). *The investments of organized crime in Italy: An exploratory analysis.* Presented at the 63rd American Society of Criminology meeting, Washington, DC.

Caneppele, S., Riccardi, M., & Standridge, P. (2013). Green energy and black economy: Mafia investments in the wind power sector in Italy. *Crime Law and Social Change, 59*(3), 319–339.

Catanzaro, R. (1988). *Il delitto come impresa. Storia sociale della mafia.* Padova: Liviana.

Centorrino, M., & Signorino, G. (Eds.). (1997). *Macroeconomia della mafia.* Roma: La Nuova Italia Scientifica.

Covello, V. T., & Merkhofer, M. W. (1993). *Risk assessment methods. Approaches for assessing health and environmental risks.* New York, NY: Plenum Press.

Daniele, V., & Marani, U. (2008). *Organized crime and foreign direct investments: The Italian case* (CESifo Working Paper Series 2416). Munich: CESifo Group Munich.

Dawe, S. (2013). Conducting national money laundering or financing of terrorism risk assessment. In B. Unger & D. van der Linde (Eds.), *Research handbook on money laundering* (pp. 110–126). Cheltenham: Edward Elgar Publishing.

Di Bono, L., Cincimino, S., Riccardi, M., & Berlusconi, G. (2015). Management strategies of infiltrated businesses. In E. U. Savona & G. Berlusconi (Eds.), *Organized crime infiltration of legitimate businesses in Europe: A pilot project in five European countries* (pp. 102–112). Trento: Transcrime – Università degli Studi di Trento.

Donato, L., Saporito, A., & Scognamiglio, A. (2013). *Aziende sequestrate alla criminalità organizzata: Le relazioni con il sistema bancario* (Occasional Papers No. 202). Roma: Banca d'Italia.

Europol. (2015). *Why cash is still king?* The Hague: European Police Office.

Fantò, E. (1999). *L'impresa a partecipazione mafiosa. Economia legale ed economia criminale.* Bari: Edizioni Dedalo.

FATF. (2004). *Report on money laundering typologies: 2003–2004.* Paris: The Financial Action Task Force.

FATF. (2006). *The misuse of corporate vehicles, including trust and company service providers.* Paris: The Financial Action Task Force.

FATF. (2010). *Specific risk factors in laundering the proceeds of corruption.* Paris: The Financial Action Task Force.

FATF. (2012). *International standards on combating money laundering and the financing of terrorism & proliferation: The FATF Recommendations.* Paris: The Financial Action Task Force.

FATF. (2013). *National money laundering and terrorist financing risk assessment*. Paris: The Financial Action Task Force.

Fiorentini, G. (2000). Organized crime and illegal markets. In B. Bouckaert & G. De Geest (Eds.), *Encyclopedia of Law & Economics* (Vol. 5). Cheltenham: Edward Elgar Publishing.

Gambetta, D., & Reuter, P. (2000). Conspiracy among the many: The mafia in legitimate industries. In N. G. Fielding, A. Clarke, & R. Witt (Eds.), *The economic dimensions of crime*. New York, NY: St. Martin's Press.

Gup, B. E., & Beekarry, N. (2009). Limited liability companies (LLCs) and financial crimes. *Journal of Money Laundering Control, 12*(1), 7–18.

Kelly, R. J. (2012). *The upperworld and the underworld: Case studies of racketeering and business infiltrations in the United States*. New York, NY: Springer.

Lavezzi, A. M. (2008). Economic structure and vulnerability to organised crime: Evidence from Sicily. *Global Crime, 9*(3), 198–220.

Marine, F. J. (2010). The effects of organized crime on legitimate businesses. *Journal of Financial Crime, 13*(2), 214–234.

Masciandro, D., & Ruozi, R. (1999). *Mercati e illegalità: Economia e rischio criminalità in Italia*. Milano: Egea.

Riccardi, M. (2014). When criminals invest in businesses: Are we looking in the right direction? An exploratory analysis of companies controlled by mafias. In F. Calderoni & S. Caneppele (Eds.), *Organized crime, corruption and crime prevention. Essays in honor of Ernesto U. Savona*. New York, NY: Springer.

Rozekrans, R., & Emde, E. J. (1996). Organized crime: Towards the preventive screening of industries: A conceptual model. *Security Journal, 7*(3), 169–176.

Ruggiero, V. (2008). 'E' l'economia, stupido!' Una classificazione dei crimini di potere. *Questione Giustizia, 3*, 188–208.

Sacco, S. (2010). *La mafia in cantiere. L'incidenza della criminalità organizzata nell'economia: Una verifica empirica nel settore delle costruzioni*. Palermo: Centro di studi ed iniziative culturali Pio La Torre.

Sarno, F. (2015). Control strategies of infiltrated businesses. In E. U. Savona & G. Berlusconi (Eds.), *Organised crime infiltration of legitimate businesses in Europe: A pilot project in five European countries* (pp. 90–101). Trento: Transcrime – Università degli Studi di Trento.

Savona, E. U., & Berlusconi, G. (2015). *Organized crime infiltration of legitimate businesses in Europe: A pilot project in five European countries*. Trento: Transcrime – Università degli Studi di Trento.

Savona, E. U., & Riccardi, M. (Eds.). (2015). *From illegal markets to legitimate businesses: The portfolio of organised crime in Europe*. Trento: Transcrime – Università degli Studi di Trento.

Schneider, F. (2010). Turnover of organized crime and money laundering: Some preliminary empirical findings. *Public Choice, 144*(3–4), 473–486.

Schneider, F., Buehn, A., & Montenegro, C. E. (2010). New estimates for the shadow economies all over the world. *International Economic Journal, 24*(4), 443–461.

Schneider, S. (2004). The incorporation and operation of criminally controlled companies in Canada. *Journal of Money Laundering Control, 7*(2), 126–138.

Sciarrone, R. (2009). *Mafie vecchie, mafie nuove: Radicamento ed espansione*. Roma: Donzelli.

Smith, D. C. (1975). *The mafia mystique*. New York, NY: Basic Books.

Smith, D. C. (1980). Paragons, pariahs, and pirates: A spectrum-based theory of enterprise. *Crime & Delinquency, 26*(3), 358–386.

Steinko, A. F. (2012). Financial channels of money laundering in Spain. *British Journal of Criminology*, *52*(5), 908–931.

Suendorf, U. (2001). *Geldwäsche: Eine kriminologische Untersuchung*. Neuwied: Hermann Luchterhand Verlag.

The Dutch Parliament. (1996). *Inzake opsporing: Enquêtecommissie opsporings-methoden*. The Hague: Tweede Kamer der Staten-Generaal.

Transcrime. (2000). *Euroshore: Protecting the EU financial system from the exploitation of financial centres and off-shore facilities by organised crime: Final report*. Trento: Transcrime – Università di Trento.

Transcrime. (2008a). Implementazione analisi criminale. Macroattività 3 – Sottoattività 3.A. Rapporto RisI.C.O. – Le interviste. Unpublished.

Transcrime. (2008b). Implementazione analisi criminale. Macroattività 3 – Sottoattività 3.B. Rapporto RisI.C.O. – I casi di studio. Unpublished.

Transcrime. (2008c). *Implementazione analisi criminale – Ris.I.C.O.* Trento: Transcrime – Università di Trento.

Transcrime. (2013a). *METRiC. Monitoraggio dell'Economia Trentina contro il Rischio Criminalità*. Trento: Transcrime – Università di Trento.

Transcrime. (2013b). *Progetto PON Sicurezza 2007–2013. Gli investimenti delle mafie*. Milano: Transcrime – Joint Research Centre on Transnational Crime.

UIF. (2015). *Casistiche di riciclaggio* (Quaderni dell'antiriciclaggio. Analisi e studi). Roma: Unità d'Informazione Finanziaria per l'Italia.

van der Does de Willebois, E., Halter, E. M., Harrison, R. A., Park, J. W., & Sharman, J. C. (2011). *The puppet masters: How the corrupt use legal structures to hide stolen assets and what to do about it*. Washington, DC: The World Bank.

van Duyne, P. C., Jager, M., von Lampe, K., & Newell, J. L. (Eds.). (2004). *Threats and phantoms of organised crime, corruption and terrorism*. Nijmegen: Wolf Legal Publishers.

Vander Beken, T. (2004). Risky business: A risk-based methodology to measure organized crime. *Crime, Law and Social Change*, *41*(5), 471–516.

Vander Beken, T. (Ed.). (2005). *Organised crime and vulnerability of economic sectors. The European transport and music sector*. Antwerp-Apeldoorn: Maklu Publishers.

Vander Beken, T. (2007). *The European waste industry and crime vulnerabilities*. Antwerp-Apeldoorn: Maklu Publishers.

Vander Beken, T., & van Daele, S. (2008). Legitimate businesses and crime vulnerabilities. *International Journal of Social Economics*, *35*(10), 739–750.

Vannucci, A. (1997). *Il mercato della corruzione. I meccanismi dello scambio occulto in Italia*. Milano: Società Aperta.

Varese, F. (2011). *Mafias on the move: How organized crime conquers new territories*. Princenton, NJ: Princeton University Press.

Conclusions

Ernesto U. Savona

This book describes the main ingredients of the complex phenomenon of infiltration of organised crime in the legitimate economy. The perception of the problem varies as one navigates among general theories and different experiences in the countries covered by the book. This explains why, at the end of this research experience, it is still difficult to operationalise the concept and state the relevant indicators and measures. Exploration of the various case studies has increased the level of knowledge, but it is not yet possible to generalise variables and their dynamics in a single interpretative model.

The concluding chapter, entitled 'From the analysis of criminal infiltration to the assessment of its risk', is a bridge between the research carried out in this book and the ongoing project 'MORE – Modelling and mapping the risk of Serious and Organised Crime infiltration in legitimate businesses across European territories and sectors', co-funded by the EU Commission, coordinated by Transcrime – Università Cattolica Sacro Cuore (www.transcrime.it) and started in January 2016. This project continues the two projects (OCP and ARIEL) from which this book derives. It will provide further knowledge about the relationships between organised crime and the economy, either legitimate or criminal. But it will do so from a different perspective.

The studies produced by Transcrime in the past few years,[1] and which are partially represented by this book, have sought to estimate criminal proceeds while identifying the drivers of criminal investments in the legitimate economy. The new project continues this analysis by moving from a descriptive or static perspective to a more dynamic one. This will be made possible by translating into risk factors what we have learned from the analyses carried out for this book and from the research conducted by Transcrime since 2011.

This requires mapping the risks of organised crime infiltration where they emerge, combining primary data with secondary ones, discussing the socio-economic factors that facilitate these risks, and considering systemic vulnerabilities. All this is part of the ongoing MORE project. With its results, the cycle will be closed by answering the two remaining questions that I raised in the introduction to this book: how can the infiltration process be interrupted and dismantled, and what policies are most effective for this purpose?

Note

1 For instance the ARIEL, OCP, IARM, 'Mafia Investments' research projects. For a full list see the Transcrime website www.transcrime.it.

Index

Page numbers in *italics* denote tables, those in **bold** denote figures.

For Product Safety Concerns and Information please contact our EU
representative GPSR@taylorandfrancis.com Taylor & Francis Verlag GmbH,
Kaufingerstraße 24, 80331 München, Germany

Printed and bound by CPI Group (UK) Ltd, Croydon, CR0 4YY
08/05/2025
01864515-0001